SAM

SAM

The German, the Officer, the Man

Samuel Meffire with Lothar Kittstein

Translated by Priscilla Layne

dialogue
books

DIALOGUE BOOKS

First published in Germany in 2023 by Ullstein Paperback Verlag
This translation published in Great Britain in 2023 by Dialogue Books

10 9 8 7 6 5 4 3 2 1

A CIP catalogue record for this book
is available from the British Library.

ISBN 978-0-349-70349-7

Typeset in Ehrhardt by M Rules
Printed and bound in Great Britain by
Clays Ltd, Elcograf S.p.A.

Papers used by Dialogue Books are from well-managed forests
and other responsible sources.

MIX
Supporting
responsible forestry
FSC® C104740

Dialogue Books
Carmelite House
50 Victoria Embankment
London EC4Y 0DZ

www.dialoguebooks.co.uk

Dialogue Books, part of Little, Brown Book Group Limited,
an Hachette UK company.

Contents

I

The Foreign Homeland

Bonn, mid-July, 2021

'Dad?'

The cry echoes through the short hallway and turns the corner in a gallop. I've just cleaned up what is left of lunch and made myself comfortable at the kitchen table. I just want to quickly catch my breath, pause for a moment and surrender to my obsession with news. But I guess there's no chance.

'Dad?'

Just ten minutes. Me and *Der Spiegel*, the online magazine. Just ten tiny minutes. That's all I dream of. But now Una is calling me, the younger of my two daughters. And my dream is over. The tone of Una's voice tells me she's caught a whale. She's discovered something big, something outrageous. So outrageous for a five-year-old that it immediately has to be announced. As quickly and as loud as possible. Telling everyone who wants to hear it.

Una, she's my scurrying, demanding, infinitely curious acrobatic *wunderkind* with corkscrew curls. Every day, I'm astonished by my offspring, always full of bliss and affectionate admiration. How she smells. How she moves.

'Dad, come! Come quickly!' Una's intuition is legendary. Nothing, absolutely nothing can stay hidden from her for long. She roots around in the lowest depths of the drawers and climbs our highest cupboards. She is an explorer. She manages to scribble on the freshly painted walls with my carefully hoarded markers. Or to beautify herself with her mother's kiss proof lipstick, to convincingly paint her face for Halloween.

'I'm coming! Just don't touch anything, please, I'm coming!'

In the middle of her bedroom, the indoor trampoline looks like an alien spaceship. Next to it there's a treehouse bed and a climbing arch. And there are a million things wildly scattered on the floor. Here one can really find everything a child could want. But no Una.

'Dad?' The voice is coming from my office. That shouldn't be the case. My office is off limits. She knows she's not allowed to go inside. At least not without my explicit permission. My office is full of my things, piled high into chaotic towers. Mountains of books, binders and an army of home-made training equipment. This is anything but childproof. And what's also in my office are the ghosts of my past, neatly put away in boxes.

'Una, what are you doing there?!' Too late. She's sitting cross-legged under my desk, an open box in front of her. She's holding a yellowed, wrinkled article from the *Bild* newspaper in her hand.

I haven't wanted to open that box. Not yet. I put it with five other boxes up on the bookcase, on the highest shelf, as far away as possible. It's a beige cardboard box full of toxic memories. But my life is now being digested by Disney+, by the immortal narrators of epic fairy tales. Yes, it's unreal. My past is best suited for a horror film, but they're turning it into a splendid drama with all the bells and whistles. Just without unicorns, wizards or singing fairies. *Merde, scheisse.* I promised to give the folks from production the toxic boxes, that's why I pulled them off the shelf. And now Una has one.

I've done a series of extremely questionable things.

Inexcusable things. And their results were … disastrous. So many errors. So many losses. So much pain. Over which time passes and so everything falls victim to becoming meaningless. But then the film people came and I made a deal with them, for money. And against forgetting. Part of this deal was, I had to remember everything. And since I can't, I got those damn boxes off the shelf. I wanted to open them. Sometime. Maybe soon. Just not now.

'What does that say, Dad?'

Una is pointing to the headline that boasts my photo beneath it. My younger self is looking back at me. With a calm, cold grimness. Yes, that's me. I could try to deny it, but it would be pointless. In the presence of the article, carefully repressed feelings flood over me. They well up like a cold, oily liquid. Bizarre photoflashes of the past.

'N——! Fucking, dirty n——!' They yell and rage in the hallway. They ram the door again. Plaster falls from the crack in white, thin crumbs onto the floor. 'Come out of there! You and your whore, you're dead!'

A loud crack! The door to the nightclub flies open from the kick. 'On the ground! Move, move, get to the ground!' someone yells. A commando. A threat. Is that my voice?

The minister's vice-like handshake. Sustained, insistent eye contact. 'I'm counting on you, Sam. Think about why you became a policeman. Think about what's on the line!'

The dying woman on the pavement. 'I'm from the press! I'm taking pictures!' The loud, tall man with the camera. The zip of the flash. 'Fuck off!' Dark, sweeping anger. I don't have it under control.

Booming bass. Techno disco hell. A hand on my forearm. 'Felix said that you're Sam. You're the ex-policeman?' She's really close. The warmth of her body surges out through her dress. Why does this girl look like Fee's twin sister? My heart pangs and jolts.

The whimpering old man on the floor. Finally. A crappy wrestling match with this giant.

'Where's the money? Where are you hiding the fucking money?'

A vase breaks on the granite tiles. I've got shards under my shoes.

The jail cell is silent. This goddamn abysmal silence. Except for the crackling neon lights and the buzzing of the ventilation. A coffin under the cellar of some official fortress. I won't last long. I want to jump at the ochre tiles. With a running start, again and again. Until everything bursts, oozes out, all of these damn feelings and memories. And everything seeps away in a small drain in the corner. And then they will come and wash away what's left of me.

'Dad?'

A little voice from afar. I try to understand where I am. And what I'm doing here. It takes a moment.

'Dad? What's written there?'

Una's face is worried and really close. Fuck, how long was I out for? She's holding the newspaper in front of my face. Oh yeah, the article! This miserable headline.

'"Enemy of the State", curly Sue.' I smile, even though I don't feel like it. 'It says: "Number One Enemy of the State Writes Books."'

'And what is an enemy of the state?'

'That's someone who attacks the state, honey. Someone who wants to destroy the state.'

'What is the state?'

'It's all of us. All of us together. That which belongs to all of us. And the rules that everyone should follow.'

'That's what you wanted to destroy?' Una looks at me incredulously.

'No, bug. I didn't want that. I never could have done that.' But it's actually not that difficult, I think. Sometimes communities destroy themselves. They just implode. Once it's started, it can happen incredibly fast. Then the angry ones come forward. The frustrated ones. All the ones whose lives feel futile anyway. And the sociopaths join them. Sometimes they wave brown flags. Sometimes red. But deep in their hearts, they are strangers to ideology. They're low-level blood suckers. They need the intoxication of the suffering of others. I experienced that twice. I don't want to again.

'Were you really in jail?'

'Yes, my love.'

'For how long?'

'Seven years.'

'Seven years?' She looks at me horrified. Then she does the maths. 'Two years longer than I've been alive!'

That's true. Half of a child's life. Una's entire lifetime.

'But you were a policeman! Do policemen go to jail?'

'If they've done something awful, then yes.'

She nods. That, she can understand. Now she wants to know what I did. She hesitates. Does she sense the abyss? The shame? Yes, there's still shame, even after almost twenty-five years have passed. Shame. After all this time. Una looks down at the ground. She has old black-and-white photos spread out there. On all the photos, the same man is visible: a guy with a brawny physique, like a wrestler on a college team. Short hair. Full lips. He's wearing a neatly trimmed beard on his chin. 'Who is that?'

In the picture that Una is holding in her hand, the man is sitting in a restaurant. His left arm is casually leaning on the armrest of a corner booth. Across from him sits a slim woman wearing sunglasses. She's got the face of a model.

There are more photos of the two of them. Cheek to cheek. Arm in arm. Intimately familiar with each other.

I want to say, *My father.* But I can't even get these two words out. I clear my throat. Once. Twice. Una is looking at me full of anticipation. That doesn't make it better.

'Your dad?'

I nod. She picks up one of the photos and scrutinises it. 'What's his name?'

'Meffire,' I say hoarsely. 'His name was Samuel Meffire.'

She laughs. It's a laugh that sounds like my grandparents' Christmas bell. 'Like you? Is that allowed? To have the same name?'

I smile. 'I think so. You know, that was common in his family. They always named their sons Samuel in every generation. People come and go. But the name lives on.'

Una nods. She pauses for a moment. If I don't end this conversation quickly, I'll be trapped.

'Samuel.' She weighs the word on her tongue with intent. By now she's in her bombard-Dad-with-questions-mode.

'What does that mean? Does that mean something?'

'It's from the Bible. It means "he whom God desired".'

Una looks at the photo. 'He's dead, right?'

Suddenly, I ask myself whether one can tell that from the pictures. Whether it's because of the faded colours or the grainy black and white. Whether she can sense, with her childish sensorium, that the man there was long ago condemned to death.

That he would never see me, his second son.

A further photo. My young daughter has dug even deeper into the box. My father again. He looks at me directly, at least it appears that way. For more than a half a century. Past the gulf of death. The way he sits there, kind of stiff, almost formally, on a crooked wooden bench. That must be in Leipzig. There was a zoo and some colleague must have thought it would be funny to place a real lion cub on his lap, the African's lap. Or did they do that with everyone back then? In any case, this oversized pussycat is perching there. And my mother is sitting to the right, next to my father. And to the left of him is a skinny young man in shorts, smiling shyly.

'That's you, Dad! Look, that's you!'

'No,' I say. 'That's my brother.'

'You don't have a brother,' Una protests with childish indignation, demanding justice. Yes, true. The past tense is true. I had a brother. I don't have one any more. I once told her that. Or didn't I? Suddenly I'm no longer sure. And if I didn't, what else have I hidden? I'm an approachable father. A relaxed, modern dad. Right? I talk to my children about nearly everything. I do. Dammit . . .

'Where is your brother?'

'Dead,' I mumble as quietly as possible. 'My brother is dead.'

She lays the photo on the floor, carefully, with an almost tender gesture. She doesn't want to disturb the dead. All of my dead. They're lying before us on my office floor. For a moment everything is quiet, except for my computer's fans whirring to themselves. The deceased lie before us. My beautiful mother. My brother. My father.

'Feli says that some men killed him.'

'Who?' Who allegedly killed him? I'm alarmed and my tone is more severe than I want. Una doesn't let herself be deterred.

'Your dad! Is that right, what Feli said?' Feli is Una's ten-year-old sister. How does she know that? Did she overhear something? Was she listening in on something? A conversation? Some telephone call? ... *that little spy.* I invest a lot of effort in shielding my children from my past. From the toxic waste. And the demons. My kids are in the here and now. They're my present. My happiness.

But protecting them isn't always possible. Apparently. Una sees her chance. Her big blue-green eyes shine eagerly. They're my mother's eyes. They're extremely effective in triggering trance-like states in me. A state of involuntary volition. This kid could make an appearance in any mentalist show. And we have time today. It's summer vacation. My wife is off work; she doesn't have to go into the office, so she's visiting some friend in a nearby town. She won't be back until late. My wife commanded me to 'sheep herder duty'. Today it's just me and the sheep. And it's been raining outside for hours. It's raining cats and dogs. What else is there to do on a day like this? I could gripe. Or I could give in to the unavoidable. I have the sheep. Outside it's hellish, wet weather. And the most important thing of all, the family squadron commander is on the road. We're stuck here. And that's how it becomes a day in the family cocoon, because ultimately no one can compete with the natural forces.

'Come on,' I say to Una. 'Let's go into the kitchen and make a hot chocolate.'

'Then you'll tell me everything?'

'Then I'll tell you everything.' I say it with a little reservation, something Una misses. She runs ahead of me into the kitchen and dives onto the purple couch. She knows that jumping on the couch isn't allowed, but I allow it. I can't let anything disturb the peace this morning. After all, I'm the one shut in with these two little goblins. I search the kitchen drawers and mix together some cocoa. We always have cocoa in the morning. It always has to be the same. Deviations unsettle me. They're harbingers of disturbance. And danger lurks behind disturbance. I have to know. I had to learn. And that's exactly why I love my new life. It's fundamentally calm. Clean. And full of familiar things.

'Who killed your dad? You were a policeman, weren't you? Did you try to find them?'

I laugh. 'One thing at a time, curly Sue! One thing at a time.'

And I tell her. From the beginning.

CHAPTER ONE

Father

My father is eleven years old and doesn't have any shoes.

None of the children in the village have any shoes. At this time, in this godforsaken corner somewhere in north-western Cameroon, only adults have shoes. Often, they're patched up shoes in faded colours. And the elderly wear sandals, so that their crooked, scarred feet will fit into some kind of covering.

That's why my father is walking barefoot across a dusty dirt road that leads from the huts to the fork in the road in the forest. From there, a different path meanders to another fork and continues further and further until, after an eternity, the trodden clay road reached the red, sandy streets of the city Foumban. That's where my father's school is.

Sometimes my father hops on one leg, to distract himself from the brooding, dusty heat. From his thirst and hurting feet. He sometimes hops, but mostly he looks to the ground, because he has to avoid stepping on the numerous sharp stones that bite painfully into the soles of his feet.

My father knows a trick against the debilitating distance of the journey to school: he solves problems from maths class, just like that, in his head. And he's good at that. The numbers float around him like the notes of a melody; music that only he can hear. When it sounds happy, almost demanding, like the song of a fork-tailed drongo bird behind the village, then the answer is right. That's how my father does maths. It's fun for him.

All his friends have long become herdsmen in the pastures. Sometimes he wonders if he'd have been better off in the pastures. Learning in the brooding heat is exhausting. And whoever gives the wrong answer or gossips in class frequently gets hit. School is no bed of roses in this country, in this remote corner of the French empire, at the beginning of the 1950s. Shouldn't he be spending his days with the other boys? Lying in the shadows of the big acacia trees, close to the peaceful, grazing cattle?

But somewhere in my father's head a voice whispered: 'There's another world, *mon petit*. Beyond the bushes and the dust. There's much more!'

A lot of people in Cameroon dream of getting out. Whoever lives in the village dreams of the provincial town. Whoever lives in the provincial town dreams of Yaondé, the seat of government. And everyone dreams of the distant, unreachable fairy-tale land called Europe – where they speak French; the elegant, tongue twisting language of the colonial masters that the whites brought, its strange sounds bravely fought by the children sitting at their desks, day after day. Everyone says in Europe there are giant towers made of steel and glass. And you eat off white plates made of ivory. Europe seems to be full of wonder. And it is endlessly far away. But it still calls and beckons you.

My father tells my grandmother about the numerical melodies

in his head. She pulls him to the side, over to her hut and puts a big piece of baked banana in his mouth. In the meantime, grandmother is wrinkled and toothless. And she stares at him like a five-hundred-year-old, two-legged turtle.

'That comes from the Lord,' she finally says. 'The voice in your head comes from Jesus. Listen to it!'

'But what should I do?'

'The Lord has a plan for each one of his children,' his grand-mother whispers to him in the semi-darkness of the hut, in which it smells so pleasantly like fried banana. 'He can motivate you as much as make it happen. That's in the letters of the apostles. Read it. And try to listen.'

'And then? What happens then?'

Listening is one thing, but doing the right thing is something else. My father is just a boy. He asks himself, what am I supposed to do, when God is calling me?

'Then do what the voices tell you. Then do what He wants.'

My father absorbs every one of her words. He hides it, deep inside, like a secret treasure. Grandmother used to carry him around when he was small. She comforted him. She told him stories with a quiet, raspy voice. She'd tell him about Jesus, the gentle Christian God, in whose name he was baptised. Samuel, the one whom God desired.

A lot of people in the village think Grandmother is crazy, because no mentally healthy person voluntarily prays to the God of the whites. But Samuel loves her to the stars and back again. He loves her more than he can love his mother, who goes to the fields at daybreak and stays there until the evening in a daily fight against hunger. His father is long gone, over the hills and far away. He wanted to look for work on the coast, in one of the port towns. He promised to return with a lot of money. But to this day, he has not been seen again. His grandmother is the only one who is always there. She's as constant as the forest behind the huts. Like the sky above the fields. Samuel believes her every word. So, he continues to walk through the pastures daily, past his old friends, until he gets to the fork between the trees, where the long path to school begins. What my father doesn't learn there: the Christian God, to whom grandmother prays, is actually German.

The French weren't the first foreigners in the area. Many decades ago, Foumban was the capital of a small kingdom. It was called Bamum and it was ruled by King Nyoja, the clever one. His father had subjected himself to the German Emperor, Wilhelm II. Nyoja planned to make the best of the dominance of foreigners that he'd inherited. As a symbol of loyalty, he gave the emperor his own holy throne as a birthday present. It was a marvel of woodcraft, adorned all over with multi-coloured pearls. The emperor determined Njoya was loyal. And this loyalty paid dividends. Njoya was allowed to pursue his visions. He would lead Bamum into a blossoming future. And the key to that was education. Every child in his empire would learn to read and write. The king even invented his own alphabet, the impulse for more trade and a more effi-cient administration. He gladly allowed Prussian missionaries to roam through the entire land. Give or take a god, what did that matter? And that's how the tall, pale-faced men reached a village near Foumban, where a girl lived who soaked up the stories about a single, loving God. That was grandmother. At least that's how she told it.

Somehow Emperor Wilhelm had a conflict with his God or

he hadn't properly prayed. Or maybe he hadn't cleaned his plate. Because he lost his empire and his dominion in the inferno of the Great War. Victorious France obtained the entire northern part of Cameroon, and with it also Bamum. The French didn't dither. A kingdom of vassals, like under the Germans? That was out of the question. The French ended this outlandishness with the stroke of a pen. The king's alphabet was outlawed. And the brick palace that Njoya had had built based on a Northern German model, now stands in the middle of Foumban like a stone postcard from a past, glamorous time.

France was determined not to lose this valuable country as shamefully as the Germans. When the mandate of the colonial power ended in 1960, Paris never thought of renouncing its influence. A puppet government was installed, allegedly to rule an 'independent' Cameroon. That was the big bosses from old families who would do anything for money. When a communist guerrilla movement was founded, the *Armée nationale de Liberation du Kamerun*, France didn't show any mercy. The decapitated heads of activists lay in the streets. No one was allowed to bury them because they posed a warning. In the villages, the dead slowly decayed in the fields, because no one dared bury them. Just the suspicion of being a 'communist' was a death sentence. Fear spread across the country like a heavy fog, suffocating everything. Only a few dared to resist, including the unions. They secretly recruited in the cities. They looked for those who were prepared to go to the Eastern bloc. Who was brave enough to seek an education behind the 'iron curtain' in the empire of the communists? Who wants to study in Warsaw or Prague, in Moscow or even in Leipzig? And who would resist the temptations of being abroad and come back afterward, to fight for change at home? Who would help the rebellion?

Qualified volunteers to study in the East were rare. Young people wanted to go out in the world but not to the East. They were driven by longing for other places. England. France. The land of milk and honey. Go to the Eastern bloc? That was more of a vision of terror. It was rumoured that there was not enough to eat. And everyone had to march to work wearing grey uniforms, in lock step singing the 'International'.

Anyone not scared off by these rumours was forbidden to tell anyone about their trip to the East. He'd be an enemy of France and his life would not be safe for long. That's why the journey had to be disguised as a trip to Paris. From there, the young men could be smuggled East; that's the socialist underground railroad. Often their families didn't even know where they were really going. Whoever took this path had to have a lot of courage. Or idealism. Samuel Meffire had both.

My father is eighteen years old by this time, still not especially tall, but with the stout stature of a prize fighter. There's no *Lycée* in Foumban, the city is too small. His relatives scraped together their last savings and sent my father to a big city to finish secondary school. That's where he got mixed up in the orbit of the leftist unions. Socialism! That sounds like a magic word to him. Finally, an alternative to the misery in the villages. To the hunger. It's also an alternative to capitalism, in which the same people always win in the end. Where only a few have everything. And the many have almost nothing. My father is a Christian. Staunch. Devout. He gets that from his grandmother. She prayed and read the Bible with him, every morning and every evening, just like the missionaries taught her so many years ago. But Jesus and Marx, that's not a contradiction! Don't they both speak about salvation? Didn't the Redeemer want a truly just world? In my father's head, faith and the socialist utopia solidified into a single, promising picture of paradise. Cameroon could one day be the promised land. One day. There was a long way to go before then, and many steps. This path has led my father to East Germany. His destination is Freiberg. A tiny town in Saxony, not far from the Czech border. There, a spot in engineering is waiting for him at the university. My father has never heard of Saxony. Certainly not of Freiberg. He only knows two things about the GDR: first, socialism rules there. And second, in the winter snow falls. A frosty, white cover settles over the land. My father doesn't yet know whether he'll like snow.

'Listen to the Lord's voice, Samuel!' His grandmother kisses his forehead softly. It's his last visit to the village, their last encounter.

'Be good and diligent, you hear?' My father nods and for a short moment he still feels secure in his grandmother's pride. Studying in Europe! Samuel is 'the chosen one', the grandmother smiles toothless, she always knew it. On a foggy autumn day, my father steps out of a rickety express train operated by the East German Railroad. He hoists his shoulders and fumbles with the top button of his trench coat. He bought it in Paris. Used. And it is clearly too thin for this city. It's cold in Leipzig.

Mother

Finally summer vacation! My mother hops down the steps in front of the main entrance of the stucco-fronted school. Christine is fourteen years old. A thin, dark-blond girl of ordinary attractiveness. Beneath the surface of her growth spurt and her beginning puberty, she is still a child. Playful and free from the world of the adults. Now she is hopping on one leg, her long skirt swaying back and forth.

She's got her report card in her bag and she's content with herself.

Maths 'very good', collaboration 'very good', organisation 'very good', cleanliness 'very good'. That's important to her father.

Otto, the bookish, pernickety civil engineer, can't stand it when people let themselves go. Especially not his child. When you build houses for a living, messiness can be deadly. And that's why she knows that there won't be any trouble when her father sees her grades. Her best grade is the 'very good' in singing. That's the best thing at her school: music class. And the best thing about her: that she can sing, that she loves singing. Then she forgets the world around her. Otherwise, her report card has two Bs, but it's hard to get better grades than that during these years. Getting an A average is reserved for geniuses, for the straight A students. But that's OK for my mother. She's happy with what she's got. And why should she be worried about the future? The teachers in school preach that things can only get better when everyone works together and diligently builds the house of socialism. There's a place for everyone. There's work for everyone. And one day, the shelves in the stores will be as full as the West's and there will be enough apartments for everyone. Enough cars. Trabis. Wartburgs. Nice vacations at the Baltic Sea and in the Harz mountains; vacations for everyone. That's how it will be. At least that's what the teachers say. And my mother has no reason to distrust them. She believes in it.

And why not? She lives with her parents on a quiet street, in a light-filled apartment. Her grandmother is in the West and every time she visits, she smuggles West German Marks in her underwear. With a sly grin, she pulls the bills out from under her skirt and winks at her granddaughter. But her family actually doesn't need this smuggling via underwear. Her mother sets the table generously. Otto earns well. For his daughter, he's like a king out of a Brothers Grimm fairy tale. He's strict, but fair. He doesn't drink. He never hits her. In this day and age, these things aren't a given. At gym class, in the changing room, she sometimes secretly peers at the red marks and black and blue spots on the backs of the other girls. Otto, her father, is a giant. And considering that he can crack the thick-shelled, German walnuts they eat at Christmas with his bare hands, mother is certain that he must also have Herculean strength. But her father never raises a hand or his voice. Not against a woman and not against his daughter. He is the strict, house-building king and she is proud of him.

But even the king has dismal days. Then he appears to be distant and barely speaks. Then he stares past his coffee into space and silently walks from the breakfast table to his office. On days like that, she's a little scared of him. On days like that it's better to leave him alone. Additionally, there are also the occasions, when, griping and carping on about something, he stomps through the apartment. Then her father complains about the lack of building material, about the senseless regulations and the 'Reds', whatever that means. Once, in an intense rampage, he slams his coffee cup on the kitchen table and mumbles something to himself about how 'back then' everything used to be different.

Back then. Her father probably meant the Nazis and their

'Third Reich'. She has naturally heard all about that in school. There are pictures of olive-green tanks and devastated land-scapes in her history book. Of boys and girls waving flags. They all wore military-style uniforms. Somehow it all seems familiar to Christine. But when the teachers talk about the Nazi period, it's as if these things happened in another country, on another planet. Yes, there were awfully horrible people there and despicable crimes. But no one who lives in the GDR could have anything to do with that. All the murderers are in the West. My mother's world is perfectly right, clearly divided and well organised in 'here' and 'there'.

Two years later. It's summer vacation again. Once again, my mother leaves school, but now she's not skipping any more. The little girl in her has disappeared. She's turning into a real woman. Only recently has she been paying more attention to her posture. She now knows that she's pretty. And a pretty girl should also act 'pretty'. At home, when she feels unobserved, she secretly practises in front of the mirror. She pushes back her hair and checks her gestures and their possible effect. Her performance in school is now just 'good'. That's just enough for her father's demands. Just as before, she sings divinely confident; in music class everyone turns to look at her.

Otherwise, she's barely able to finish her high school diploma with a B-average, then study at university – if the authorities allow it. It's not just a case of having good enough grades, you also have to be politically reliable and have the right background. My mother has long sensed that Otto won't break his back to enable her to study. If he had a son, he would definitely want to make him his successor at the drafting table. But a girl? He's not concerned about her.

She's secretly been fostering her own dream for a long time: she wants to be an actress. She loves to sing. She loves the stage. To touch the audience with gestures and movement. To be seen. That's why she wants to study acting. She heard that with singing, only talent counts, not your diploma. She can perform. Isn't everyone's gaze drawn to her when she performs a solo in the school choir? Even in the lay group of the school, people tell her she's gifted. She's chosen to apply to the most ambitious acting school in the country. Her studies would be in Leipzig, but that doesn't bother her – on the contrary. She's ready for the next step. She's never been to Leipzig. The city is only an hour away by train. So, she's able to go to the auditions without anyone noticing. One morning, she just has to sneak out of the house, and then she'll be back home by the evening. That's the plan.

My mother's been practising for months. Secretly, at home. And in the empty girls' bathroom at the school. The range of strong women's roles is limited, so she chooses a Gretchen monologue from *Faust*. She speaks in front of the bathroom mirror, practicing her lines. She puts as much expression in as it's possible to when whispering in secret.

Her high school exams come like the overdue end of a long drizzle. Unspectacular, inevitable. She works for a few summer months as an assistant at an insurance office, to earn a little money. In a sticky, hot office, she sticks contribution stamps into insurance booklets. It's monotonous. She bores herself to death. Is she supposed to squat in some office and inhale dust from files into her lungs until she retires? No way. So the well-behaved girl secretly goes to Lepizig. She sits in the train with a racing heart and yet can't do anything else. She has to try. Against all expectations, against all likelihood that she might be admitted. Provided her parents agree to it. My mother is only seventeen years old. Reality brings her back to earth.

'What do you want to be? An actress?' Otto laughs, incredulous, almost mockingly. 'What kind of silly idea is that?'

The tears fill her eyes. Otto stares at her. Only now does he notice that it's serious. Suddenly, he's beside himself with anger. He screams: 'An artist? They don't want to work! Antisocial! Perverted! Not as long as I live!'

He turns around, goes into his office and slams the door shut. Her mother sits silently at the table and looks out the window, then she leaves while averting her gaze. In the living room, she begins to wipe imaginary dust off furniture. Her mother won't help her.

In the winter, Christine sits at the insurance office again, sticking stamps into notebooks. Before, she used to hum to herself, sometimes she sang at home, just like that. Folk songs or songs from school. Snappy socialist marches. Whatever came to mind. Her father always liked to hear them. Now she's silent. In Berlin, the wall is built in 1961. And her father, the builder in a country with a lack of building materials, he built a wall, too. Around his own child.

For three long months, she doesn't speak a word to him. For three long months, she floats like a ghost through her parents' apartment. She feels hurt. Maimed. She feels like she's changed. In these days, she discovers an unknown severity in herself. A new decision matures inside her: she's going to leave home. Get away from her father. Get out of Dresden, any way she can. She'll live her own life. She'll be free.

Why is she studying gas production of all things? Is it the

expression of a cool calculation? The subject seems promising. The young GDR economy is hungry for energy. Brown coal excavators are eating their way across the land. This year, Walther Ulrbricht has requested a large-scale search for crude oil. Maybe she just wants to say to her father, *I'm going to Leipzig. Regardless of what I do there.* Because there's also an engineering school in Leipzig where she'll study. After that, she can call herself a skilled labourer. That's as good as a high school diploma. Then she can study at a real university. But for the moment, only one thing counts: not to end up in the insurance office! Not to end up in Dresden, with her parents!

My mother is nineteen years old. Her small room is in the south of Leipzig, Lenin Street 29. It has a tiny bed, a rickety wardrobe and an old wine crate as a table. Her fellowship is barely enough to live off. When she visits home on the weekends, her father lays money on the kitchen table without comment. It's his way of showing her his approval. Gas engineering, that's a real job. He thinks she's come to her senses. Finally, she's his obedient, well-behaved girl again. Boy did he deceive himself!

One day, sometime in the autumn, my mother is on her way home. She barely knows anyone in Leipzig. She travels alone. The sky is overcast, a sallow light is shining on the yard strewn with rubble that she walks past near Lenin Street. These 'gifts' from the war are all over Leipzig. She's familiar with it from Dresden. Traces of bomb-burning hell. My mother's mother barely escaped the inferno. Even today, she still avoids the old market where mountains of corpses burned. But for the children born after the war, the rubble is merely the ugly present. No one wastes any time thinking about it. What for? The war is over. A troop of young men are working on the property that my mother is hurrying past. Shovels and hoes rattle against the stone. The Free German Youth remove the rubble. She once did that, too; it's a back-breaking job. Bits of wall land in the wheelbarrows with a crash. Mother is holding her hand over her mouth and nose. The air is full of dirt and dust. One can barely recognise the youthful faces beneath the whitish grease of limestone and sweat. That's why she at first doesn't notice, that some of the faces actually aren't white. They're Black. She quickens her stride.

Father and Mother

'Who's travelling to Leipzig tomorrow?'

Out on the grey corridor of the house for visiting students, a whistle resounds again.

'Leipzig, who's travelling to Leipzig?'

My father sticks his head through the crack of the door, he wants to know what the whistling is all about. He's already been away from his homeland for several months. He fought his way through the preparatory course. It was like running a marathon through the loamy mud of the village pond. Daily he studied vocabulary until late at night. Success, that's his mandate, and he takes it seriously. Not even a year after he got off the train, he had already reached the requisite language level for his studies, had moved to the campus in Freiberg and moved into the dormitory. To him the sparse room there was like heaven on earth. The little barefoot boy from the village of herdsmen has made it.

There's a boy wearing a blue shirt in the hallway. My father knows what blue shirts mean. He's a pioneer in the Free German Youth, the recruiting organisation for the socialists. The blue shirt looks at the line of heads sticking out of doors. By now hands follow the heads. Many people are volunteering. A day in Leipzig? That sounds like a welcome diversion, a chance to escape the eternal routine of learning. And the isolation on campus.

'We're clearing rubble! Put on your work clothes – understood?'

Disillusionment spreads across the faces in the hallway. There's no soft serve or campfire. Only work. The blue shirt looks at the faces in the hallway and tries to improve the mood with a roll call.

'You'll even be in the newspaper! You're sending a message to the youth of the world! We're taking photos of you!'

My father doesn't need a roll call. He doesn't even need to be convinced. For him, it's not a question of honour or of decency; as a guest, he pitches in. There's a war going on and the slaughter at home in Cameroon is only a tiny part. My father already understands that much for himself. It's a new kind of war. It's a fight against the system on all possible fronts. And since Father believes in the great promises of socialism, he wants to do his part. Whether in the lecture hall or during an extra shift. And so he marches off campus in a small delegation. The group heads to Leipzig.

After a walk to the train station, and a two-hour trip by train and several stops on the streetcar, someone puts a pickaxe in my father's hand and shows him an absurdly large pile of stones:

'Clean it up, OK? Clean everything up nicely!'

After hours of drudgery the pile of stones is still the same size as it was before. It's like Albert Einstein's theory of time: the faster everyone digs, the slower the seconds and moments pass. The time has become rubbery, like dripping tar. His back hurts, his hands are sore. It's like the stones are growing out of the ground. When the photographer gets there, everyone enthusiastically throws down their tools, it's a welcome break.

The photographer picks out my father. He 'adjusts' him carefully. 'Put the pickaxe on your shoulder,' he says. 'Shoulder!'

He acts it out in pantomime just to be sure. My father obeys.

'And smile. Smile!'

The photographer twists his face into an exaggerated grin, so that the foreigner can really understand everything. My father obeys.

A loud mechanical 'click'. The camera lens shuts.

At this moment, he sees my mother.

She's walking along the site, striding through the cloud of smoke he caused. My father drops the axe. He hurriedly climbs down a mountain of rubble, as fast as he can. It's not easy, the bits of rubble lie loosely and treacherously on top of each other. He climbs and slips and makes it down without having an accident. The girl is almost past the site. He speeds up.

What happens next can't be recalled with certainty. Did something fall out of my mother's jacket pocket? A handkerchief maybe? A note? Later, she can't really remember.

'Excuse me?'

She turns around and is briefly startled. She looks at a sweaty, ghostly face smeared with white. His skin, which peeks through the chalk in patches, appears as black as night. Not brown, but black.

'Did you drop this, miss?' Maybe something like that. Language-instruction German. Polite. Very correct.

She laughs.

'Yes, I dropped it. I'm beholden to you, sir!'

My father gives my mother back her handkerchief. Their hands touch for a brief moment. Both of them are new to the city. She is from Dresden, always been looked after, never even been away from her parents for a year. He has travelled halfway around the world, fleeing a civil war. Both so different. Both so alone. And united in their loneliness?

My father plucks up the courage. He hectically searches his head for vocabulary. 'Would you like to look at the sun on Sunday?'

She looks confused. She searches her head for a possible meaning. Then she laughs. Look at the sun on Sunday? Why not?

'My name is Christine,' she says. 'Sunday?' He nods eagerly. Settled!

Maybe it happened like that. Like a Hollywood romance. My mother would in later years only speak well of my father. There are other kinds of guys in the GDR. Visiting students, driven by the illusion of meaning, products of patriarchal upbringing in semi-feudal societies. Guys who fathered children in diverse cities in the East and then left them behind like meaningless rubbish. And these men and their needs fit nicely with certain women who feel lost among the grey ordinariness. Women who, in the empty post-war years, hope to experience something extraordinary, something exotic. Something that helps to break through the sad uniformity of these times. And a short, even if fleeting freedom.

It's different for these two. They feel inexplicably united, ignoring all reason and probability. My father and my mother are more than two differently gendered puzzle pieces, more than two animals in jungle fever. They really see each other. They make each other complete. At least more complete. The photos from back then are proof. A photographer in some studio took a close-up of the romantic pair: pale skin next to black skin. My mother next to my father. Both huddled up to one another. She looks into the distance, to some place she longs for. The picture eternalizes the moment like a scene out of an old romance film.

And like in every good film drama, the lovers have many enemies: for the GDR authorities, these 'mixed couples' are disturbing their fulfilment of the plan. For the higher good. They are and will always be the 'N' word. They're impossible to integrate. But no one says it openly, because it neither reflects the desired socialist mindset nor language use in public. In the 1960s, nearly the entire social elite of the GDR consists of the transformed. Of pre-war mindsets. Generations moulded by the Emperor and the Führer. And the longing for a German formula. For a unifying identity. And with all the internationalist solidarity: sex with Blacks? This kind of international understanding breaks the mould. My father and my mother are being monitored. His letters take an unusually long time to reach her. Hers to him, too. And that, even though the GDR is not a very big country. Both of them know: the letters are being intercepted and searched. And what else is there? And which of their classmates is spying on them? Who can they still trust? The happiness of the two lovers is no longer a private matter. My grandfather is beside himself. He goes to Leipzig to see my mother; he's never done that. In her tiny student room, he talks to her insistently, implores her: 'Do you know what you're getting yourself into?'

She stubbornly keeps silent.

'People will gossip. They're probably already doing that at your university. And in the end, you'll have his child. Then you'll be branded! Forever! How can you be so crazy?'

Silence is her weapon. She averts her eyes and doesn't say a word. She just sits there. That's how you confuse a superior opponent. Her father suddenly jumps up. She's certain he'll lunge at her now. But instead, his fist lands with a thump against the closet door. Just once, but it's like a bomb exploded in the small room. It's booming. And then there's also the silence. Now her father is silent too. And suddenly she realises how helpless he is. She senses her power.

In the end he leaves without having achieved anything. He leaves without saying anything. He won't see his daughter for ten years. For ten years, it's like he's standing at the edge of a chasm. Ten years of silence. Ten years of a merciless trench war and irreconcilable hardness, inherited by another generation.

Now my mother is alone a lot. Sometimes she doesn't see her lover for weeks at a time. He's way up north, at the Baltic Sea. The growing GDR economy has a frantic hunger for gas and crude oil. My father is supposed to lure traces of oil out of boreholes. That's why he's up north. Sometimes he strides around in spring meadows. Then he'll be underneath the torrid summer sun. And in the whipping autumn rain. There's no winter in Cameroon. The unfamiliar change of the seasons bothers my father. He sends photos of himself to his love. One shows him in overalls smeared with oil and mud in front of an apparently endless snowy wasteland. The address is Drilling Facility 133.

Sometimes my mother gets a visit from her mother. Secretly.

She stays one or two hours. That's too little but it's better than nothing. Her father can't know about the visits. Or does he sense something and just keep quiet?

'I'm expecting,' my mother says very quietly and looks at the ground.

Her mother understands every word, but she still asks to be sure.

'You're what?'

A child. A child from a Black man. And logically the child will be Black, too. Or at best light brown. Who knows? The mother looks at her daughter for a long while. Inspecting her.

My mother wants the child. She's excited. She's crying. She's desperate. She throws up in the morning. She searches the stores for fish. And dill pickles. She's afraid that Samuel will leave her. Although on the good days she's sure that he loves her, on bad days her doubts grow boundlessly. She drops out of college. In the fall of 1963, my brother Moïse is born. That's French for 'Moses'.

The neighbours gossip. And on the street, people stare at my mother, whisper when they walk by her; things like: 'N——whore', or 'Gas them'.

No one speaks openly. No one says it to her face.

'Racial hatred' isn't tolerated by the state. But subconscious hatred is almost worse. My mother notices how she's thinking about her father's warnings. He's not allowed to be right. Let the people stare on the street. And let the old Nazi witch next door spy on her. She hasn't done anything wrong.

She pours herself into work. What else is she supposed to do? Maternal leave? No chance. In socialism, women aren't supposed to sit around at home. Everyone is needed. And child care is taken care of, from toddlers upwards. Two months after Moïse's birth, my mother signs a contract with the Leipzig Gas Company as an assistant lab tech. She's completely starting over. In the morning, she brings Moïse to day-care. Goes to work. Takes classes and is soon certified as a lab tech. With iron determination she sets aside her meagre pay, whatever she can go without, because she desperately wants to study again: computer science this time. She wants to be a part of the cybernetic revolution. That's the big new thing, both in the East and the West. They calculate using punch cards made of paper. And computers aren't the handy plastic boxes of the next millennium, rather they're enormous, complicated machines that fill entire office floors. Nevertheless, for most contemporaries, they seem like science fiction come true. Computers are modern alchemy. Magic created with wires, transistors and buttons.

My mother's honours thesis is entitled: 'Proposals for the Use of Punch Card Technology in Operational Production Planning and Checking the Status of Contract Fulfilment'. That sounds really dry, but it addresses an existential topic: the future of the republic depends on supplying the masses. Depends on socialism. My mother hasn't created any groundbreaking inventions. She's not breaking any records. She's just a tiny uniform wheel in a large mechanism. However, she's still part of an awakening and she feels lively and needed, like never before.

Now my father spends more time at home, and my parents are finally getting married. They're not the East German perfect couple. But who cares? Ultimately, my father is doing his part drilling in the north. It's a back-breaking job. And my mother is doing her part in cybernetics. Additionally, my parents have a lively, happy child. Isn't this little family living proof of that better world the government is always grandiosely raving about? A world without poverty or racist arrogance or some other bullshit. But none of that seems to matter. The neighbours still gossip. They're still being surveilled. Once, my mother sees an old neighbour sitting on a bench near the graveyard. The man has a bureaucrat's face and is wearing one of those remarkably unremarkable suits. He's one of the secret watchdogs of the Ministry for State Security. My mother is sure of that. And beyond that: wake the child up, day-care, work, pick the child up, put the child to bed, fall asleep. Is that all there is to life? It's too much. It's too little. My mother isn't sure herself why she always has the feeling that something is missing.

My father is home again, on vacation from the drilling station. My mother is cooking something. My brother's already asleep. Do my parents talk after dinner until deep into the night? Did they already have words for what they'd have to do? Did they have a plan? My mother is crying tonight. She doesn't know exactly why. My father holds her in his arms, he needs to promise her things will be better, but he doesn't know how. At some point, the heavy feeling of sleep overcomes them both. They fall asleep on the couch. Half sitting, half falling over.

Holding onto each other. Escaping their daily troubles for just a few hours.

Next morning. The breakfast table. My brother is still sleeping. 'Why don't we go to Cameroon?'

My mother's heart jolts agitatedly in her chest. She's finally said it out loud. She knows that Samuel, her unexpected, unhoped-for, most favourite person in the world, once so foreign to her, this devout believer in socialist utopias and biblical promises, has always wanted to return to his homeland. But they have never spoken about it. And now she's suddenly afraid that her sweetheart might want to stay here forever.

'You want to go to Cameroon?' My father seems surprised. My mother nods.

'You're coming? With Moïse? All three of us, together?'

She nods and repeats his slightly quirky German that she loves: 'All three of us.'

That's how it was decided. She's euphoric. Maybe they can move around freer in Africa compared to the GDR, she thinks. Does Cameroon even have a large-capacity computer? And if not, maybe she could help build a facility like that. She can already see it in spirit: how the punch-card machines pull in strips of paper, she can hear their clattering like sewing machines. Deep in her stomach, she can feel the buzzing of the perforated tape being read and the fans for cooling the transistors. They can plan the electricity usage. For the farm work in the regions. They can coordinate healthcare. The vaccines. The medicine production. Everything is possible, if you can calculate it. Her heart is lifted. Leaving feels like liberation.

When my mother becomes pregnant again in the autumn, she's of the firm opinion that it's only a little derailment. She'll get over the birth quickly the following summer. She thinks to herself: as soon as she's back on her feet, they'll go. Everything will be fine.

Bonn, mid-July 2021

'And then he died, right?'

Felicitas is standing in the kitchen doorway. We all call her Feli. These days she's in Harry Potter fever and is happy for every undisturbed minute with her book. Little sisters can be really annoying if you're ten years old and want to read in peace. But Feli somehow realises that something is going on here, something that seems more interesting than bearded wizards and evil.

'Come in, Feli,' I say. 'Do you want some cocoa?'

Why did I say that? It sounds as if I'm planning to be a storyteller all day. But I'm not. No way. I just wanted to explain who my father was. Nothing more.

'Feli, Dad is telling me his whole life story,' Una announces with a grave expression.

I have to smile over her pride-filled, dirty little trick. The two girls love each other. But at the same time, everyone takes what they can get. And that's just life, I guess. It's the eternal sibling destiny, unparalleled love as well as competition.

'The cocoa is really tasty,' Una says. That's also a little bit of 'sisterly teasing'. *I got cocoa, you didn't.*

Feli shrugs her shoulders, in a way that means, *big deal.* But I think I've actually made the very best cocoa in this and all other universes. My cocoa flatters the tongue. I make it with soy cream. And Ghanaian beans. And brown crumbs of raw sugar and a dash of salt with lots of cinnamon. In addition to that, it's creamy thanks to the help of some pudding powder.

'Oh, come on.' I wave Feli over and put the pot back on the stove. 'I'll make some more.'

Feli moves over to the window. She probably won't sit down

for another five minutes. She has her pride. She's standing as straight as an arrow at the large window that looks out onto the backyard. She's standing there and staring into the rain. That's not normal weather, I think. That doesn't fit here, I don't associate something like that with Germany. Syria, Afghanistan, Libya, the Congo. The whole damn world is acting crazy. And now the weather is too.

'I found the photos,' Una explains with a serious expression. 'Dad was telling me about his father. He's dead.'

'I already knew that!' Feli said. 'They killed grandpa Samuel.' With that she makes a face at Una.

'But I'm the one who found the pictures!' Una is drumming angrily with her little fists on the table.

'Quiet, you two,' I say sternly. 'Whoever wants cocoa needs to be quiet.'

I use the chipped wooden spoon to stir the cocoa. I do the little things with a lot of joy. Just water that circles a pot. A warm strudel with tiny shaft rings. When I see that, I have to think of the mud-brown Congo distributary, somewhere in Zaire. And the fever. The priest's worried face as he bends over me. The Latin words that he mumbles. The dark dreams on this damn, eternally rocking boat, of this rusty, overloaded caricature of a boat. On the eve before the slaughter. Suddenly I'm in the kitchen again. I notice the stillness. I notice Una's glances. How long have I been standing here stirring this pot? I pour two full cups.

'What happened to him?' Feli asks. She's turned around and is looking at me.

Last exit. This is my last opportunity. It's the last chance for me to say that I have to work. *Drink your cocoa and be still. I love you, but leave me alone.* I should say that now. 'Yeah exactly,' Una says. 'What happened to grandpa?'

I've had to endure many stares before, from emotionally stunted, robot-like enforcement bureaucrats. Downright omnipotent prosecutors and judges. Unpredictable Congolese secret police. Vampires, pumped full with hate and cheap drugs. But Feli's stare is something else. It's playing in a totally different league. I've got no chance. I give up. A man has to know when he's lost. I sit down on the kitchen stool and start to talk.

CHAPTER TWO

Leipzig. It's summer. It's 1970. The work week is ending. With a warm night, Friday flows into Saturday. Hanging low over the horizon, the half-moon lies on its round back, large and shimmering greyish yellow. The swimming pools have been full all afternoon. People poured into the ice cream parlours and into the few parks that exist, with their shady trees. The city is only now settling down. The hellish glow of the day is slowly leaving the asphalt, the houses and the people. It's an exhale of relief. Just not everywhere. Unfortunately. At the hospital, the heat has entrenched itself between the brick walls and doesn't want to budge. The maternity ward is like an oven.

Sweat is running down my mother's face. She spent the night thinking about the next contraction. And then the next. And then the one after that. She wants to finally get this birth over with. She wants to be finished with the pain. But it keeps going and going. And the waiting is gnawing on her flesh and her spirit – until the next contraction comes and every rational thought in her head floats away. Other women are also lying in the labour ward, separated from each other only by movable screens. It gives the impression of an assembly line. Pelvis against pelvis, destiny on destiny: narrowly pushed together, as if they were all working to fulfil the great plan. No one in this place is interested in my mother's beauty. Here, life is reduced to pure substance, to its innermost core. And for my mother, this core is: pain. It's as if her womb is constantly being pressed together by a giant in a bad mood. With increasing strength and in shorter and shorter intervals.

My mother senses that we are now approaching the home stretch. It will soon be over. Soon, someone will place the being that grows inside of her onto her chest. Tiny. Smeared with blood. Unknowing. Soon she will be exhausted and be able to exhale. Soon she can sleep. But not yet. She's still stuck in this sheer, unending, unspeakable pain. Why does she have to lie on her back, like an absurd form of crucifixion? Her aunts can get splendidly worked up about that. They didn't use to do that back in the day, they complain. You used to just squat somewhere. And push. And gravity did the rest. But the doctors, who have long demanded sovereignty from the midwives over births, don't like to bend down. Yes, back in the day, one may have done that in villages in Brandenburg, but here you lie down on your back properly when you're giving birth. We're not Hottentots after all; that's the argument of the doctors.

My father isn't here. That's normal in these days. Fathers won't be included in the birth for a while, neither in the East nor in the West. Fathers wait at home near the telephone. Or at work. Or in the bar. At best they wait in the hospital, bashfully standing in a corner in some hallway.

But my father isn't waiting at home. He's not waiting outside on the steps in front of the entrance. He hasn't got her flowers that are wilting in his hand because it's taking so long. Also his college town of Freiberg isn't endlessly far away. Even the notoriously unpunctual 'East German Railroad' would manage to get someone from there to Leipzig during an hours' long labour.

My mother thinks briefly about her husband's condition, before the next contraction washes away this thought. She can't hold on to anything, not with this pain. The last time she was allowed to see him a few days ago, he wasn't doing well. He was doing worse than in prior weeks. The doctors had advised her not to bring her first child with her. Her husband was virtually blind, a secondary effect of organ failure. Little Moïse couldn't understand why he couldn't go into the room. A nurse lured my crying brother down the hallway with the promise of some sweets.

Out of the corner of her eye, my mother peers at the small commotion at the delivery room door. The head midwife is speaking insistently to the ward physician. He promptly hurries away. And not long afterwards, a man in a suit appears. A man with a shiny party insignia on his lapel. A whole throng of doctors is following him. They confer with each other in whispers, with helpless expressions. *Is something wrong with the child?* An abrupt wave of fear rushes through my mother. It's the one, the only feeling that's stronger than the pain of labour. Tears fill her eyes. She's going to push the child into the world somehow, regardless of the pain. She's going to hold the child in her arms. That's her reward, she's not going to let anyone take that.

She can feel the tiny life pushing forward little by little through the narrow canal, in which it must then perform the absurd feat of a quarter turn. My mother pushes. And screams. That's not expected either. In 1970: 'Birth is class struggle, not a three-ring-circus.' A comrade is supposed to just grit her teeth and bear it. But my mother screams. Regardless of the party's expectation and 'public morality'. And then the giant fist, that she makes with her hand, suddenly disappears. And someone else screams. It's a little, hungry, crowing bird. My mother doesn't suspect that not only has she just given birth to another child, but has become a widow at almost the same time.

A Thursday, a few weeks earlier. My father rashly takes a few bites of his marmalade sandwich in the student dormitory. Then he washes everything down with the rest of the lemonade from the bottle he opened on the day before. He has to go, the lecture won't wait for him. My father is full of zest for action this morning, despite the troubled night with his stomach ache and his sweat-soaked sheets. His studies are going well. Soon his second child will be born. Soon he'll have his diploma. Soon he'll have his final deployment up north, at the drilling station. Soon he'll write his final reports. Then he'll go on a trip with his sweetheart and his children. He longs for the tranquil smell of charcoal in the morning, that the peddlers use to cook tea in Foumban. Longs for the smell of dusty, reddish earth. He longs for the familiar faces of his homeland.

My father is just about to leave his room when he throws up his breakfast. Retching, he runs to the sink. The chyme, barely digested, gathers in the drain. He tries to settle down. He probably ate something bad yesterday. No big deal. He should have skipped breakfast. He washes his mouth out, brushes his teeth and goes out into the hallway on unsteady legs, making for the stairway as fast as he can. My father has no idea what else he swallowed in the sticky sweet of the lemonade.

Halfway to the lecture hall, the cramps start. His legs give way. He breaks down on the pavement. He retches, but he can't throw up any more. People stop and stare at him from a safe distance. No one helps him. Down there on the ground, lying on the large stone slabs, a terrible idea enters his mind. Scraps of conversation he overheard in the hallway suddenly take on a whole new meaning. Clues and fragments come together to form an image. All of a sudden, my father also has to think of the stories of the Gangas, the medicine men at home. And think of their devastating mixtures that don't just magically heal, but can also kill. Whoever hates a neighbour or is driven by jealousy can pay a little money and have a poisonous drink made that no one can survive.

My father doesn't go to the university lecture hall, rather he goes to Markkleeberg, to his wife, and takes himself to the nearest police station. He has to throw up on the steps. Inside, he tries to explain to the annoyed, scowling policemen. He doesn't talk about Gangas or magical potions. Instead, he puts his passport on the counter in the lobby. His student ID too. He speaks as calmly and quietly as he can. But the policemen's gazes are everything from annoyed to sceptical. My father holds on to the counter. Then he throws up green-yellowish liquid. This doesn't exactly cheer the policemen. But no one swears here. They remain formal in all circumstances, even when a Black man who's sick to his stomach throws up in the station. That's what they learn in the police academy. You urge the foreigner, in correct socialist German, to leave the station and in the future, to be a little more careful with his accusation. The food probably didn't agree with him. Or the unfamiliar climate. They know this about exchange students. Cabin fever. Maybe some stomach medicine or a long walk would help?

The Black man has gone crazy. A busybody looking to appear important. A work-shy malingerer. But none of these theses hold up for long. His high fever alone is life threatening. Are they going to have to reconsider his claim that he's been poisoned? A flurry of activity spreads. If the Black man dies, there will be hell to pay. Western guests are holy cows. What kind of an impression will they make? What kinds of headlines will be in the foreign press? An ambulance races through Leipzig with a screaming siren. It brings the patient to the best equipped hospital in the city. Too late, as they'll soon learn. His organ failure can no longer be stopped. As strong as the young, bullnecked man appears, the poison is stronger.

'Has the stuff already worked?' That's what my father heard from the mumbling of voices in front of his door the previous evening. They were the voices of two of his fellow students. My father had just thrown up in the hallway and was tossing and turning in the darkness in his bed, unable to sleep due to stomach pains. My father whispers the description of these events to his sweetheart. But my mother can't do anything but sit next to his hospital bed, and helplessly hold his sweaty, feverish hand.

Now my father is dead. A week before his thirtieth birthday. Two hours before my birth. In the end he was blind. Alone. And far away from home.

'Mrs Meffire?'

By now my mother suspects what has happened; it is a few hours after my birth and the man in the suit is looking through the door of her hospital room. It's extremely uncomfortable for him to have to bring this news. It's a shitty job that no one in the world wants. How does one do it?

'I regret to inform you that your husband unfortunately passed away this evening. The party sends their condolences, Mrs Meffire.'

Embarrassed, he fiddles with his suit. There are no flowers, no greeting cards and no other visitors at her bed. Politeness wouldn't allow any congratulations.

'Con ... Congrat ... Congratulations for your son, Mrs Meffire,' the suit adds, stuttering. He bows again and hastily retreats. My mother watches him. For a long time. Somewhere plates are rattling in the hallway. Nurses' shoes are squeaking in the distance on the linoleum.

What can be saved? My mother knows about the transfer of the paternal name that is tradition. Samuel. She wants to name her second son that. Maybe she can hold on to a piece of her husband in her thoughts. But mother has done her reckoning without bureaucracy. The people in the administration know that they have a woman before them who's tired to death. A woman without any reserves or support.

'Samuel?' The head nurse doesn't budge. She's supposed to write the name on the form now. Instead, she's tapping with the pen on the clipboard in her left hand. Samuel? She has to discuss this name with her superiors first. One can't just do that. In the higher tiers, the name causes head scratching: *Samuel? That doesn't fit here. A Thomas, OK. Or at least a Johannes. Can't that women pick a normal name for her child?*

'Samuel' isn't possible. Wherever there are Jewish names, Zionism can't be far behind. And the GDR is strictly on the side of the Palestinians. It had been a mistake to allow for 'Moïse'. It was negligence. Someone had overlooked that the name is the French equivalent of 'Moses'. And Jewish too. These names aren't socialist. A threat to the state. They won't allow that again.

When at some point the birth certificate comes, my mother doesn't know whether she should laugh, or scream from anger. The head nurse had written something down that appeared to be acceptable to her and her bosses. 'Sam'. In this variation no more Zionists were hiding. *Basta*. The end. That's it. My mother gave birth to me, despite all of the adversity, and I was perfectly healthy. And yet, I am still maimed. They turned my melodious name from the Old Testament prophet into a politically correct neutrality. Of course, later on, people didn't call me 'Sam' like in English, the language of the American class enemy. I was called staunchly in German 'Samm'. Just like *Samstag*, the day of my birth. I'm a half-orphan. And even my name has been halved.

Nothing of my father remains besides a lightly used shoebox full of photos and articles. WORLD DAY FOR YOUTH AGAINST COLONIALISM reads one newspaper headline. Next to that is a photo of a rubble pile in Leipzig. My father beams with a smile across his entire face. There's a caption of the photo. The usual, staid stuff. About a world without racial hatred and about international solidarity. The students from Africa are our siblings in the socialist class war. And one day, they'll return to their homeland with 'superior knowledge', in order to make the world a better place. But my father won't be returning home. Since his death, the GDR is extremely clingy. They won't be giving up the deceased Black mischief-maker. Regardless of whether he wanted to be buried in his homeland, his corpse is now a matter of the state. His widow certainly won't get it. And flying it back to Cameroon? That won't be approved.

Many others would have given up at this point, but not my mother. She lost her sweetheart. And with him, the hope for a different life. She's on the other side of the red line. At the end of August, she personally complained to the Berlin ministry responsible for visiting students. *A citizen dares to make trouble. And in this way! It's outrageous.* The ministers' reaction is immediate: after the conversation they suggest hiding the deceased immediately in the earth at the Leipzig central cemetery. Anonymously. Just as executed murderers and enemies of the state would be buried. Without a funeral service. Without last words.

For a long time, my mother learns nothing about it. And the autopsy previously arranged by the state rendered the desired result: cause of death uncertain, no trace of foul play. The GDR has no use for a 'homicide case Meffire'. There's no racial hatred in socialism. The case is closed.

That was at least the plan. But my mother speaks with my father's colleagues, with his superiors and other Cameroonian students. She makes notes. She tries to make connections. It's virtually an investigation; it's scandalous and raises a stink. My mother surprises the authorities with the power of her doubt. She has two kids to take care of, one of whom is an infant. She works full time. And in the end, her protest forces a second autopsy. This time, Dr Matip takes part, a Cameroonian doctor who just happens to be residing in the GDR. What Matip finds appears to concern him in such a way that he heads to Moscow with my mother. There's no Cameroonian embassy in the GDR and the mail is naturally monitored. Dr Matip goes to Moscow because he wants to speak with the ambassador personally. But after they land, men in plain clothes detain the good doctor and, without any explanation or accusation of misconduct, they send him right back to East Berlin. Who harbours that kind of fear?

Two years later, in 1972, during a strictly secret initiative, in the sparse headlights of a utility van, the coffin and the dead are dug up from the deep. In the dawn, a Soviet plane takes off from Berlin-Schönefeld airport; its destination is Cameroon. The coffin is on board. My father is finally allowed to leave. Without his wife. And without his children.

A few days later, my unsuspecting mother goes to the cemetery. She wants to have a gravestone installed with the help of the administration. The grave of her beloved husband cannot remain permanently unfinished, one wouldn't wish such a circumstance on one's worst enemy. My mother stares at the cold autumn earth, bewildered. There, where her loved one once lay, is now a gaping hole, patchily covered with a few boards. The unexpected absence sticks her in her chest like a hot glowing needle. Now her sweetheart is gone forever.

The next day, she returns with a camera. She photographs the hole. She documents her pain.

Mystifyingly, my mother wasn't arrested in Moscow at the airport. She got as far as the ambassador. His excellency had, of course, already heard of the matter. And he was full of sympathy. But he couldn't do anything. The entire story was a minefield; pure, convoluted politics. She has to understand that, the ambassador begged her. But to give her some consolation, after waiting so long in the embassy: a Cameroonian passport. A greenish little book with the number 09-71-ACM. With her photo inside: deeply shaded, sunken cheeks, conspicuous circles under her eyes, an empty glance. My mother appears as if she were one of an odd number of survivors from a ship disaster. Her appearance no longer corresponds with her still youthful age. She's aged in a time-lapse. She's used up the reserves of her body and spirit. Next to hers are the passport photos of her children. Two little black heads sticking out of white sweaters. Moïse is smiling. I look astonished, somehow. I still don't understand the abyss, but I will soon.

This Cameroonian passport, issued in Moscow, is until today the only official certificate I have that shows my full name: I'm the second son of Christine Njankouo Meffire, maiden name Klemm, born on 11 July, 1970 in Leipzig, the German Democratic Republic. I'm the half-orphan, the one who wasn't envisaged in the socialist fulfilment of the plan, and the one whom my parents had long waited for. And I'm named after my father: 'the desired one'. My name is Samuel.

Bonn, mid-July 2021

'You have a beautiful name, Dad.'

I smile. 'Thanks, Una.' I immediately wash up the cocoa cups. They're untethered objects clattering in the chaotic stream of life. That's why cleaning and putting them tidily away is a little victory.

'And what name is on your ID now?' Feli asks.

'Sam.' I shrug my shoulders. For years after reunification, I asked around to see if my name could still be corrected. There was nothing to be done. In the East, it was possible to reassign pieces of land that had been wrongfully expropriated. But not wrongfully expropriated names.

'Hey, Dad!' Feli is standing next to me and gives me a shove. 'When you were little, did you never want to run away from the GDR?'

'What's a GDR?' Una interrupts.

'It was a kind of prison,' Feli explains with a serious expression. 'It was terrible. You weren't allowed to do anything. You weren't even allowed to leave.'

'Nothing at all?' The little one's eyes grow big.

'Nonsense,' I say. 'There were all sorts of things. And first and foremost, it was my home. Your home is always the most important thing in the world. The most beautiful.'

I should have told the kids about the long-lost country of my childhood. Some people take strolls through their memories like through a meadow of flowers, until they reach the earliest days of their life. But for me remembering is an abyss. I avoid any trips into the past. I'm a master of avoiding memories. But sometimes it happens suddenly, just like that, like an accident at work. Like right now. Chunks from a distant memory are stirred up. A storm of puzzling retrospection in momentary images.

I'm staring out from the stroller. The water in the large tub is glittering greenish in front of me, behind that a mountain of grey stone is piled up. It's the Monument to the Battle of the Nations.

Moïse and I have a bag of peanut puffs. We're hunkering deep in a hedge cave in front of the grey house in Markkleeberg. Raindrops explode on the leaves above us, but we're sitting almost entirely in a dry spot. Nothing can happen to me here, in my big brother's secret hiding spot!

In the backyard. We're chasing each other through our neighbours' laundry hanging on the line. We run around and I'm so happy and carefree. Our machine guns are making a hellish noise. They're the toy versions of Soviet submachine guns. My heart is beating up to my throat. Then Moïse jumps up behind me: ratatat. 'You're dead!' 'No I'm not!' 'Yes you are!'

Evenings in our narrow kids' room. The walls were always a little damp, like in so many of the apartments back then. In the darkness, Moïse is telling scary stories. I'm crying from fear.

The waiting room of the speech therapist in Leipzig. I stutter a lot. And increasingly when my mother is nearby, I completely fall silent. There's a beige phone on the therapist's desk. One with buttons. That's like something from a sci-fi film come to life. I marvel at it. I could tell the therapist: 'My mother often gets angry.' Strictly speaking she beats me black and blue. But I don't say anything about it. You don't tell strangers anything. That's the iron rule. My mother taught me that. I'm a well-dressed little pet. I keep quiet.

The breakfast table: oatmeal cooked with milk. With sliced apples on top and small pieces of bread and on top of that a layer of sugar. Everything gets eaten up. I need to grow big. And strong. Even my mother's care is a weapon.

Mother and I are at the photographer's. My mother's wearing colourful bell bottoms with stitching that looks like it was edged with a ruler. Her hair sits perfectly styled. Me, in colourful Seventies children's clothes, looking like a child out of a catalogue. I lay the photos on the kitchen table. There's a whole series of them. The photographer in Leipzig was evidently enthusiastic about his exotic subjects.

'Dad, you were cute!' Una screams.

'The clothes are weird,' Feli comments expertly. 'Everything has such crazy patterns. Look at that coat!'

The coat my mother's used for photographs looks like snakeskin. Her showpiece. No idea where she got that.

'Oh, you were so cute!' Una screams again.

Today when I look at these pictures, I can see the abyss

shimmering from her eyes. And I can smell her breath, sour from alcohol, when she'd give me a good night kiss in the unprotected darkness of my childhood room. I'd get a kiss on good days. And they were as seldom as a six-leaf clover.

1975. I'm in the hospital. They think I have scarlet fever. Highly contagious outbreaks abound at this time.

My grandmother is sitting at my bedside. She's a giant woman, with a towering, blue-coloured helmet of hair. When I see her I immediately think of the gigantic wolf from the fairy tale, the one with Red Riding Hood. Grandmother looks at me for a long time. It's a hard, scrutinising, deliberate look. I look up to the painted white ceiling. The fever in me glows and prevents me from thinking too much. Meanwhile, the gigantic grandmother-wolf is taking her time with her assessment.

Then comes the judgement: 'It smells. This can't go on. I'm taking you with me. You're going to live with us.'

Feli is standing with her mouth open. Her pupils are as big as saucers. Fuck, I never wanted to tell my children that. At least not like that. But why not? Is it shame? Still this sting, after all these years. Still this doubt, after all these years. Was it my fault? My mother's angry outbursts? Her beatings? And everything that was lost or missing?

'Why did your mother do that?' Feli wants to know.

I shrug my shoulders. How do you explain to a child what it means when your life breaks apart, like a biscuit in a bag that's been shaken up? How am I supposed to explain to Feli that my mother tried to smash me against the tiled stove? And that I owe my life to a random visit from my grandmother, who intervened at the last second?

'My mother was very sad,' I say. 'You know, when parents are very, very sad, they sometimes get very, very angry.'

'But why?' Una asks.

'Maybe because then you don't feel the sadness. You just feel anger.'

'That so stupid!'

I smile. Yes, it's stupid. People are sometimes stupid. My poor, angry mother, who was in danger of drinking herself to death from her sadness, and her responsibility, she was so goddamn stupid. And nevertheless, I feel guilty. Even now.

'How was at with your grandma and grandpa?' Una asks.

'Better?' Una is just incorrigibly curious. I have to laugh.

'Better? You have no idea, dear. It was paradise!'

CHAPTER THREE

Autumn 1975

A small cluster of houses that crouch high up on the slope above Dresden appear white. Giant poplars tower above the dense fog of the early morning. Pallid light falls through the crowns of trees, whose branches have only a few half-withered leaves clinging to them.

Once again, I feel this vague strain in my breast. It's the time of transition. Summer is making its way south, and up north, winter is already pulling on its boots. Otto, my grandfather, likes to hike. He would probably hike all the time, from someplace to somewhere or other, if only his job allowed it. He tells whoever asks about all of this wandering about that he inherited his joy of hiking from his parents. That's true. But that's only half of the story.

Deep inside, behind the paper-thin exterior of his friendliness, this gigantic man doesn't wander across the peaceful moor before the gates of Dresden. In his head, my grandfather still marches through streets full of bullet holes and the muddy fields of war somewhere in France. He's marching towards the enemy.

Or away from the enemy. One often doesn't know exactly on the front. His bruised feet can't feel anything any more. His back, sore from the weight of his field luggage, can't feel anything any more. My grandfather practically never speaks about the war. Like most of them; the ones who were there for the major battles.

But for me, his five-year-old grandson who loves him more than anything and would never judge him, grandfather-man is willing to break his silence. He tells me that they once conquered a mill. There had been rats living in there, so big that they chased the cats. And then his unit blew up the mill. Those are the kind of stories he tells. Grandfather makes sure that no blood flows in his story. Comrades are never torn to pieces by *Panzerfausts*. No one dies. Is he protecting me? Or is he protecting himself, since his fingers start to tremble whenever he remembers how he tried to fill the clips with bullets in the middle of a fight?

We hike to my grandparents' garden house, up the hills of Weißig, a suburb of Dresden, toward the distant, evergreen poplars that resist the autumn wind like unconquerable giants. Now he's standing still. I look up to him. I'm five years and three months old. And to me he looks like a benevolent giant from a fairy-tale world.

We turn around and look in the other direction, where the city is supposed to be, beyond the fog. What's my grandfather thinking about? About lunch? The autumn storms? Or the bomb inferno? Is he thinking about a war once waged down there, a firestorm from which his wife, my grandmother, barely escaped?

As a five-year-old, I know nearly nothing about my grandfather's abyss. But nevertheless I understand everything. That's just how love is. Dresden still has the scars of war, over which autumn has laid its merciful fog blanket. I hug my grandfather's legs. It's a wild, affectionate gesture. It's pure love. He lays his hand on my head. For me, the touch of his giant hand means absolute comfort. There's nothing better. I'm protected, sheltered. I'm safe.

We reach the dacha, the garden house. There's a porch swing behind the house. Naptime. He puts me in the swing. The blanket is old and heavy and a little scratchy. It smells like my grandfather. He sits down next to the swing and nudges it with his foot. After a few minutes I'm in dreamland. Grandfather watches over my sleep like a mythical giant dog. I'm his unsought, late awakening. His grandson. The son of his daughter. For years he fought a trench war with her. In a time full of shortcomings.

Grandfather has little to gain from socialism. He's a really competent engineer; for him, whatever plans you make have to work. Otherwise the house will break apart. But in this damn system of incompetent party bureaucrats and idealistic nutcases, nothing works the way it should. And you're not even allowed to speak about it. Grandfather abhors the blood and fire of war. And the 'Bohemian corporal' who climbed the ranks from a buffoon to a murderer and then to the 'Führer' was, to put it mildly, a case for the insane asylum. But at least things got built back then. And my grandfather is a master-builder after all. Building is his world.

After 1945, the communists made the city halfway inhabitable. And look at it now! Once the Venice of the East, Dresden now is misshapen by legions of ugly new buildings. Everything looks the same. All sombre.

Grandfather shares his opinion at the kitchen table within the family circle. His daughter, my mother, once called him a 'revanchist' there. That sounds well thought out, but it's really just another word for Nazi. I think: he's supposed to be a Nazi? Just because he didn't want his only child to get mixed up with a Black man? You see what that leads to. Now she's sitting there. A widow. Isolated and half crazy from worry. And that's exactly what he wants to prevent. (And today she levels this charge against him even more aggressively.)

But what kind of leverage does a father have when his child is grown? Threatening to stop speaking to her seems like the only way. And as Grandfather learned in the war, if you make a threat, you don't dare back down in the face of danger. Grandfather didn't speak a word to my mother until his foreign son-in-law unexpectedly croaked. Grandfather doesn't feel triumphant. He didn't wish death on the boy. But since being alone again, everything between father and daughter is slightly better. At least they're speaking again. They scrutinise each other suspiciously. Watch each other furtively. It's a fragile ceasefire. A cold war.

Does grandfather think about that when he sits next to me? I'm lying on the porch swing, wrapped up in the blanket. And grandfather watches and listens to the rustling of the poplars. I'm the son that he never had, that's what grandma says sometimes. And during remarks like that, she wears a scrutinising wolf face.

On the way home, grandfather and I sometimes go to the dive bars on the moor. There, grandfather orders us an early dinner. The innkeeper brings us delicious meatloaf. He manages to get it from a butcher in convoluted, inscrutable ways that make it through the desert of the socialist economy of scarcity. Golden brown onions, a fried egg on top, with fried potatoes and spinach. The butcher knows the innkeeper. The innkeeper knows my grandfather. And my grandfather loves me and that's why I've been gifted this meatloaf. And naturally my grandfather likes to be praised because of me. How politely and grown-up I speak. How well I sit up straight. How well I can eat with a knife and fork. My grandfather enjoys the attention he's given from the innkeeper. I smile timidly. Maybe I really am my grandfather's son.

Next morning in Dresden. Outside, behind the closed window shutters, the tinny puttering of the Trabant's motor announces a new day. Grandfather goes into his office where he'll sit at his drafting table until noon. That's why it has to be very quiet in the house. I draw and play in the kitchen.

Behind three closed doors, through the hallway, behind the living room, in the office, grandfather scratches with his pencil on the large, rolled out paper. After hours of absolute concentration, the image of a bungalow emerges from his hands – smooth lines, modern and timelessly appealing. A house for one of the privileged who is more equal than all of his other equals in this nation of workers and farmers.

My grandfather is only allowed to work from home thanks to his relationships with the people who offer such contracts. That's the only way grandfather could buy himself the dacha in Weißig. And that's the only way I can get my meatloaf with a fried egg. My five-year-old self doesn't care about that. I simmer with excitement about the moment when my grandfather comes out of his office. Then he'll have time for me and we can do something together.

Tuesdays and Fridays we go to the butcher. The butcher greets him politely and weighs some slices of grey cervelat sausage. Inconspicuously, he lays another small package on the counter. 'Your order, Mr Klemm.'

My grandfather takes his 'order' and winks at me impishly. In the carefully wrapped package, there's a treasure hidden: sausage made of ground pork and some steak tartare called 'Hackepeter' for my grandmother to spread on her roll at breakfast. Not everyone gets things like that here. We hurry home, happily, with our loot.

Friday, in the afternoon, we take all of the sausage to the dacha and grandfather barbecues. I marvel at the crackling of the charcoal fire. And how, momentarily, a piece of fat from the sausage falls into the embers. There's also a record player at the dacha. Grandfather puts on a record while we eat. The needle falls onto the vinyl and turns the static and scratching into music. We listen to grandfather's favourite song one more time. It's Brahms. The *Requiem*. I don't understand the puzzling verses, and nevertheless I am awestruck:

> *Lord, teach me*
> *That I must have an end*
> *And my life has a purpose*
> *and I must accept this.*
>
> *See, my days are*
> *The span of a hand before Thee*
> *And my life is like nothing before Thee*

Sausages and the supernatural Brahms. That's how grandfather planned it. He's happy. I'm happy. Nothing is missing.

Wednesday is Cousteau day. Each Wednesday evening Jacques Cousteau comes on TV. Right after *Aktuelle Kamera*, the GDR news, promptly at 8 p.m. Grandfather and I love this Frenchman in a red hat. And we marvel at the *Calypso*, the ship Cousteau uses to roam the world's oceans. On his trips, he encounters giant whales and octopi and sharks. And in remote places, he encounters indigenous people, whom almost no one has seen before. Grandfather lets me sit on his knees. And without this support, I would probably run out of the living room as soon as I saw the murderous shark teeth and shrunken heads. That's the big, wide world, about which you're only allowed to dream from here, this city on the Elbe river, deep inside the GDR.

The next morning, I wake up in the giant bed made from oak. I must have spent the night there, lying next to grandfather's back; he towers before me like an always warm, protective wall. And grandfather himself? Maybe he also longs for a safe place. Maybe we're protecting each other. He protects me during the day from my mother. I protect him at night, from the demons of the battlefields.

I'm carried from my grandparents' bedroom to the kitchen table, to hot cocoa and honey on toast. *My grandfather, a Nazi?*

Two years of peace. Two years of grace. My grandparents' paradise lies far away from the dark queen. I was always afraid of her. Gruesome fear that makes me pee myself just at the thought of her.

At night, I peed my bed. The biting stench was hard to hide. I got beaten when I wet the bed. And I got beaten for being slow. And for all of mother's stomach cramps, which she says my mistakes have caused. Later, it was a beating for bad grades. And 'bad' was anything that wasn't an 'A+'. And sometimes my mother would storm into the room. Lessons couldn't be easier. 'I rule everywhere. You're not safe anywhere. Never.'

'Could you sleep at your mother's house sometimes? Maybe

it'd be easier for you to settle down there.' That's what my grand-mother asks me every morning. The wolf looks at me across the kitchen table.

'Nnnnoooo!' Just the thought of it is horrifying to me. Sleep at my mother's? My fingers start to tremble, the bread roll falls to the floor honey-butter side down. I drop my head down past my shoulders and await the unavoidable. But it doesn't come. Instead, the grandmother-wolf takes me in her arms. Holds me. Until the trembling stops. After that I have to cry from relief.

Months go by. Grandfather decides it would be for the best if I just move in with them permanently. There's a school nearby. They have enough room at home. What started as temporary accommodation will become more permanent.

Sometime, during a weekly Sunday visit for coffee and cake, grandfather brings up the idea. He presents the plan to my mother. I'm doing well there. And she can visit me anytime. And it would make less work for her. And she can take better care of my brother. She could go back to her studies. It's all for the best! But this time my grandfather, the gifted civil engineer, has mis-judged the situation. Incensed, my mother explodes. She jumps up from cake and coffee, the cups rattle. And me, as a precaution I slide behind the wing chair in the next room.

My mother snorts nearby with her voice cracking. For her, the offer is nothing more than a hostage situation. And a hidden reproach. Her father abandoned her, left her alone. And now he wants to take her child?

'I was having a bad time,' my mother says, after a long silence. 'But now that's over. I can do it.' After that, she grabs her purse and stands up.

I'm just a child, not even seven years old. I live in the now. I'm happy. I only recognise the complete danger when my mother pulls me out of the apartment door behind her. In any other situation, even the slightest rebellion against her would have seemed like sacrilege to me. Simply impossible. But my instinct realises what my childish intellect can't understand: when I leave this apartment, paradise will be lost forever. So I scream. I thrash about. And crying, I beg my grandfather for help, until, in the end, snot is hanging out of my nose in long strands.

Grandfather has dug his hands deep into his pockets.

And the doors of the otherwise friendly neighbours remain closed. No one helps.

I manage to tear myself away one more time. I rush over to grandfather and grab onto his legs. My grandfather leaves his hands where they are. And grandmother doesn't come to the hallway.

'Please! Please! Please!' I plead. I beg. My grandfather's trusted face is high above me. It's inexplicably rigid and numb. That finishes me. All resistance inside me breaks down. My mother pulls me away from my grandfather. That man towers over her by two feet. And next to his massive body, my mother seems tiny, almost like a child. And yet, grandfather still doesn't intervene. Mother drags me away down the wooden stairs, while I thrash about. The door to the building closes.

CHAPTER FOUR

Dresden – the Prohlis district

An area under development. Buildings made of concrete as far as the eye can see. I'm standing next to the wide-open window in my bedroom and look outside. To the left and right of me there are endless rows of apartment buildings; it's anonymous, large-scale housing. Ten stories high. Here, socialism stacks its citizens ten stories high. Living space is a scarce commodity. This new district on the city's margins was developed in record time. Concrete. And even more concrete. And what's between the houses, or more precisely, what's supposed to be between the houses, has been totally forgotten. Behind me a desert landscape stretches out, with irregular walls of earth and weeds. Wooden planks bridge the pits of this chaotic, muddy, no man's land. Everything conveys the feeling of a callous, abandoned construction site. As abandoned as I feel. Moïse left. My brother is gone. I don't understand it.

No one has explained anything to me. I'm eleven years old. I'm alone. My brother is gone. And the abyss appears even more tempting than before. With all my strength, I cling to my last bit of hope, and to the window frame I'm standing inside. The pavement, ten stories down, calls me and tempts me. My mother seems unaffected by Moïse's disappearance. She perches proudly in her new apartment. Two bedrooms in a newly constructed building – that's like winning the lotto. Most of the people who live here think so. This is widely coveted progress. No one wants to live in the partially rotted nineteenth-century apartments that survived the war. Here, in the new development, there's even a garbage chute: you go down the hall, open the hatch, throw the bag inside and it's gone. When we moved in, it felt like I was living in one of my utopian sci-fi novels. Stanislaw Lem. Asimov. Strugazki. Science fiction realised in new construction. Yet from the balcony, you can see the fruit grove to the south of the city, you can see as far as the poplars in Babisnau, a green attraction of branches and leaves that has been around since the Austro-Prussian war.

The room that had belonged to Moïse and me is now mine alone. I could go around the big spruce wood bookcase that provisionally divided the room. No one will yell at me: 'Get out!' I could look for his precious treasure, a wristwatch from our grandfather. But the watch is gone. My mother packed all of his things in bags and carried them away. The only thing left is the bed. There's a mattress without sheets, like a skinned animal. My brother is gone. 'Expatriated,' that's what my mother finally told me. I know that word. In my imagination, it only applies to people who have done unspeakable things. Really awful criminals. They're sent to the West and they probably feel pretty good there with all of the other predators. And, of course, I understand why people like that have to be taken away. But what does that have to do with my brother?

Once, on the long way home through the concrete buildings, after a late afterschool club, a group of boys discovered me. They were big. And they were all pumped up on meanness. First, they started throwing clumps of dirt at me from the other side of the street, then they chased me. I ran as fast as I could. Despite my fear, I was a lot slower with a full back-pack and a sports bag than a group of sociopaths on wheels. I don't have a bike because of my mother's anxiety that I could fall. Topple. Die. Every now and again you hear about something like that. About children who were ground to mush on the street.

I didn't have a bike, so I ran. My feet flew across the flagged path until my lungs burned and my legs felt like stilts made of concrete. Then I suddenly heard the rattling of pedals behind me. I slowed down and then finally stood still. I wheezed. Choked. Let my book bag and sports bag fall. When I turned around there was no one there. Far away, at the other end of the path, I saw my pursuers disappear. And next to me was a familiar figure. Moïse. Straddle-legged. And squatting. And in his right hand he held a piece of reinforced steel that looked like a rusty club.

'One monkey alone is a victim. Two monkeys are a gang. And who knows what the parents of those savages will do. Maybe they put white kids in pots. Or stuff like that.'

Sometimes the absurd ideas in people's heads work like a magic fix. And sometimes it helps to have an older brother with an improvised cudgel. Moïse is seven years older than me. And for quite some time now, our father's bullheadness has been protecting him from my mother's beatings. Moïse is no longer small and weak. He doesn't avoid brawls on the street. And this fact allows him to think up foolhardy ideas at home. When our mother leaves the house to go shopping one day, only carrying her wallet, my brother sees our chance has come.

My mother's holy black handbag is lying on the couch in the living room, unprotected from our curiosity. Mother keeps silent. She only tells us that she works in 'data processing'. And that it's none of our business. She hides her files. She hides her calendar. And she is even better at hiding her bag. And now the thing is just lying around, almost like an invitation.

I'm naturally too scared, but not Moïse. There's not really anything interesting inside. A coin purse with a lot of dollar coins and pennies, a whole clump of coins. And mother's scribbled notes stuck inside her calendar. There are reminders of meetings and errands. Finally, Moïse takes a narrow, brown wallet out of a side pocket. There's a small card inside there. And inside the card there's only a single word, written neatly in capital letters:

'Larkspur.'

'What is that?' I ask.

'It's a password, man!'

'What's a password?'

'Oh man, you're so dumb.' My brother hits me across the forehead with the back of his hand. 'Everybody knows that. It's like with Ali Baba and his forty thieves.'

'Oh yeah. Of course.' I'm angry at my stupidity. 'Is something like that secret?'

'Of course, man. A password is always secret!'

I'm incredibly excited. Is mother a kind of spy?

Or is my brother just making fun of me? He does that all the time. And he enjoys it. I don't really buy his story. We put the card, including the wallet, back in the small pocket of her purse.

Then comes that Sunday, a half year later. Sometime during the spring of 1980. Sunday is holy. All stores and businesses are closed. No one bothers anyone before 10 a.m. Our doorbell rings unexpectedly. More than once. Mother is taking a shower. Moïse is outside on the street loitering. Maybe he forgot his key. But he would never risk ringing the bell like that. Or would he? What should I do? For a long, fearful moment, I struggle with making a decision. Just don't make a mistake that would cause mother to storm angrily out of the bathroom. I work up my courage and use the intercom.

'Yes?' I can't get anything else out.

An unknown male voice is on the other side. 'Is your mother there?'

'She's in the shower.'

'Listen, son, tell your mother: Larkspur. I repeat: Larkspur.'

My mother is already standing in the doorway of the bathroom with wet hair and demands from me: 'Who was that?'

Did I make a mistake? I cower. 'A man. Larkspur. I'm supposed to tell you: Larkspur.'

I could have saved myself repeating the word. For a half of a second, my mother is standing there, like a ghost, paler than usual. Then movement comes into her. She hurries into the bedroom and in under a minute she's back in the hallway fully clothed. I've never experienced that. It was like a magic trick. Mother rushes out.

The door slams shut.

I look out the window. Downstairs, in the courtyard the size of a stadium, I can't see anyone. The flagstone paths between the building entrances have long been abandoned. Typical Sunday morning. But the usual void seems strangely loaded. Fearfully, I think about what they told us at school, at the Young Pioneers' meeting. How the imperialists want to destroy us. Wipe us out, at any cost. 'When something happens, it will happen suddenly. And unexpected. That's why we always have to be watchful.' Suddenly and unexpected. That's what they told us in school after all.

Where has everyone gone? Did they warn her and forget me?

A bang shakes the house, I cower horrified under the window. Directly above the buildings, two fighter planes have just broken the sound barrier. The crying of their engines disappears behind the roofs. Then everything is quiet again. Except for the sound in the hallway. I can hear a key turning in the lock of the apartment door. I shiver scared. It's so dumb. As if imperialists would come through the door, with a key.

Of course it's Moïse. And I tell him excitedly what happened. My brother just brushes me off and throws himself on his bed, still wearing his gym trainers.

'I was just outside. Nothing's happening.' He yawns.

'How do you know that nothing's happening?'

'Because otherwise we'd hear sirens, idiot. Do you hear sirens?'

Actually, there aren't any sirens. Just Sunday and silence. We wait. But the class enemy never appears. There's no cry of sirens.

My mother doesn't return until evening. Tired. And irritable. She mumbles something about a drill, then disappears into her bedroom. For weeks, I dream about atom bombs that ascend in the distance and head for the city.

A real emergency happens a year later: Moïse is away. Gone. Just like that. Now the entire room belongs to me, though I'd rather share it with my brother. Mother sits at the living room table. She's writing something on a piece of paper, then she raises her head.

Her gaze is frigid.

Years later I learn what she wasn't ready to tell me that day. Moïse had punched some boy at his trade school. There was a fight and my brother lost control. The boy had to be taken to the hospital, his injuries proved to be life threatening.

My brother is no longer the cavalier hero as I'd like to see him. I sense that our father's death mangled him something awful, inside. And I only find out a little more about my brother's past many years after he moved out. My mother tells me, as always really late at night, crying and kneeling before the dark king of her drinking, how Moïse's behaviour had begun to have repercussions. He became increasingly wild. Increasingly resistant. How he must have got into a fight. And worse yet: how he had got hold of Nazi books and showed them around. He even drew swastikas in the bathroom of his technical college. A Black Neo-Nazi, that was really the ultimate provocation.

And then he nearly beat a classmate to death. That was enough. They arrested him and locked him up. And no one asked about his dead father or any kind of pain. They took my brother to Bautzen II, the detention centre of the state ministry. They took him to hell. Whatever wasn't yet broken in him broke there. The boy that I knew died there. His 'remains' were negotiated for during a prisoner exchange with West Germany. Hard cash for progressives, troublemakers and other undesirable elements. My brother was expatriated to the West. I'd never see him again.

Murderers killed my father. And they maimed my mother

and left her traumatised. Just like her oldest son. These are the uncanny, destructive resonances of this crime. And so, on this day, mother sits at the living room table and tries to commit words to paper.

'I hereby declare and promise that . . . that on my part there is no contact between myself and . . . my son.'

My mother pauses, ponders. Then her pen continues to scratch across the paper.

'His negative political attitude . . . as well as the criminal acts he committed in connection to them are the main cause why I renounce him.'

Mother looks at the paper for a long time. Is she hesitating? Is she disgusted by herself, in the face of her treason? Or does she simply not have any other choice, if she doesn't want to lose me, too, due to 'incompetent childrearing'?

My mother fought her way to the top. She had to rehabilitate herself with the party after her insurrection following my father's death. And she did it through hard work. Walter Ulbricht, the top circus director of the GDR made 'cybernetics', automatic information processing, a matter for discussion at the top level. *Machine progress will rescue socialism.* Cybernetics is supposed to help them achieve the perfect plan. My mother is now part of an IT team, part of a task force that's working under secretive conditions: they want to create software that collects so much information about citizens that they become transparent. They'll analyse the activities of comrades, their habits and routines. And that's how they'll identify their desires. Their longing. And then they'll know how many jeans have to be produced and how many shoes. And which sizes and colours. Everything according to the push of a button, with the help of a computerised planning matrix. The population's happiness will bend itself to the disturbances of collective phasing. Cybernetics is the future. The experts are sure of it. And my mother is along for this ride to progress. A small cog out of many, but she won't let herself be put down.

She formally renounces her son, totally. With pen and paper and an explanation. He's lost anyway. She'll never see him again. She never says his name again. Now she's alone with me. And I'm alone with her.

For thirty years I feel strangely rootless. Lost. It began in those days, this feeling that I don't truly belong to anyone. That I have no meaning for anyone. That as far as I'm concerned, no one wants me. Back then, I was almost a completely normal boy, with good grades, athletic and well-read. I liked to go to school. And four times a week I played football in a club. But I didn't have a single friend. And I soon wouldn't be able to visit grandfather at all any more.

My mother is driven. And I'm one of her projects – why would I need a grandfather? Why would I need friends? That's all excessive luxury. My father didn't make it. My brother didn't either. One is dead. The other was exorcised and disappeared. I *have* to make it. I can't fail. And that's why she pushes me. And that's why I try hard. But one would have to be a mixture of Superman and Jesus Christ to fulfil all her expectations.

Just trying becomes a daily marathon of exertion. And the sum of these efforts cuts me into many little pieces; severely worn, barely useable individual fragments. My body and mind digest the fictional resistance turning it into a bizarre head-game about suicide and redemption. My childhood bedroom is high up, ten floors above the concrete pavement and my room's windowsill develops an appeal I find increasingly difficult to resist. Streetcars also magically tempt me. From now on, I often have to use all my strength to cling to the streetcar stop before the car arrives. Or my childhood bedroom window frame. Why don't I jump? I'm mostly afraid of the pain on impact. And I'm afraid of my mother's nagging because I've done something wrong.

Increasingly, I slip away from reality into the dark forest of my mind. And my mother drinks. Every evening she binges to forget the dreariness of the days. Every evening she bends her will to the rule of the dark king. He promises her relief. My mother drinks. And naturally she has everything under control. As if. When evening comes and the king takes his seat on the throne, I'm no longer a human being for my mother. When she's under the influence, I'm only ever a little bug. A reflection of her failure, the enemy of her success. Mother is haunted by demons. And when she's drunk, she becomes one, too. She hits me increasingly often. Increasingly harder. And I become more desperate to find a way to fulfil all her expectations.

At school, I shine with the best grades. And at home I dream of utopia, that all injustices are eliminated. After that, I have yearnings. Communism will certainly promise what I can't have today. I just have to persevere today. And that's easier said than done. Erratically, I pee myself and smell like pee. I stutter a lot. I'm a freak. My only escape from all of this is the world of sci-fi and sports. Sport silence the voices in my head. Sport makes me faster. Stronger. Sport gives me recognition and patience, at least in the short term. And since I'm big for my age, one day a trainer notices me.

My path leads directly from school to a training assessment.

And from there to the sports academy. I become a kayakist. I don't know anything about this sport and I've never been in a kayak. And that's why I have no idea what I'm getting myself into. But it's my ticket out of the eternal grind. I've never sat in a boat before. But I'm used to eating shit. And pain. From now on, I'm on the water. Or in the water whenever I once again fall out of the boat and involuntarily take a bath.

I'm often in the weight room too. Elbe and iron. I become obsessed with the fight against the river and the fight against the weights. On the water, the strain drives away any other thoughts and any other head games. I'm only concerned with the kilometres and the rhythm. It's like a kind of prayer service. The boat is the church. And my coach is the priest. And the pain is the choir.

There are no longer voices. There's no longer longing. For my grandfather. Or my brother. But my grades become progressively worse. I only dream of representing my country as a 'diplomat in a tracksuit', that's the official convention of speech. But I'm simply not good enough in order to be an 'ambassador'. I continue.

One evening, my mother snarls at me because I dropped an egg. 'What'd you do that for? Are you trying to trash the kitchen?'

I look at my mother like through an inverted telescope. This woman, of whom I was once afraid, is suddenly more than a foot smaller than me. She doesn't come closer. She doesn't touch me. My mother, my dark queen, is afraid of me. Late at night, I wake up from sleep. My heart is racing and jolting. Beyond the head of the bed, the open window gapes. All around me, there's a cement mountain in near total darkness. My gaze goes towards the roofs far away, and I hazily sense the outline of the old waterworks. It's shining in the distance like a barely formed giant who fell asleep while standing.

'Come,' a voice deep inside me whispers. 'It's easy.'

CHAPTER FIVE

'Heil Hitler! What kind of Jewish nonsense is that, Meffire?'

The Führer is staring at me with bloodshot eyes. He's wearing poorly fitting overalls, has greasy hair and doesn't smell very fresh, one could say.

'Mornin', Ulf.' I have to smile.

'That's *mornin', my Führer*!' Ulf waves in my direction with his forefinger. 'Stand up straight, comrade! And greet me properly. We aren't in the bushlands here.' Half-heartedly I raise my right arm.

The Führer's gaze wanders around. 'Now, how does it look here?' I turn my head from side to side. The Führer is right, the construction site looks as if its troop of workers gave up in a panicked rush. And especially because what I built with bricks yesterday, when I was alone for a day here, gives the impression of being a pile of shit.

'Meffire! What you built looks like shit! It's pathetic! You're not supposed to build a Wailing Wall! German walls are straight!'

Admittedly, the wall was crooked.

It's shit. There's no more fitting word for it. Comrade Meffire, meaning I, built a leaning and crooked wall. Not sure how. Yesterday it looked straight, I thought. We're going to have to dismantle part of the wall. That doesn't change the fact that our leader is just as bad a bricklayer as I am.

We stare at the disaster together. 'Were you thinking about your girl again?' the leader asks.

'No.' I shake my head hastily. It's not like that. At least not just that. 'I had to go to training.'

'You need to make a decision, man. Do you want to rescue the world in your paddle boat or do you want to finally become an honest comrade?'

I need to decide, but it's not that simple. I never wanted to be a bricklayer. This apprenticeship was kind of an accident. I'm doing it because everyone has to play the game. There are no professional athletes in the GDR. There are only 'farmers and workers who play sport' secondarily. And with the right convictions, they have the strength to win medals.

'How far along is she?' The leader means Silke, my girlfriend. 'Six months.'

'And?' He grins suggestively. 'Are you getting any? I mean, you know what I mean.' I sense what's going through the leader's head. He's a real dirtbag. He's also the closest thing I have to a friend at the moment.

'Don't be so coy! I've never got anyone pregnant. I don't know! Tell me.'

I throw a trowel down in the sand after him. More half-assed. I'm definitely not going to talk to this clown about my sex life with Silke. For a little longer, the leader looks at me expectantly, then he waves it off. We are both silent. Together we look at the crooked wall.

To our relief, comrade Wattmilch comes along; the bull-necked boss of our brigade with the full beard. A little later than usual. In the already difficult territory of class struggle and craftsmanship, we're a burden to him.

Being a bricklayer in the GDR is not a rewarding job. It's a kind of magician's job in a zone that's constantly under-supplied. Every day something's missing on the construction site. Or everything. Cement. Steel joists for the windows. The hoses for the hydraulic system of our excavator. Well, we're able to solve the problem of the excavator: Wattmilch, the foreman, lets us apprentices dig the goddamn stone blocks out of the earth ourselves instead of using an excavator. The earth is as hard as concrete and some of the stones are so big that they could've been used to build the pyramids. It's the only day I skip my kayak training. After work, I get on the streetcar and at home, I let my half-dead body fall into bed.

Nevertheless, I have a good boss in Wattmilch. Others would have long since ratted me out to the central office because of my unwillingness and inability. He gives me such simple tasks that I could complete them even if brain dead. The days are always the same. Get up. Mix the cement, move stones somewhere. Shovel. Make piles. Carry. Without a doubt, I am the worst bricklayer there, but definitely not the only cause of worry.

Wattmilch is leading a brigade with up-and-coming slobs assembled from the entire Kombinat. We're the leftovers who actually weren't earmarked for full employment in the social-ist policy.

There is Ron, who had once drunk himself halfway across Dresden's small punk scene. And fucked everything. That's how he got syphilis. Twice. We were all allowed to share in his pus-filled symptoms. His stories are simply epic.

In addition to Ron, there is Karl, the ex-priest. Ex-aspiring priest. At some point he just quit the seminary. Karl still seems to be a little doubtful. Still a little spaced out. Maybe you can take the priest out of the seminary, but you can't take the seminary out of the priest.

Then there's Ulf, the 'leader'. Hyperintelligent. At least I suspect there's a rather clever brain hiding behind the mean Nazi-clown that he's always letting hang out. The clown and his malicious tongue ensured he had to flee the only Christian secondary school in the city.

And then there's Erik, who I just called Slimo because of his submissive snake-like nature. He's the son of a high up, party-affiliated bigwig in the Kombinat and his favourite thing to do is recite boa-constrictor sentences from *Capital*, that cryptic outpouring from Karl Marx. But otherwise, there's nothing he likes more than watching me work. I'd love to punch him. But I know that the secret watchdogs will come and pick up anyone who lays a hand on the spawn of a party bigwig. So I don't risk the slap in the face.

Dammit, what am I doing here? According to my mother's ideas, I should have completed my A-levels, but in my half-childish training-fanaticism, my 'I'm getting out and will be free' fanaticism, I had fallen so far behind at school that even the most benevolent look at my grades wouldn't have convinced anyone that I was right for higher education. At least not for competition with the A-students who can generally be found in all the higher classes. When it finally became clear to my mother and me that I could only hope to return to sport training if I found an apprenticeship, it was already too late. My mother then hectically plumbed the depths of her network and found an apprenticeship for me. As a bricklayer.

With little enthusiasm, I went to a dirty old grey building and was enthusiastically greeted by the Kombinat administration there. I was committed with a handshake. Powerful working drones ... Welcome.

Wattmilch believes in Jesus. I know that from the leader, although I have no idea how he knows that. Christians are a strange species. Their belief is one of the hallucinogens that numbs the masses, so that they're not quick to revolt against their oppressors. That's what they taught us at school.

Wattmilch believes in Jesus. But he doesn't appear like a remote-controlled hostage to me, quite the contrary. But what do I know? OK, the parents of a classmate were Jehovah's Witnesses. They were confusingly against everything. Against being a pioneer. Against the Free German Youth. Against celebrating Christmas. And birthdays. And, of course, against paramilitary sports. They'd rather be picked up and thrown in jail. The Witnesses are so crazy, that I secretly admire them for it. But Wattmilch is different. He conducts himself totally inconspicuously. No one would get the idea that he's anything more than a normal guy who's doing his job.

For some reason, he reminds me of my grandfather – of his favourite record, and how when he'd listen to it, he'd thoughtfully stare off into space and quote from the Psalms: 'You see, my days lie a hand wide in front of you, and my life seems like nothing before you.' Why do people take such effort to think about things like that? Why does Wattmilch seem like he's in such a good mood every day, even though his job consists of overseeing a group of crazy idiots and failures?

'Tell me,' the leader interrupts my thoughts. 'What do you want to do with the thing, when it's hatched?'

This guy and his metaphors. 'No idea,' I respond. 'We'll feed it. Or something like that.'

He looks at me for a long time. Then he hits himself on the forehead. 'Man, you're totally clueless.'

Exactly. I'm clueless. I'm tired. Not only because it's 5.53 a.m. I'm also tired because yesterday at 5.56 a.m. I was already at the construction site. That's how it is every goddamn day.

In the morning I get up at 4.30 a.m. And I work until noon. Then I wolf down my lunch. Or I'm already on the train, on my way to Blasewitz and I wolf down my lunch on the train. I stay in Blasewitz until the evening. Three training sessions. That's my daily routine. The construction site is only closed on the weekend. So the only thing on Saturday is training. And I'm only free on Sunday. That's my life.

My little hamster wheel is always turning. And the fact that I have to struggle in this kayak on this stinking river doesn't make things better. Other people take their kayak on the lake in Brandenburg on glassy water. But I have to go out on the Elbe. It's a gigantic river, a greenish-brown brew that smells terrible. The river is a turbulent stage for daily training. I avoid maelstroms and flows as best I can, and I break my paddle on the stones in the shallow water. But my doubts are even worse than the shallow water, the maelstroms, and the stink. It takes ever more effort to suppress the facts.

I may be able to propel myself forward quickly in a racing kayak, but that will never be good enough, not even for the second tier national team. Failure. I hear my mother's commentary somewhere in the back of my mind. And her reproach is sitting there like a sardonic, grinning demon. But the coach hasn't fired me yet. I paddle against it. I torture myself for kilometres down the river, often full of anger at myself.

It was one of those days. I'm on the way home. I'm tired. Hungry. My hands are shivering and holding the pole in the streetcar. Strain and hyperglycaemia. Somehow, I drag myself from the streetcar towards my apartment, over endless crooked pavestones overgrown with weeds. In the building foyer a feeling of dizziness suddenly floods over me and I have to lean against the wall. I'm standing in the partial darkness of the hallway and even with my eyes closed, the world around me turns in circles. And in the meantime, I'm sweating and shaking with grotesque intensity.

'Can I help you?' A voice. Quiet. Friendly. I don't dare open my eyes. The nausea is only a millimetre away. The voice is accompanied by a hand and an arm. I'm led to the landing on shaky legs and sat down. It feels good.

'Food,' I finally say. 'I have low blood sugar. I need something, anything . . .'

I hear footsteps moving away from me. Then a key in a lock, close by, on the ground floor. Shortly thereafter a piece of rusk is placed in my mouth. I chew it. Then another piece. I'm being fed like a baby. Chewing and chewing. The rusk becomes a slightly sweet purée and greedily my body sucks out the carbohydrates. With that, I try to begin again. Slowly and carefully.

I open my eyes and what I see is shocking beauty. The hand and rusk are coupled to dark, almost black eyes. And curls of the same colour, shoulder-length. This girl is breathtakingly beautiful. I can at least understand that much, despite my nausea and the rusk crumbs in my mouth. And slowly I realise that in my confusion I must have ended up in the wrong building. This isn't the building in which, a few months ago, I fled from my mother in a bout of angry desperation. Right street. Wrong house. The fairy-tale princess leads me through a poorly lit door on the ground floor. Beyond the tiny hallway, a group of people are sitting in a kitchen. They're young. And they laugh.

Many of them are holding teacups, several others knit. They're mostly long-hairs. I suspect some kind of activists for flower meadows and world peace. Thoroughly trained and short-haired I fit in here as well as a wolf in a herd of summer sheep. And it occurs to me that all sorts of subversive ideas must have come together in this room. Ideas from environmentalism to pacifism. They would probably even decorate the wall with daisies if they got the chance to. If I'd listened properly at the party school, I'd know that ultimately there can only be a single system in the world. The other one, with inequality and virtual slavery. Or ours. Marx, Luxemburg and Liebknecht knew that. And Stalin too. And the people over there know it, too. So they'll come. And when they do, I don't want to stand there with daisies. Or knitting tools. I stare with squinty eyes at the long-hairs.

The girl gently pushes me onto a chair in the corner. My knee unavoidably touches one of the hippies' knees. Discomfort runs through me as if I'd slurped too-hot soup. I want to run away, but I can't find the strength. Someone hands me some tea. I hesitatingly take the cup that has something green swimming inside.

'That's a hop-peppermint-daisy infusion.' She smiles encouragingly. A strong-smelling steam wafts up from the cup. I'm definitely not going to drink this stuff. I'd rather someone had cooked all the old socks from the changing room at the training centre.

'By the way, I'm Silke.' The girl reaches out her hand to me. She's warm and surprisingly strong. She smiles. I should probably smile back now. I try to. And I sip my tea with tightly pressed lips.

What happened then? Who said what? Who did what?

I wake up the next morning next to Silke. In everything she does, Silke is relaxed and matter of fact. She likes her body. And, inscrutably, she likes mine too. At least she likes to fumble around with it. I, of course, know my body well. I know every variation of rotation and contraction. And I can estimate my pulse and my blood pressure exactly, regardless of the level of strain. The body is an instrument. A tool with a purpose. But what me and the black, curly-haired fairy-tale princess do at night (and sometimes also in the morning) doesn't have anything to do with rotation or pulse frequency. And it's impossible to calculate. In general, 'being touched' is somehow strange.

Sure, I've had other people touch me. During doctor's visits. Or during physical therapy after injuries. And, of course, in the ugliest manifestations: during my mother's beatings. Being touched, apart from examinations or injuries, that feels strange to me. With her hands, the fairy-tale princess teaches me a new, strange language. I feel exposed. Directed. Like an extra in someone else's film. It's unbelievably beautiful. Incredibly intense. I hate it. I love it. And in between I'd like to jump out of bed completely naked and run away.

April 87. Once again, I turn up at Silke's completely starving. But instead of a meal and a long hug, a really special surprise is waiting for me: a group meeting for the pre-Easter fast. Silke had raved about it to me for days, but I forgot. I repressed it. I'm so unbelievably hungry. I could eat the bark off a tree. But the only thing I get is herbal tea. The minutes pass by too slowly. And the hours are even worse. The group discusses everything that finally needs to be changed in the republic. And about recipes for herb bread and homemade butter. My stomach growls audibly, just like my teddy bear from my childhood. I'm acutely lacking about 1,000 calories. And my muscles, warmed after a good four hours of training, are making sure that this deficit matters more with each minute. I'm in pain. I'm like a starving zombie. None of the hippies in the room can sense what danger they're in.

It's 2 a.m. Finally, the last of the fasting fanatics are gone. I jump at the cupboards and start looking for something to eat. Relieved, I find the remains of a loaf of bread. I cram as much as possible into my mouth and start chewing.

'Sam? We need to talk.'

I turn hastily. The fairy-tale princess is standing in the kitchen door. She's holding onto her cup.

'What are you? But ...' My heartbeat clatters like a sewing machine.

'I'm having a child.' And she says: 'I'm pretty sure.'

The bread is suddenly a cement-like clump in my mouth, and I can't swallow.

I've never worried about protection. Silke didn't want to take the pill. And in the heat of our encounters, I was simply too insistent to use condoms. 'We'll use a natural form of birth control,' Silke decided. And with that she meant a method that seemed complicated and confusing to me, consisting of calculating the fertile and infertile days of her cycle and supplementing that with feeling the consistency of her mucous. Like a weatherman, Silke announces every day whether or not I get permission to land. 'Today you can.' Or, if I get too close during an inopportune moment: 'Today I'm closed.' But sometimes she was open on fertile days. And sometimes, despite being 'closed', we couldn't keep our hands off each other. And on those days, I get assigned a very special and awful task: pulling out. *But who am I?* In the sagas, the Greek Titans failed under much more favourable conditions. I tried it. I really tried. But, in a dangerous state of exhilaration, my urges wouldn't listen to any commands. Not to mention a few completely unplanned encounters. Long story short: we were fucking like rabbits and were relying on a wall calendar and my ability to control myself. That sounded like a really good idea.

Four weeks later. It's an ice cold, grey November Saturday on the Elbe. I rush towards the jetty with the others and in the throng. I try to get my boat into the water as fast as possible. The first people have already pulled their spray decks onto the entryway and cross the river to the other side. The spray decks are essential. They hang from a strong elastic band around the waist, like a kind of strange, orange-coloured dress made of waterproof material. The spray deck is stretched across the entire entryway and prevents the residual water from permeating the material on the back – and so you don't drown in the wave peaks of a passing boat. At these temperatures, getting water in your boat would also mean catching a cold.

I pull and tear at the spray deck but I can't get it over the entryway. I can't allow these eager, paddle-swinging super men to beat me. I won't, can't, and will not be the last comrade left on this side of the river. I finally get the orange thing over the entryway and propel my boat across the water. Despite all my efforts I am the last one, and now I have to sacrifice all my energy in order to catch up. I'm annoyed with myself.

There is a headwind, and without a bow wave I can use, it's all tenacious drudgery, trying to make my way up the river at a snail's pace. Two or three times, I chop the ground with my paddle. I have no other choice than to stay close to the riverbank to avoid the back current, but this also means the paddle keeps hitting rocks under the surface. The boat master is going to lecture me when I bring my battered paddle to his workshop. I paddle with all my strength. I stretch forward. I make long movements.

And then it happens: I get stuck between two rocks. With all of my strength on the paddle, I accidentally pull to the left side. The boat immediately responds, faster than I can. It's a goddamn racing kayak after all, and so narrow that I have to squeeze my butt painfully into the opening. This thing doesn't forgive any mistakes. I fall. The boat veers with a swooping movement and I'm in the water. The water bites into my body like an angry watchdog biting an unwanted visitor. I can't see anything but the green, cloudy broth and risk being immediately pulled under because the current inflates the rubberised spray deck like a sail.

I'm being pulled away faster and faster. Shit. Shit. Shit. I struggle. I want to get back on top. I gasp for air. On top of the water, I turn onto my back and try to push the spray deck off of my hips. In the meantime, the boat floats further and further out to the middle of the river. The water is five degrees Celsius. Maybe six. I'm in the middle of the river. My muscles are hypothermic. The last thing I had planned to do today was drown. I wouldn't be the first one the river takes. I swim and swim, filled with fear and adrenalin.

On the riverbank, far away, a long line of people are waiting at a bakery. My last bit of strength is gone, I can see more and more heads turn toward me. I only consist of cold and panic. I sink. The water is above me. I come back up. Try to fight. The three-layer, wool training outfit is fully soaked. Shirts. Pants. Everything is pulling me into the river. Shit. Shit. Shit. And then a strong rumble comes out of nowhere.

The motorboat makes a sharp turn around me. Then a hand grabs me. It's a determined iron grip. My trainer, my rescuer, is pissed off. He's beside himself. And he's right. His tirade continues when we're back on the riverbank and have fastened the motorboat to the dock. I climb wordlessly onto the dock and mount the concrete embankment. I go on and on, while my trainer's voice gets softer and softer. I'm so damn tired.

I go home. Home is with my fairy princess, with Silke. I moved in with her months ago. It felt right. Appropriate. But now that I'm frozen and half in shock, it doesn't seem to make sense any more. I stare out of the bus window and see nothing. With heavy steps I climb the small half-landing into the foyer. This is my home. And yet, I don't belong anywhere. I walk through the narrow hallway past Silke wordlessly and lay myself shivering under all over the covers.

I'm no longer a kayaker. I didn't give it much thought, I know that now. I'm also no longer a bricklayer, at least soon I won't be. My time there is up and I'll never set foot on a construction site again; I swear to myself. No kayaker. No bricklayer. No father. I can't do it. Getting up every day at 4.30 a.m. and shovel, tow and chop. And eat. And talk about dumb shit. And fall into bed. And fuck. And soon change the new baby's diaper. And have bloody dreams at night. And go pee twice.

And then it's 4.30 a.m. again; the alarm rings. I just can't do it.

'We need a name,' Silke declares.

I shrug my shoulders. Nod. Sure, I guess we do. Silke has a bunch of girls' names up her sleeve, but what if it's a boy? 'What about Samuel? Like your father.'

'Sure,' I say. And I put on a smile. But my joy is merely an old, loose-sitting tapestry. I'm a goddamn traitor, ready to desert. 'Samuel is good,' I say.

I can't bring myself to move out. And I can't bring myself to say how broken I feel. How completely destroyed and burned out. I can't even bring myself to admit it to myself. I'm a damn coward. I let a doctor give me a sick note for a week. For me, that's the ultimate admission of failure. Of weakness.

These days I talk less and less. And Silke and I don't do much, apart from a few rare, fleeting embraces. Not because the fairy-tale princess is now as round as a ball, rather because I know about my 'high treason' and I'm ashamed of it. Every evening, I refer to my 'headache' and I turn over towards the wall. I'm a piece of shit.

A week later. My sick note is no longer good. The doctor refuses to extend it. So I go back to the construction site. There, everyone is just sitting around and waiting for material to be delivered but doesn't come. Some play cards. In the background, a cassette recorder blasts frivolous Schlager.

In the afternoon, I take refuge in running. I don't run any more for kayaking. And I no longer do it to please my ambitious mother. I run, because I'm used to running, for as long as I can remember. I run, kilometre for kilometre, restless. Until I can crawl underneath the covers exhausted. I run along the football field, down by the river. And then across the bridge by the courthouse and turn right, towards the municipal precinct.

The secret watchmen are sitting there, not so secretly, on the Elbe slope visible from afar. If you dare, you can see the terraces, from the path by the meadows. There's a high fence on every terrace. And barbed wire. And on a plane between them, dogs led by long chain straps and steel cables hurry along, just as restless as I am.

I keep running along the river. Until I reach the Blaues Wunder, the old, studded bridge below the slopes. I walk over to the other bank. And from there, back towards the university clinic. I run. And run. And run.

Days turn into weeks. I roam through Dresden and the surrounding area, making larger and larger circles. I run past brand-new, desolate, grey stony tower blocks. And all the villas in different states of decay. I run past post-war barracks covered in overgrown weeds and I overtake the swaying, rumbling street-cars that struggle forwards at a walking pace on one of the many ailing track sections.

I run in the Großen Garten until I reach the Zschernitz Peak. I run until I reach Weißig, to the limits of the city and then along Pappelallee. The trees still tower up in the sky. Now it's only two minutes of easy jogging until I reach the house. I stand up high, at the top. And don't dare go back down.

Grandfather is gone, he's dead. Cancer cut down the giant of my childhood. It ate him up. I was with him, in the end. The wheezing. The fight. The waning. And now I can't come back down. It's just too much. Words can't describe how much I miss him. Even up here, I can still hear his grumpy voice. I can feel his giant hand, consolingly on top of my head. I smell the smoke of the charcoal on the grill. Somehow, it'll always be there, behind the fence.

I turn around and run away. And run back to the city; it seems to be dissolving into more and more individual parts. More frequently, I see the yellow painted moving trucks roll past me. They will cart away the things of those who are leaving. Going over there, to the West. It's been like that for years. But for months now, it feels like wave after wave has been rolling. Even our sports' doctor in the watercraft centre, who drives the Volvo, went West. He just never turned up again after his last vacation. Why would someone like that leave? He had everything. Or apparently not.

It's an overcast, unnaturally warm early spring day in May 1989. I'm walking through a park with sweaty hands and what looks like a caricature of a bouquet of flowers that I picked in the park. Towards the hospital room. Past many different rooms. Continuing past the signs, along the green linoleum floor, down the hallway.

In the hallway, already from afar, I hear his voice through the open door. It sounds like a bird that just hatched from an egg, croaking and impatient. Hungry. The fairy-tale princess is expecting me. She's pale. Seems tired. Very tired. She places the little guy in my arms. He has been sleeping next to Silke. Now he opens the eyes for a moment. They're milky and cloudy, searching for something. Barely moments after I've arranged him in my arms, his eyes fall shut again.

'What do you think of him?' Silke whispers.

Good question. What do I think of him? What am I supposed to think of him? I don't know. My son is a clump of flesh
buried under many layers of clothing. He weighs less than the
smallest block dumbbell in the weight room. He's as light as a
feather. Defenceless. What a joke. What responsibility. What an
oppressive weight.

'He's great. So cute,' I answer. I think, that's what she wants
to hear right now. Has to hear.

Strange, he feels strange, that's what I should have answered.
He's poorly put together. So small and lightweight, too. That's shit.
I should have said: *How are you supposed to protect something like
that? It's impossible! I can't do it!*

I should have said all of that. But who does something like
that, straight after the mother of *your* child has given birth? But
maybe the truth would have been less horrible than my awkward
lies. The head nurse strides into the room with a clipboard. She
smiles curtly. And compulsorily. 'So, what are we supposed to
call the little one?'

'Samuel,' the fairy-tale princess says with a hoarse voice. 'His
name should be Samuel.'

The nurse looks up to me briefly. I feel exposed under her
gaze. I feel like she's seen through me. I'm confident that an
experienced professional like her would have long realised that
I'm on the way out.

'Steve. I'd like his middle name to be Steve,' Silke says, without looking away from me.

'First name Samuel. Middle name Steve. Understood. I'll
write that down,' the head nurse says. She scribbles something
on her clip board.

Nine weeks later I move out.

II

Kids of the Revolution

Bonn, mid-July 2021

I'm sitting alone in the kitchen and staring outside. Remembering is eating through all of my layers. Through years and walls and graves. Inside and outside. I suggested we take a break, that was enough for today. The girls have holed themselves up. In the protection of a cave made of blankets, underneath the loft bed, once again they're listening to *Rusty the Knight*, their favourite audio book. It's the story about a petty, cowardly and nevertheless exceedingly lovable knight named Rusty. And about his courageous damsel Bö. Feli has gotten too big for it, but sometimes, like today, she still likes to listen reverently, closely entwined with her loved-above-all, sisterly archenemy. Sometimes we all need these old stories.

I try again to call my wife, but her number still can't be reached. Her friend lives over the hills and far away and there's probably no reception there. I stare into the rain and get worried. The city has never gotten this much water. It's like Petrus' wickedness has turned into water. A wet grave. The manholes will soon run over. Streets, paths and underpasses will then turn into tearing torrents. I stare dumbstruck out of the window. Someone up there, in the bureaucracy of the weather gods, must have made a mistake. My fingers search for my telephone. I hurriedly swipe the display, searching the notifications. The weather: rain. Nothing but rain. And otherwise *Spiegel* online doesn't report much good news. In Afghanistan, another border crossing has fallen into the hands of the Taliban. Palma, the biggest oil-producing city in Mozambique, was overrun by Islamists. And only silence echoes from the Vatican in response to the child abuse, while the newspapers are full of revelations. Fuck. There's a bit of action every day, but this? The world seems to be out of joint. Or has it always been like this that one catastrophe follows the next?

'Dad?' Feli is standing in the doorway.

'What's up, sweetheart? Not interested in *Rusty the Knight* any more?'

'That's for babies.' Feli waves me off patronisingly and sits down next to me.

'Papa, the woman you told us about. Samuel's mother.'

I nod. I wait. I know what she wants to know about the mother of her big brother.

'Wasn't she sad? And mad at you?'

I nod. Oh yes. She was. Rightly so. The fairy-tale princess was verily and truthfully pissed off. Feli is silent. We look at the rain together. Feli is probably wondering, what else she can get out of this day. Even more loot.

'Yes,' I say as relaxed as possible. But I'm nervous. I sense the old shame. 'She was very, very mad at me. I disappointed her terribly.'

Feli looks at me. Very urgently, very seriously.

'And then? Then you met mum?'

I shake my head. I have long been hooked on Feli's curiosity. Now I have to deliver. I have to remember.

CHAPTER SIX

Dresden, October 89

'We want out! We want out! We want out!'

Thousands of throats are engaged in a furious competition. If Fee knew that I was among all of these people, in the middle, she would crucify me. At the very least. I drift with an incalculable mass that pushes towards the train station. Many are bitter. Many are desperate. And many are holding hands in order not to lose each other. A woman next to me, with sparse, white hair, screams her heart out, projecting her voice. A feverish glow shines in her eyes. The woman is small and old, but her anger is big and young. And in the crowd, she is just one of many furious shapes. The turmoil of people is like a giant animal that's almost insane from hunger after being locked up for a long time. Hungry for something, that they won't get today. Or only for a terrible price.

I didn't even want to participate in this demonstration. I just wanted to watch, from a safe distance. For days people have been talking about how the trains will roll through Dresden. They're trains coming from Prague, where citizens of the GDR allegedly entrenched themselves en masse at the West German embassy. Now they're apparently allowed to leave the embassy and head West. With the train. And these trains are now rolling through Dresden. They're not going to stop, just pass through. Everyone's talking about how people are going to throw themselves on the tracks, in order to stop the trains. It's pure desperation.

I can't imagine just running off 'over there'. Running away, just with whatever I happen to have on my person. And leaving everything behind. Escaping can't be the solution. Us and the people over there, we're completely different kinds of folks. It's a completely foreign country over there. They have completely different ideas. And probably completely different dreams. The people over there, they're being led by powerful bosses. And by the large amount of assets that have been collected by these bosses. Over there, there's unemployment. Homelessness. Drug addiction. Over there is the country that devoured my brother. Lured him there and devoured him. I'm not longing to go there, to the West. Nothing that I think I know about the country on the other side of the wall is suited for motivating me to leave. In the pictures in my head, the West is colourful, dazzling and has a toxic attraction, like a giant trap for worker drones. The West, that's the great seducer. The mass of bodies carries me away.

I try to get to the edge, but it's useless. The mass surges with an unstoppable force towards the train station. A giant water fountain whips water over our heads and hits somebody further back. Then spreads out from the middle towards the left, and from there back to the middle. And then to the right. Soon a lot of the people are wet. Meanwhile, I'm standing so far to the front, that I can see the giant green metal monsters that are supposed to drive the demonstrators away. Their cold streams of water are supposed to wash the protest away from the square in front of the train station.

But it's not working. And then the soldiers march up, wearing battle dress, lined up in rows of three. Their boots stomp on the asphalt in unison. It's an immense sweeper made of uniforms. Smoke is drifting. Stones are flying. Night sticks are flying. A woman in uniform drags a giant rioting demonstrator by the feet, as if he was just a crash test dummy, and sends him flying. The guy spins around and then hits the pavement. Air escapes him with a sharp hissing sound. I'd never experienced anything like that. I couldn't have even imagined something like that. I'm rigid from fright. I want to throw up. I want to throw myself on the ground and cry.

'Hands up!' someone screams. Two or three seconds later, hundreds of people around are screaming together as if bewitched: 'Up! Up!'

They mean the train platforms on the upper level. The people on the small square in front of the train station scream and rage. A pressure that's been building up for years relieves itself. Building up for decades. All the grievances small and great, all of the affronts and the unfulfilled wishes, all of that wants to get out. The leap onto the train tracks seems like a leap into freedom, into paradise.

'Up! Up! Up!'

It is a collective need, the strongest desire imaginable, almost a madness. Out. Now. Whatever it takes – now. Someone is bumping into me from behind heavily. I grab someone's arm. Too late. I'm almost down. People are pushing and shoving, I am afraid they will simply trample over me to make me part of the asphalt, right there, in front of the station. I picture myself with broken bones, collateral damage. People are shoving. And I am thrashing desperately on the ground.

While the mob is standing still for a second, I somehow manage to get up again. I want to get away. But no muscle strength, no fitness in this world can protect me from this panicking mass around me. I keep left. I'm stuck. Propelled by growing fear, I push to the right, and finally, I succeed in forcibly clearing a path between the bodies. I stumble over something. Over someone. Get yelled at. Hurry even more. Just out. Away from here. And I manage to get out. I stumble along the fringes of the mob while suddenly it starts dissolving. All of a sudden there is no fringe any more. Everyone's running. The mob, that roaring, charging monster, evaporates and turns into a thousand individuals, so many panicking rabbits looking for their earth holes. I hit a metal bollard that I overlooked in my panicky escape. Its upper end bores into my stomach like a spear. Pain everywhere. My sight grows dim. I don't even experience my body hitting the ground any more.

And then, a thin, cold October rain is falling. My cheek and the back of my head are wet. I carefully feel around me. The wetness isn't blood. How long was I unconscious? Seconds? Minutes? My abdominal muscles might have a tear, the pain is strong. With difficulty, I squat on one knee. Finally, I support myself on the bollard. And then, while curled up, I drag myself further away from the train station. Fearful, I search my surroundings. No one notices me in any way. But I can't just sneak around here alone. Dirty and hurt. That would certainly be an invitation to arrest me.

I leave the side street and return to Prager Street. It's the biggest street in the city centre. There are people here. Many,

many people into whose bustling mass I can disappear. On this flagship street of Dresden at this evening hour, I stand out most because of the state of my clothing. To the right of me, towards the train station, is the Interhotel, fully lit up and luxurious. A distant, unreachable world with soft carpets and lighting. A world just for party functionaries and businesspeople. They've probably got their faces glued to the windows of their rooms and the restaurant and are enjoying this spectacle of the people who are tearing themselves apart.

How fast can I go, without someone noticing that I'm running away? I won't be very fast anyway with the pain in my stomach.

The pain has let up a little, and that's how I make it to the August bridge and over the Elbe after a good half hour. The more I get away from the chaos at the train station, the more my pulse quietens. I stand still in the middle of the bridge. The Elbe flows below me. To the right of me, there's the baroque silhouette of Brühl's Terraces and the towers of the castle and the Semper opera house. Crouching to my left are the tower block fortresses of Johannstadt, near the riverbank. And behind the tower blocks, the fairy-tale princess lives with our baby.

Suddenly, I have an unspeakable longing for them both. And yet I can't go back. I've single-handedly cut myself out of my little family. Expatriated. And even if I wanted to return, the fairy-tale princess doesn't want that. Not any more. She protects her little paradise, suspicious and watchful, a mother angel with her sword of flames.

It's all the same to the river. It doesn't care that in this time-honoured – but bombed and then provisionally cobbled together city – a riot is brewing. It doesn't care that on this day at the train station, someone will throw themselves on the tracks in front of one of the trains and will lose a leg. This river already flowed unimpressed into the same riverbed toward the northwest, when the city had to pay for the unleashed, bloodthirsty Führer and his madness, and descended into the fiery inferno of the firebombs. And as long as its sources don't dry up, this river will still flow through the land, when all of the people and their madness are no longer there.

I have to learn from the serenity of this river. But it's not that easy. I'm worried. I'm scared. Over there, on the other side, Neustadt is waiting for me. The ruinous old district of Dresden, the rundown stepchild of the city planner that they're allowing to rot, because all the poor resources are being pumped into the fancy, newly built tower blocks in the test-tube cities of the green meadow. Places without a history. Without a soul. But they're necessary, if the people aren't going to completely lose their beliefs in socialism and its blessings.

Increasingly more tower-block UFOs land in the wasteland around Dresden, while Neustadt has been practically given up. With all of its townhouses and their provisionally patched, often damaged roofs. It's common to encounter roof trusses that are partially collapsed and the house beneath it irretrievably rotted. Neustadt, those are the cracked, sooty facades. Those are the warped, swollen window panes with the colour peeling off. And the backyard with overgrown weeds. Neustadt is doomed. In these decaying piles of stones you find the authority of all those who don't properly belong. That's where the '249ers' live, the 'workshy antisocials' and the ex-convicts. And the eternal troublemakers who stir up the people with their complaining and their concerns. They're joined by students who can't find a room anywhere else. And artists, of whom many would rather live on the margins of society and pursue their art, rather than moving into the tower block fortresses. And me.

By every conceivable standard, my life is a complete disaster. I failed at my sports career. My relationship is in ruins and my child is growing up without a father. I didn't get a new work contract after finishing my apprenticeship, instead I received a warning notice because of the 'danger of antisocial behaviour', including a summons. Just hang around? I wish! I'm not even capable of that.

My mother's voice is breathing down my neck. 'Failure, you're a failure! Whoever doesn't work shouldn't eat!' By the time I show up for the meeting, where I'm supposed to promise improvement, I've long since found a job as a warehouse worker. The work is only half as difficult as on the construction site. And it's dry. And the pay is enough for an apartment the size of a shoe box with an old coal oven, for which I can't find any coal, and which has a tendency to spit out stinking, black clouds of smoke when the autumn wind presses against the roof vent. The toilet is located at the end of the hallway, on the half landing. The little window is just a placeholder without glass and the toilet is correspondingly draughty. The job at the warehouse is a killer. Every day the monotony burns away entire fields of brain cells. This work is something for braindead chimpanzees.

In the end, I enquire about something in the 'Barn'. That's what we call the cultural centre across the street from my apartment. As it happens, the comrades there are looking for an assistant. Someone who doesn't have to know how to do anything and isn't afraid of getting dirty. They put on theatre at the Barn. They have readings. And there are a lot of live concerts featuring East German bands. And naturally there are also LPs.

There I schlep tons of beer crates here and there. And wine crates. Or some other crates full of stuff. Or I clean the floor after the events are over. I pick up the garbage from the stairs and the courtyard. Or I plunge the toilets filled with vomit. Or filled with rolls of toilet paper. Or both. In exchange for my work, I get to eat in the cafeteria. And my pay is a little extra pocket money.

But somehow, it's enough. I don't drink. I don't smoke. I don't pray. I work. Train. And read a lot. While my country holds its breath. Between all this, a haze of change wafts. And then this October day and this night happened, at the train station.

'I wanted to take your picture today. Where were you?' Fee asks. Reproach resounds in her voice. It's got late. And in all that chaos I forgot that we were supposed to meet. Fee is what you could call a friend to me, if I wasn't so fiercely and very secretly in love with her. Fee is a lot of things. She's a photographer with a brilliant eye for details. And she's a mathematical genius. She's just finishing her Abitur, a year before the standard time. In addition, she's also taking some courses at the university. Maybe she's some kind of *wunderkind*, maybe she has two brains or something. In any case, she is so busy with everything that she doesn't have time for anything else. Like for a boyfriend. And definitely not a maths dud like me.

I know Fee from an event at the Barn. Fee was allowed to take pictures there. And now and again she took photos of me, without asking and always with a cheeky grin on her lips. I wasn't sure if I should rip the camera out of her fingers, or just look away shyly. But no one in the world can stop Fee. She takes photos of everything that happens in front of her lens. She takes pictures of dead pigeons that lie on the pavement with bizarrely twisted wings in front of the Barn. She takes pictures of the little piles of garbage at the foot of the solders' monument, in front of the intersection. And she takes pictures of all the toothless guys that stare out of the ground-floor windows like ghosts. And today she wanted to take photos of me. But I wasn't there. And maybe I subconsciously thwarted our meeting. Sabotaged it. Because I don't like photography.

All these photos are illusions. I know that from photos of my father. In one picture, he sits there smiling and in love in the park, right next to my mother. And a little later he's dead. But no, you can't change the photo any more. Death outsmarted the photo. I don't want to be outsmarted. I don't want time to laugh at me, because it created another reality a long time ago. A different reality than you can see in the pictures. I only had a photo-father, a dead one. His example is a warning to me. That's why there are hardly any pictures of my childhood, besides the ones to which my mother dragged me. They are, of course, tall tales documented by a time catcher. Lies about a well-dressed, happy boy that never existed. Fee is staring at me. First without comment, but it doesn't stay that way for long.

'Why don't you want to take some pictures with me?'

'I just don't want to. I always look like a fat hamster in those. Or like a serial killer who frequents his favourite café too often. The one with the butter cream cake.' That is nonsense, but I can't tell her that I'm afraid of the photos.

'You're not fat. And in my book, there's not the slightest indication that photos make slim people look fat.' She gets quite upset over my sheep-headed stubbornness. 'The area of the square over the hypotenuse is the same as the sum of the surface area of the square above both catheti.'

I shake my head. Is she really telling me the Pythagorean theorem right now?

'What does that have to do with the photos? I just don't want to.'

In the meantime, Fee has a swollen carotid artery. 'It's about logic! About the laws of nature. The earth isn't flat. Rain falls from the sky down below. And photos don't make people look fat.'

I shake my head again.

'How can someone be so pretty? And yet so dumb.' Fee smacks her hand against her forehead. Pretty? Why pretty, I'm not a girl. No one has ever said that to me.

I smile, embarrassed. What does she like about me? She knows so many people, many more interesting ones. In her apartment there's a regular hustle of people who are so enthusiastically and doggedly crazy about her art as she is about maths. I meet musicians there. Theatre people. And self-proclaimed professional revolutionaries. And usually, I only understand a fraction of what is spoken about and lectured about on those long evenings. And all the chewed-over shit in their heads didn't really interest me anyway.

But Fee sees something in me. She's like a drill at the dentist. She pushes through the rotten part until she gets to the nerve. Goddamn Fee. I don't need any female friends. And I don't need any butterflies in my stomach. And I don't need any secret ones, because then I don't run the risk of being rejected.

Goddamn Fee. Goddamn logic. Goddamn photos. And yet, her belief in me isn't without effect. I write on old newspapers. I write with gnawed-on pencils and some pieces of paper. And, of course, I write secretly. It's just scribbles. Just scraps of thoughts. Bits of something. Only a few sentences long, not even that. One could hardly call it prose. I've always written. Doodled. Always in secret. For fear of my mother's malice. And the malice of my German teacher. Both were fiery fans of socialist realism and they have no interest in my childish, scrambled texts.

Goddamn Fee. I had thought I had left writing behind me. I throw a lot of the texts directly in the oven, some of them a little later. I seldom keep anything. I'm ashamed of all the emotional alphabet soup.

> *Hold me, when I fall,*
> *Hold me*
> *If dark clouds come*
> *And the waves carry away the land*
> *So far.*
> *Hold me, when I fall.*

Goddamn longing. Goddamn Fee. Ultimately, I let her take pictures of me.

'Did you hear what happened at the train station? Someone fell in front of a train. Horrible!' The camera clicks.

'I was there.'

'Where?' Fee puts the camera down. She wrinkles her forehead.

'At the demonstration, at the train station.'

This will cause a fight. Maybe I want this fight. Maybe I need this fight. Fee's face changes colour in a fraction of a second. She's beside herself with anger. 'Have you completely lost your mind? They bagged hundreds of people. And no one knows where they took them.'

I shrug my shoulders. I know she's right, but I'll never admit it. Not for gummy bears and not for cookies. 'They trampled some people to death in front of the train station. That could have been you!' She's mad as hell about so much carelessness. 'Do you not care about any of that?'

You! I want to tell her, *I care about you*. But feeling something and saying it out loud are two different things. I want to, but I can't. But Fee can and she wants to. She wants to talk. She wants me to do more than just relief work in the Barn. She wants me to take a walk with her. She wants me to stay away from the upheaval at the train station. She's such an adult. So organised. And now she's angrily walking back and forth. In the middle of the movement, her step remains in the air. And then this sentence comes.

'I was in Berlin.'

'Why?' I'm confused.

'There's a church there. They secretly make flyers.'

'Excuse me?' This can only be a joke.

'I have some with me. I brought them.'

I don't know what I should say.

'Will you help me distribute them?' she asks. Just like that, as if she was talking about chocolate for children.

I feel dizzy. That's even worse than going to some demonstration. I stumbled into that. But Fee wants to participate in a conspiracy! My conditioned brain is rebelling in the shrillest colours and tones. You don't resist. You don't revolt. At least not if you can avoid it.

'Stop!' I hear my mother call. 'Sam! Stop it now! Go to your room!' Fee wants to be part of a rebellion. I should say no, I don't want to be a part of something like that. No, no and once more no!

'I hope they don't catch us.' My voice sounds hoarse, strange, like the voice of someone else. Inside, I smack my hand against my forehead. How dumb can you be? We're all going to end up in jail. Or even worse, in the basement of the secret police. We go outside. It dawns. We walk together in the rain down Alaun Street, the trashy, cracked main artery of the neighbourhood. Fee tells me about the 'Democratic Beginning', that's the group that she wants to support with flyers from Berlin. *Democratic Beginning*, that sounds like it's been dreamed up. By the SED. The Socialist Unity Party of Germany. Sounds official. Totally uncool, but official. Democratic Beginning. It sounds like the hobby club of some crazy people.

'What do they want?' I ask Fee.

'They want something to finally get moving again.'

I look extra dimwitted. 'Get moving? So are they some kind of new training collective?'

'You're an asshole. You know exactly what I mean.' Fee makes a vague movement with her arms. 'It's like everything here is dead. Everything here is eternally standing still.'

Tell me something new. I've known that for a long time. That nothing is moving, and everything is falling apart. And the public pronouncements are getting increasingly absurd. It's like in Tarkovsky's 'Zone'. Just as beautiful, and just as broken. Fee reaches for my hand.

'Let's try to keep the good things alive. And we'll tear down what's bad. And we'll make the ugly things beautiful.'

I stop dead and stare at Fee. I'm stunned. This girl says such crazy things. Things that throw me out of my eternal rut. Sometimes I could just start to cry. She should go and be with the poets, not me. And yes, she's right. Of course. It's our home. And it should be full of life. Colourful. And full of progress, technology, and stuff. And everyone here should want to stay and not leave.

I stare bewildered at Fee and her clever words. Ravens are circling above us, looking for something. Fee and I have walked in a giant circle. Down Bautzner Street and then left, towards the city library.

Somehow, we've arrived at the army museum, that giant chunk made of grey stone. No one is up here. The area is empty. These restless days probably don't provide the best occasion for visiting a museum. And definitely not one that's surrounded by Russian tanks. Even if these glowing, army-green monsters won't be able to move their steel anywhere any more. They're old. They've been placed here as a memorial to the last great battle. Fee leans against a base. The rain has stopped, but the remaining drops make the metal shine and shimmer surreally in the last minutes of daylight. Fee keeps her eyes on me. Then she wordlessly takes my hand and pulls me to her. Fee leads and I follow. The kiss is little more than brief contact. And yet it's a kind of mathematical proof. It can't be refuted.

'We're going change everything. Do you understand?' No, I don't understand it. But I still nod. 'Are you with me?'

I would sit on the tip of a cannonball with this woman and let myself be shot to the moon. I would do anything.

'Sure. I'm in.' My words sound more like a despondent, evasive whisper. And Fee isn't convinced. 'I'm in. Really.' I quickly follow up. Fee examines me with her gazes and ultimately nods. And I have no idea what's going to come.

CHAPTER SEVEN

In Fee's attic room there's a tiny desk. I'm sitting there and writing. I admire the world. And I'm also organising a club. Because, these days, not just the wall is coming down. For me, life with colour blindness is also ending. I am who I am. I can no longer deny that some ex-comrades are extremely displeased. Suddenly it seems to bother a lot of people.

The reactions on the street range from grim, unsmiling faces to overtly hateful looks and the hissing of slogans. I should run away. I should leave. I'm just a dirty n—— . . . At first, I consider this to be just ordinary day-to-day resentment. And sometimes a joke. After all, I've lived among these comrades for nineteen years without any of this. Maybe it's a virus? Or a kind of mass psychosis. Or the result of food intolerance that has simultaneously affected many people at once? But unfortunately, the problem seems to go deeper and it's not disappearing into thin air or being solved by complacency.

There have always been dumb comments, but socialism expected its citizens to have solidarity with the oppressed of the world. And because the state didn't express any sense of humour towards the attitudes of its workers and farmers, we were all colour blind. That how I grew up. I was protected through the party's position. The party had iron brooms and men in uniforms who knew how to swing them. And that's why I could walk around my hometown at every hour of the day and night unaffected.

That's over now. The wall is in pieces, the party is gone and their former uniformed authorised representatives are suddenly occupied with their own survival. And that's why I'm sitting at Fee's desk and that's why I'm spending the time and trouble to found this club.

We, those who can't be overlooked without the state-imposed colour blindness, have to take our livelihood, our survival, into our own hands. We, who were born here. And Angolans. And Mozambicans. Vietnamese. Algerians. Some Caucasus Russians. And all around there are also those who just want the world to be a flower meadow. Want the world to be just. Without the stupid hatred from another century.

So, out of necessity, I have become the midwife of a multicultural club that is meeting in the Barn in November and December. There, Russians are crouching next to Vietnamese and Africans next to Afro-Germans, and they are naturally surrounded by the pale-faced indigenous population. The few benevolent ones.

The collapse of the GDR affected the contract workers the worst. Now they are officially unwanted, and consequently, fair game. Most of the businesses are on the brink of ruin. They don't need any more foreign stooges. No one cares where they will work in the future, where they'll live and what they'll eat. And angry parts of the core workforce let their resentment out on their foreign colleagues. There are threats and fights. Many of the 'borrowed ones' are packed on to collective flights and sent back to their homeland.

Others hurriedly pack their few belongings and hide in West Germany.

'Help, please? You help, yes? Write letter, please.'

At the end of a meeting, someone behind me is tugging on my jacket. I turn around. A small, dark-haired man is standing there. One of many desperate Vietnamese worker drones that they're trying to get rid of. One of many from the 'socialist brother state', who are now afraid. Of deportation. Of poverty. Of misery. Now because of his fear he's turning to someone who's also afraid.

How can someone like me help? I lack all qualifications for the surprising end of my world that's just arrived. Regardless of this fact, I soon climb the stairs of a seventeen-storey apartment building at the edge of Johannstadt. It smells like cat piss and oil that's been reheated one too many times. I'm wearing my only shirt, freshly ironed. And carrying a briefcase that I borrowed especially for this day. A briefcase always seems important; it shows empowerment. Which is something I don't have and that's why poor people have to pretend.

There's a Vietnamese woman waiting in the living room. And a Vietnamese man. And their Vietnamese baby. The baby is dressed in just a nappy and seemingly has no worries, because he's sleeping on his mother's shoulder.

'Help, yes?' says the man who spoke to me in the Barn. I clear my throat. Both of them look at me. They think I'm now going to tell them what they should do.

'Dear comrades,' I start, out of habit.

The host nods at me expectantly, I'm supposed to keep talking. But I have no idea what I should say. More Vietnamese people come out of the room next door. Five. Six. Seven. Excuse me, how many people live in this shoe box of an apartment?

I open my briefcase. Inside there is a yawning emptiness. I packed a pen and a few pieces of paper. I can't think of anything other than passing out writing materials, so everyone can write out their names. I promise to write a letter to the officers responsible. But who in the hell is responsible here?

My hosts have smiles frozen on their faces. I think they can sense my embarrassment. I sip the lemonade made in my honour. At the end, I sneak away with my briefcase, completely sweaty, heading back towards Neustadt.

Next day, I write to the local office of the FDJ. The district office. I know someone from my school days who knows someone there. Back then, the FDJ guys never really had anything to report. But they have connections all the way at the top. I can't think of anything better. Weeks later, I get a friendly answer. Meaningless. They support my issue, they have solidarity, they'll see what they can do. The whole thing gets lost in the sand. Quicksand, I think. We are all sticking in quicksand.

The wall is gone. The FDJ is even more meaningless than before. The party, dissolving. The security on the streets, gone. But now we have white bread as soft as paper and disgusting sweet nut-nougat spread.

Fee infected me with her dream of hip socialism. A just world, without old stubborn rich men and the many hunger songs beneath them. A science fiction world, with food concentrates from vending machines. A world with talking computers. Flying cars. And to repair illnesses, you put people in healing machines. That's what Fee dreams about. But unfortunately, that's not what people want. The republic is bleeding out. The tower block fortresses are emptying like a carton of milk in which some bad-tempered person has stuck several large holes. A young hippie guy, a Neustadt resident like me, whom I met on the margins of a band performance, takes me back to his tower block. He needs someone to help him carry something. I have no idea where he got the key to this abandoned apartment. The whole undertaking makes me feel queasy. Is it his parents' apartment? The guy doesn't want to talk about it, but he moves through the rooms like he's familiar with them. In the corner of the living room across from the kitchen, there are two neatly arranged breakfast sets. Ceramic bowls next to oatmeal. And spoons. Big. Cups of tea. With small spoons. The fridge hums. On the kitchen window, a fly is crawling until it gets to the top. Then it falls back down again. The fly starts again. It wants to get out, I think. Everyone wants to get out. Get away.

I open the window and cold autumn air flows into the kitchen. Behind me there's a scratching sound. I spin around, but there's just a black cat in the hallway. A tiny, skinny thing with white markings. She's staring at me angrily. The owners of the apartment have disappeared, and they left the cat here. She arches her back and hisses. Her black fur bristles. The cat is visibly angry about her owner's betrayal and now she transfers her understandable hatred to anyone on two legs. But at the sight of the hippie, she meows heart-warmingly. The hippie picks up the cat, while I use a laundry basket to carry a super modern looking record player and a truckload of records out of the apartment. The hippie carries the cat almost like a baby, hidden beneath his jacket, wrapped up in a cloth. Now the apartment only belongs to the ghosts.

*

Fee and I defy reality. We don't want to give up our dream of utopia. We are still hoping. We go to one of the last Monday demonstrations at Fučík Square. We get there late, the atmosphere is heated. A speaker named Dr So-and-So from the Ardenne Institute is trying to convince the people gathered there that a fast unification is the wrong way. It would be a real 'the-shit-hit-the-fan' moment. There's a threat that the entire East German market could be destroyed. Millions of people could become unemployed. We should wait. Be patient. Ten years. Even better fifteen.

But the crowd doesn't want to hear that. The crowd boos and rages. It's not long before they drag the poor doctor off the stage and beat him up. Fee points to the flags. On the edge of the demonstration there are some imperial war flags waving. These red-and-black things didn't escape me. And the ones carrying them didn't either. And if that hate-filled, bo-wearing army and these flags prevail even once, God help me. I know a few different skinheads and other variations of these 'neo-somethings', from Neustadt, of course. I know them from the concerts of different ska bands. And from their drunken nights running through the neighbourhood. But these flags, this is new.

'Look,' says Fee and she shows me a small group of policemen.

They're standing far away at the edge and seem as if their presence there is unpleasant to them.

'Why aren't they doing anything?' Fee asks.

What kind of question is that? What can five old men do against an army?

'They should protect us! Goddammit, why aren't they doing anything?'

Fee wants to go over to the policemen and talk to them. But I just want to get off the street. I want to crawl under my blankets. And shut out the world.

Fee is someone who is rising up. Every day is new. I'm someone who's sometimes just happy that I was able to experience what the evening had in store. And didn't kill myself. 'This woman is out of your league. She's too good for you,' a familiar voice from my childhood whispers to me. 'Too good for you. Just forget it.' See, there he is again. The eternal complainer. Inappropriate and unwelcome. I'm no longer a little boy. And there are no windowsills at dizzying heights in my life either. But my love for Fee is a sufficiently high abyss into which I can plunge. I'm so angry. I'm so lost.

The neo-something is now part of the normal cityscape during the day, too. The vampires are bound to the night for longer. Or to the weekends. They have acquitted themselves from this spell. And the well-behaved, demoralised citizens applauded them. The mayor denies the problem on television, while his Commissioner for Foreigners, just a few rooms down, expresses warnings in front of the assembled press cameras. Whoever is visibly foreign, should no longer leave the house after dark. The mayor rages and denies, but his servants are right and he's not. The most everyday activities have become a kind of Russian roulette. Even the way to the sweet shop, 150 metres up Louisen Street. Neustadt is now an urban combat area. Every night someone is lying on the streets. Every morning there's blood on the asphalt. And on the pavement and in building corridors. Fear lives with all of us in this quarter.

*

Sometime in March. Another concert in the Barn. It's the usual colourful motley crew. At some point I make my rounds through the hustle, searching for something to eat upstairs in the kitchen area. Even here it's completely full. Even the band is making the closed glass doors of the bar vibrate. One of the office ladies pushes herself, annoyed, through the guests in my direction. She gestures and indicates with wide open eyes downward, towards the ground floor.

There is complete chaos. Someone is pressing a tissue against someone else's forehead. It's soaked in blood. I find Dirk, the director of the Barn, in the crowd. I gesture with my arms and try to get his attention. Without success. The director disappears through the main entrance, heading outside.

Outside is where the vampires of neo-something are waiting. They are standing crowded together next to the short rise to the main path. They build a mumbling, dark mass. And their shaved bald heads are glowing like polished bowling balls in the twilight of the streetlamps. Someone throws a bottle. It scuttles past me, a tumbling shadow, and breaks on the building's facade in a thousand pieces. A joyful hoot resounds from the group of vampires. The people over there, they're not all from here, I'm sure of it. In the group there are a lot of West German dialects. Shit squared.

I don't know any of their faces. I haven't encountered a single one of them as a guest at a concert. I've never leaned one of them against the wall of the club, when they were lying around totally wasted. I don't know any of them, they don't owe me anything. And Westerners have a devastating reputation as roughnecks. They're even more fanatic than our own problem children. I turn toward the door. The door seems like an abandoned entrance to a bear cave, overgrown and tiny. There is no one behind me who could help me. There is no one behind me at all.

On the first floor I see countless faces against the windows but outside with the monsters, it's just the director and me. In my head, the complainer is already howling gloatingly: 'You're gonna die, you dog. Now you're going to die. And before that they're going to hurt you really badly.' Dirk tries to talk to them at a distance. He wants to stall until the police come. If they come. But these days that's highly unlikely. Behind me something moves, very close by. I swirl around. My fear is pushing the adrenalin through my canals. My heart stings like after an electric shock.

Behind me, it looks like Hannes just ascended from the small area of grass in front of the club. A blessing in disguise. It's just Hannes. He recently joined the staff at the Barn. And he's like me. Or I'm like him, whichever way you take it. His father came from Africa to study, too, and then fell in love here. Hannes was born in the GDR. Shaped, educated and drilled. A model GDR citizen. Well, now he's a citizen of nowhere. Hannes helps out behind the bar. And recently, since the office ladies have more frequently been dealing with difficult clientele while selling tickets, Hannes is more frequently at the door, just like me. He's nearly two metres tall and where normal mortals usually have a throat, he has a neck shaped like an anvil, a block of tendons and muscle strands. Hannes was at the sports school, too. A wrestler. A bull. A machine. He tried to teach me some basic terms from wrestling. That was a nice gesture. I barely survived the workout though, utterly exhausted, and completely demolished.

Unlike me, Hannes is a real man. He talks and dresses and walks like a real man. I, on the other hand, just play the role of an adult. Deep down inside, I'm still a boy. I want to watch the clouds. Jump in puddles and play with sticks. I want to run around the houses screaming. The only thing that stops me is fear of the stares from real adults. I admire Hannes. If I had something like a best friend, he would be it.

Dirk talks. Hannes and I keep a short distance behind him. The vampires are staring at us. Apparently, they reckoned with a lot of things in the Barn, but certainly not two exemplars like us. With shaved heads like them. Well-trained. And maybe we remind them a little of Teofilo Stevenson, the gigantic Afro-Cuban Boxer who regularly destroyed his white opponents. Everyone in the GDR knows Stevenson. And we probably look the same anyway. Regardless of the reason, the unquestionably superior troop don't immediately proceed to execute their plans, they discuss first. My knees shake and my teeth chatter like an army of woodpeckers at work. My panic is all-encompassing. But I'm still standing. I don't fall to the ground. That's my only accomplishment.

'Eh!'

The shout echoes down Alaun Street. A hard voice, clearly used to commanding.

'What's going on here?'

The voice belongs to someone in a field service suit. The tattooed vampires make room for him, as if they were just some fifth formers in the school yard of the big kids. The guy in the military suit appears to be a policeman, but the guy is wearing a beret and doesn't at all look like the national guardsmen, whom I'm used to running into. It's as if someone put a clone of Hannes in uniform and told him to look evil. The furrowed look on his face is the only thing that betrays his age. He could truly compete with any Shar Pei. Is he sixty? But that's not possible. Not with that body. I squint at Hannes who shrugs his shoulders.

'You're gonna get out of here now. And I mean immediately.'

The Shar Pei says it quietly. Behind him, several car doors open with a rolling ratchet. Now I see it too. There are three Barkas vans, and hooded figures are climbing out of the vans. What are those helmets they're wearing? Parachuter helmets? I once saw something like that in a magazine for soldiers, in a report about parachuters. Parachuters in Neustadt? Is this twisted logic from a minister who's decided this is the way to save the city?

'Billy clubs out!'

The command that the Shar Pei shouts makes me wince. Like a perfect group of synchronised swimmers, the hooded figures pull black billy clubs out of their vests.

'And now I'm gonna tell you one last time: disappear. Immediately.'

I can already hear a kind of cold boredom in the Shar Pei's voice. And a threat. The vampires don't have long to decide. Their group starts to dissolve. Backing away, stumbling. Then running. Apparently, no one wants to be the last one there. No one wants to find out what the giant in uniform will command his small army to do next. Not a minute later, we're alone with him, as if the whole thing never happened. The giant turns to Dirk, Hannes and me. There's a hint of a smile on his face.

'So, good evening, everyone. My name is Müller.'

He tips the short end of his beret.

'I'm sorry to say this, but I need you all to fuck off, too. I don't want to have anyone on the street. We have other things to do today.'

Hannes and I look at Dirk. Dirk looks at the man in uniform.

'In a straight line.' That's what Shar Pei-face says, almost like a father to his children and he points towards the entrance. Dirk, director and boss, just grins, turns around and strolls into the Barn. Hannes and I follow him obediently. I can hardly believe my luck. So there is something like a merciful God.

A few weeks later. It's the birthday of the crazy, moustachioed Austrian and for that reason, a welcome big drinking day for all the young men who are neo-something. It's not a good idea to be out on the street in Neustadt. Because today, it's just a question of time until the drunk hordes show up. That's why Hannes and I hire ourselves out as roadies at a concert at the Junge Garde, the open-air theatre in the big park. That's the Central Park in the heart of the city. Some popular, crazy Western band is playing. The Garde will be full.

Sweating, Hannes and I schlep stuff onto the stage and the technicians screw it together. As far as I'm concerned, I would like to be done with everything, then I could return to the security of the mansard. I think about Fee's embrace. About the smell of her hair. And how we lie in the room under the roof slope and this wonderful warmth flows out of the tiles of the oven. But Hannes wants to at least watch the first part of the concert.

The band is highly praised but I'm not interested in their punk crap, and hope for some variety. Maybe they know some tricks, have a fire-breathing dragon or let long-bearded dwarves with war hammers come on stage. I hop on the spot. Hop up and down. Marking time. And this wet, April cold. Disgusting. The band has barely started their noise when unrest begins in a few different spots in the audience. Next to me, a student is bleeding, and moans. Her companions desperately call for help. The darkness lays a diffuse veil over the scenery. I turn around several times. What's happening here? What's wrong? Hannes and I are standing way up high in the stands. He hurries to the left. I move to the right. My steps search for steps in the semi-darkness. Fear is affecting my balance and coordination. I start to slip and land halfway on the floor. I am rattled. Hannes is far, far left in the stands. Between us, there's a fine-grained curtain of rain. And I finally see it.

Tiny shadows flicker across the wall. Someone from outside is throwing stones into the ground. Big ugly pieces. I rush. I trip. There's a boy who's lying on the ground. My hand reaches down below, grabs a damp leather jacket. I pull my hand back immediately, but that's not blood stuck to it, it's vomit. The guy has thrown up. He's giving off a really bad smell. I leave him on the floor and press my way through the exit. Bam! Somebody knocks into me sideways. I fall. In my panic I immediately begin to struggle and roll onto the floor. Someone above me starts to stammer apologies and runs away.

'I'm sorry. I'm really sorry. Really. Really.'

Then Hannes is suddenly towering over me. He has perfectly mastered the art of appearing out of nowhere. He's probably secretly a magician. In the meantime, the vampires are everywhere and nowhere all at once. Someone is jostling with someone else. Hannes pulls me to the left toward the main entrance. Yes, run. Away from here. Just get away. A policeman is even standing around near the trees. This has to be a goddamn joke. A single man? We're still running in that direction. When we reach the man in uniform, I'm astonished to recognise that he's a former classmate.

'Rico?'

Some things have zero probability. This is definitely one of those things.

'Sam?! Dude, what are you doing here?' Rico stares at me.

I point to Hannes. 'We helped with the construction.'

Rico keeps staring. We haven't seen each other for years. I could just as easily have introduced him as Santa Claus. 'Here, come away from there!' Rico pulls me around the corner. Hannes follows. And then suddenly we find ourselves in the middle of a déjà vu. Those uniformed superheroes are back, the ones from Neustadt. Confusingly, they're wearing new field suits with police badges. But there's no doubt about it. They're the same ones. And again, there's no more than two dozen of them. And all around us a strong, bloodthirsty enemy is encroaching. But at least the comrades have their fearless leader with them, the one with the wrinkly face. He stares at us for a moment, incredulous.

'What are you two idiots doing here?'

Once again, we're in the wrong place at the wrong time.

'They're OK.' Rico pats me on the shoulder. 'I even went to school with him.'

Pacified, the wrinkly face nods. 'Just don't get in the way. Understood? We're going in now.'

With that, the man in uniform points to the dense vegetation that surrounds the open-air theatre. In the darkness they look like a wall of black and grey. The man must be joking. Or did I misunderstand something? I pull on Rico's sleeve.

'They're far too few,' I whisper in his ear.

In the meantime, the first hooded ones disappear into the darkness. They're like ghosts. But this wasn't just a few drunk nutcases on Alaun Street. This was several hundred vampires in bloodlust. You could hear their bawling and howling in the darkness. Their combined strength appeared like a gigantic meat grinder. What are two dozen men supposed to do about that? Other than collectively die by suicide and have a nice state funeral?

'That's the ninth,' Rico says. As if there wasn't anything more to say. He pats me on the back, like an old man overwhelmed by traffic.

'That's the ninth. Don't worry about them. I'll explain everything. Come on, I'll take you both with me.'

He gestures to the police car. Hannes and I jump into the backseat. With its tyres crunching against the gravel, the Lada starts moving forward. We roll across the narrow path, then to the right. A blinking avalanche comes toward us. I stare at the police lights until the end of the avenue. It's an endless row of trucks.

'That's the riot police. They have too much stuff and always take forever,' Rico says. So the cavalry is finally here after all. We roll slowly past the column, down the rain-drenched street, towards the city centre.

'And the ones with the weird helmets?' I want to know. These guys saved my ass twice. 'Who are they?' I have to know. I must. I must. I must.

'That's the ninth!' Rico says, as if that would explain everything. But in my head nothing has been explained. The ninth of what, please?

'They're the secret ones,' Rico follows up. 'Anti-terror and the like. They're sitting over there, on the Neustadt side.'

I'm perplexed. 'They're part of the Stasi? I thought they'd dissolved. Are you one of them, too – part of the Stasi?'

Rico groans. I probably broke through the idiot sound barrier. 'They're police. Special units. Like the Russians have. And I'm certainly not one of them.' He laughs out loud, almost frightened by the idea. 'I only brief them. That corner belongs to our precinct.'

We've reached Neustadt. Rico kicks Hannes and me out. Hannes shuffles off. And I go home, still with a grumbling in my stomach. There's a punk girl with fiery red hair crouching at the corner of Alaun and Böhmische Street. She's buried her face in her hands.

'Everything OK?' I bend down to her. She flinches from me, as if I had a contagious disease. My shoes probably still smell unbearably like the vomit I accidentally stepped on.

I think about the hooded ones, sent into a fight outnumbered, a fight they can't win. They know the cost and still they do their duty. They stand their ground. That's my simple and naive understanding of the word 'heroism'. I still don't comprehend how so many sacrifices need to be made in these stories, when it's reality writing them.

I sneak up the stairs, into the roof. Fee is already sleeping. I'm as quiet as I can be. We don't have hot water; I still fill a bowl. I soap my head, my face and skull, the familiar smell calms me. Florina soap. Florina cream. I wash the stink of the Garde way. Those men, who supposedly are fighting a losing battle. I can't stop thinking about them. Probably because I'm the exact opposite of them. Frightened. And rushed. Prey. I can't keep living like this. There must be some hope. Some morning. My path must lead somewhere, it must have some kind of goal. There has to be something beyond the fact that everything in my world is falling apart. Disappearing. And apparently the only ones who care and who are still fighting, who are standing their ground, are the hooded ones. I have to find out what they're made of. And how they were able to ascend, far away from any fear.

I run away from Neustadt. It smells like early-morning fog and the rest of the night. The street glistens newly cleaned, black, and moist. I run and run. And as I run, I'm as weightless as someone like me can be these days. The Military Substitute Office is only about two kilometres up the hill. It's a run-down, old grey building. At the entrance, a uniformed officer crouches behind a high counter. The man has a carefully fed, round stomach and a thick pair of glasses. With his moustache, he looks a lot like a walrus.

'Good morning. I'd like to report for military service.'

He stares at me and doesn't say anything. His gaze is full of warmth, just as if I was a blood-smeared storm trooper from our West German class enemies. Who can blame him. No sane person marches willingly in here.

'Good morning,' I say again. 'I'd like to apply for a position in the riot police.'

The man in uniform opens his mouth and closes it again. His mind is clearly working behind his furrowed brow.

'Why?' The walrus growls, more bored than annoyed.

I know that Rico's path is the way. That's the only way to come to the ninth. First the military service. And then you become a career soldier. As long as you perform well, your bones can hold out and you don't fail the psychiatric test.

'Just don't say anything about the ninth,' Rico warned me. 'You're not even supposed to know about that!'

So I answer the walrus as imprecisely as possible.

'I want to become a career soldier at the Ministry of the Interior. Someone told me that for that I must complete my military service at a police precinct with a barracks.'

The man in uniform sends me to a wooden bench nearby. I sit down, as commanded. The walrus makes a phone call. His accent belongs to the Prussians. The pretentious Prussians who always know better and were eaten up by the conceit of the capital city, they are the natural archenemies of all Saxons. I really shouldn't let someone like that tell me anything. But fuck it, you can't always be picky. The man is ultimately the doorman to paradise. He's on the phone. Intense and short. Then he slams down the phone and dials a different number.

'Hmm. Yeah, a special case, Comrade Captain.'

Pause, the walrus listens to the voice on the other end.

'Hmm. Yes, that's what I thought.'

Pause. Listening.

'I already called him, Comrade Captain. He sent me to you.'

It goes back and forth for a while. Then the phone call ends abruptly. I sit on the hard wooden bench. I wait, as commanded. The walrus flips through a newspaper. I sweat. No one comes into the grey building. No one goes. The whole thing takes minutes. I'm sent to the captain. He wordlessly presses a piece of stamped paper into my hand.

Two days later I have a draft notice in my mailbox. With that I come back and go down the endless hallway of the grey building. From room to room. From question to question. A man in a white coat feels around on my balls and makes a disturbingly content face. After my testicles are praised, I'm classified as fit for service. I'm inspected. What will Fee say about this? I don't want to imagine it. I don't want to think about it. This is what I wanted. There's no turning back.

CHAPTER EIGHT

'Uh-uh-uh! Uh-uh-uh! Uh-uh-uh!'

Those sounds over there are no longer human. They are like an organism that has grown out of a thousand bodies, and with one single goal: screaming. Spreading fear. It's an angry, stomping, amazing collective. A violent horde. And it has a big problem with impulse control.

I've only been with the riot police for a few weeks and still fresh from the shortened basic training. Even so, I've already been sent on an operation. Over there, in the guest block, craziness is waiting. The horde is jumping up and down. They scream and scream, just a damn stone's throw away from me. I'm on the empty stands of the neighbouring block, kept free for expendable fresh meat like me.

Dresden and soccer, those things have always evoked big emotions, violent ones. And today I'm experiencing that live for the first time. The game surges back and forth. And soon the final whistle will blow. Leipzig can no longer catch up. That's great for Dynamo, of course, but when the game is over, the beatings afterwards will be all the uglier.

Our barracks are half empty. Many of the guys just aren't

showing up for duty. Why should they keep fighting for a country that soon won't exist? All those still here despite that are the dumb ones, the lazy ones, or the idealists. Too dumb to see through everything. Too lazy to take off like the others. Or just too idealistic and naïve to want to cop out of duty. Just like me. This entire mission is one big pile of bollocks. They put us in nice uniforms and dress shoes and fit us with some shields and billy clubs. The term 'billy club' being an indulgent euphemism for these black, shiny, bendable rubber sausages.

I'm nineteen and together with other nineteen-year-olds I'm manning an empty block. The opposing group is throwing stones over our heads, right in the middle of the indigenous population. The poorly aimed ones naturally hit us. There's a short, ugly 'tack' sound. And that's when you know that a stone hit something. The veterans warned us. It's no coincidence that internally our shields are called 'mission-cookies'. If they get hit really hard, they break apart into many different pieces, and then you're just standing there holding the handle.

What a fucking miserable situation. Our platoon is a long thin line, from the edge of the field to the edge of the stands. A single train, against hundreds of young men with a lot of enthusiasm for having a good time, it's just ridiculous. The only reason the group from Leipzig doesn't climb over the fence and make their way through us to the enemy is because of the comrades from the Trapo, the transportation police.

They're still standing a few metres behind us. And thank God they're not standing there alone. To be honest, their involvement is causing me just as much of a headache as a relief. The comrades from Trapo have their crazy police tools with them. Some would call them dogs, others demons, or whatever these creatures from Frankenstein's laboratory were supposed to have been. They are certainly monstrous, bulky, curmudgeonly beasts as big as horses with necks like steers. Using a giant schnauzer as a police dog is one of the many peculiarities of the GDR. The horde from Leipzig doesn't climb over the fence. These battle-tested veterans certainly aren't afraid of our platoon of clowns in uniform, I'm sure of that. But they're afraid of the dogs. And that's why the comrades would rather move to a safe distance and throw rocks. Tack. Tack. Tack.

Then the whistle. Violent cheering. Dynamo Dresden just became the second to last champions of the GDR premier league. No, actually the last. Because by the end of the next football season, there won't be any GDR. That already seems as certain as hearing 'Amen' in church.

We gather outside, in front of the central gate. We, the B-company. Second platoon. Eighteen amateurs. Eighteen very young conscripts and an officer. We all have fear in our bones. If that was just the warm-up round, what on earth is coming now? In the meantime, we're all running on panic, except for comrade Hemmerle, the former competitive judoka in our unit. Hemmerle is calm. He's waiting for whatever comes. And they come quickly.

First you just hear a rumbling behind the curve, followed shortly after by a wall of bodies. Shoulder to shoulder. Pressed together so tightly between the stadium wall and the railing that it appears like one single human clump, with many arms and legs. The clump isn't running. It's also not sneaking away. Instead, there's a constant, scraping, screaming shoving forwards. Our chain is becoming a descending line. And it's beginning to quickly dissolve. To the left and right of me are gaps.

I hold on to Hemmerle. And finally, we're standing there alone. Suddenly no one is there. No B-company. No second platoon. Just Hemmerle and me. And only a distance of about eighty metres separates us from the many-legged, many-armed screaming mass of hate. We could still run away. We still have a chance. But somehow Hemmerle doesn't make any moves at all. And I hold on to him. We really are two spectacular idiots. And as such, the meat grinder would certainly allow us to ascend to Manitu, after a short, painful death. What saves us are the were-wolves camouflaged as service dogs of the Trapo. They jump against the hostile wall of people. They don't growl, they don't bark, they have a mission to fulfil. A few people running in panicked haste, tripping and screaming, break away from the mass.

Then everything is over.

The country is dissolving increasingly faster and whoever still hasn't left or quit their service, is being deployed somewhere messed up.

Our sergeant is a man with a soft voice and a big drinking problem. Probably also a marital problem. I never found out which one came first. On weekdays, Uffz wears a troubled face with yellow colouring. A pale, troglodyte face, even though he can't be much older than we are. Uffz is our compass. He tells us how things operate when he's not too drunk. Apparently, Uffz used to give dreaded training sessions, a hail of facts like the onslought from a machine gun. Rattatatam. Now he talks in a confused way and takes a lot of unnecessary breaks, often in the middle of a sentence. Then he looks out of the window onto the tree crowns of the main avenue in front of the barracks.

Uffz is a nice guy and somehow terribly broken. We drag ourselves through the days with him. The weeks. We march.

And march. And march some more. We jump into a truck. And jump out again. We set up tables in the company hallway and take apart our weapons to clean them as fast as possible. And put them back together again. And then do the whole thing again from the beginning. Again and again. And we learn that we can only go out when all the usual crap is done. The checks on the bedsheets have to be perfectly lined up, as if they'd been set with a ruler. The things in the closet have to be stacked vertically, with smoothed-down folded edges. And our buttoned collar bands shine snow white. Even before the weekend, our company floor glows with wax polish. External order is an expression of internal discipline. Yes sir. That's what Ufz teaches us, if he happens to be sober again.

For me the most important thing is that they let us race. We run across the storm track. We run wearing sports clothes. We run in our field service suit. We run in the wobbly, squeaky rubber skin of Hazmat suits. We run with and without gas masks. As long as I have to run, and climb and crawl and march, it's easy. I can do that. Sweat. And consume the pain. I don't like the pain. But the pain helps me be in the here-and-now world that I don't have to feel any more.

The company is a home. A family. Here no one makes any kind of jokes about me. Here there are only comrades. The neo-something that is so popular right now naturally also has numerous guys in the barracks. But for them, I'm just someone who has to eat shit with them every day. Yes, in the barracks there are a lot of vampires, but they're all colour blind here.

Somehow, I contract the flu, with a fever and everything that comes with it. In slow motion, I walk towards the bathroom, down the company floor. And I can barely do even that. The doctor on location gives me a sick note. I'm supposed to rest, lie down in bed. Theoretically I could leave. I could go to Fee and lay down next to her. Theoretically we're still together. Somehow. And even this 'somehow' has become vague over the past weeks. Fee hates the cops, the common life form of 'le flic'. In mathematics she keeps things in strict order, but in society she prefers anarchy. 'The benefits of living righteously without rules.' First, she dragged me to this lecture to all the wannabe hippies. Then we yelled at each other in the mansard. We hacked away at each other. Fee wanted to talk some sense into me. Her sense.

This beautiful, clever girl is adored by more long-haired students than some boy groups are by their teenage fans, and it would seem that my basic capacity to 'have feelings' is really crap. I can hardly summon up enough reason not to go up in flames twice a day out of sheer jealousy. Love and reason have little to do with each other. All kinds of little things make me snap. Fear. I carry this fear around with me every day that Fee could leave me. Fee is a woman; she has the needs of a woman. But the sense of butterflies in the stomach isn't enough for her. She wants to feel love like an adult. And it's exactly that that I don't know anything about. Fee wants to live. But my goddamn fear turns every moment into something fearfully unpredictable. That's the way it is. Love is stressful. Love is longing. Love is doubt. Love is wonderful. Love is saying goodbye. The latest visit to Fee's ended with doors slamming. And she probably would have liked to spit on me while I went down the stairs. *Le flic*. She hates me.

So I stay at the barracks during the weekend and sweat out the flu. And sleep. If the others even let me sleep. There's constant unrest in the hallway. Twice an alarm for the DHE, the duty unit, is triggered. This goddamn tramping and running around. That's just the way it is when the city is burning. They can still let the duty unit fly to the front. But even that becomes more and more of a piece of art. Our barracks is barely half full. There have been masses of terminations and illegal departures. Why not, since they can't be prosecuted by anyone? We are the last, unplanned offer to a dying republic. The great collapse has suddenly made us 'heroes of work'. But maybe we are also just a band of idiots who, like a pirate troupe without a captain, have to steer a sinking ship.

After the fever, I return to my usual routines. Running. Crawling. Marching. And on afternoons I go to the mess hall, just like today. On the green, mossy surface in front of the car workshop, some guy is doing somersaults in a field service suit. Cracked rollovers on concrete, the guy clearly isn't of his right mind. I like that. I remain still and treat myself to the performance. It's a comrade from the staff company. After he has rolled around enough on the floor, in all possible acrobatic twists, and brushed off the dirt from his field service suit, I go over to him. The comrade appears happy, like a circus clown after a successful high wire act. When the clown looks up, I immediately snap to attention.

'Sergeant Meffire. B-Company. Second Platoon, Chief Constable, Sir.'

The other guy waves me off. 'Come, forget it.' He reaches his hand out. 'I'm Udo.'

'I'm Samuel.'

'You and your friend, you're the two idiots who didn't run away, when the fans from Leipzig were rioting? Are you dumb or just stupid?'

So word has got around about the action in the stadium. 'I'm definitely both', that's what I'd like to say, but I'm afraid to. Instead, I ask, 'What were you just doing there?'

Udo grins. 'The fall school from Gjogsul.'

'What?' Gjogsul? Never heard of it. Comrade Udo might be making a joke at my cost.

'I'm not messing with you.' As well as doing somersaults, Udo can read minds. 'That's a North Korean technique.' I'm confused. North Korean? Everyone here has been condemned to learn police jiu-jitsu.

'Aren't you from the staff company?' I ask. Udo nods.

'Are you doing something else there?'

The comrade grins. And waves me off. 'No, in the staff company we're doing the same as everyone else. But I used to be in the ninth. And they do Gjogsul.'

My jaw drops. Comrade Udo was with the ninth. I can hardly believe my luck.

'You were in the ninth service unit? Crazy!'

He waves it off.

'No, not in the service unit. They're in each district. I was in Potsdam-Eiche. With the ninth People's Police on-call duty.'

I've heard as little about that as about the service unit.

'They're set up for anti-terror missions,' Udo explains. 'Just like the Russians have.'

He scrutinises me for a moment, noting my obvious enthusiasm. 'If you're so eager, just apply.'

He makes a grand gesture towards the company building, the parade ground and everything else. 'It's over here anyway. Do you want to be the last one, to turn the light off?'

Udo's right. Everything here really is going down the drain.

Even the weapons are getting picked up. Just last week we loaded up a truck with hand grenades and RPGs and other stuff. And then they took it all away.

'It doesn't have to be Potsdam,' Udo says. 'Just apply here in Dresden.' He shrugs his shoulders. 'What could happen? They have completely different problems here.'

Why not? The worst they could do is say no. *Whoever does what he already can, always remains what he already is.* This saying hung in a wooden frame over my grandfather's drafting desk. Apparently, it is a quote from that grand duke of capitalism Henry Ford, but that didn't bother my grandfather. It goes through my head when I'm lying in my bunk at night.

The district authority is a giant stone block near the Elbe. It has the charming charisma of a promotion for the Nazi capital city Germanic. I shyly go through the main gate and leave my official paper on the counter at the station, a form, stamped and signed by the company boss himself.

The post sends me to the first floor. On the left side, an armoured door is awaiting me. Next to the door there's a keypad for the access code. Under that there's a doorbell. I press it. Shortly thereafter, the door opens a narrow crack.

'Constable Meffire at your command.'

I stand my ground. *Just don't do anything wrong. Don't screw anything up.* A giant blond guy is leaning against the door. He scrutinises me for a moment and then waves me inside, ignoring my announcement. Inside, a long hallway stretches out, with blank sealed floorboards. It looks like the director's floor of a construction company.

'Whaddya want?'

'I want to apply.'

'For what?'

I start to hesitate. Well, up here. Or is this the wrong secret floor? The wrong secret unit?

'Well, I thought . . .'

The blond guy's eyes now look threatening somehow. Shit. It's not going as planned.

'And who the hell told you we're up here? He must be crazy!'

Now I'm sweating like crazy in my uniform. Bloody hell. What am I supposed to answer?

'I'm just fucking with you! Sorry.' He takes a swing and I duck my head. Then his first just lands on my shoulder. 'You should have seen your face.' The blond laughs and laughs. What a wanker.

'Come here. Sit down.' He pulls me through a door and pushes me onto a chair. 'So the idiots from on call send you here, even though they know we're knee deep in shit.'

The blond scratches himself between his raspy short hair.

'This is all a huge pile of shit. Huge.' He stares through the blinds outside. 'They're shutting us down. Ah nonsense, they're shutting down the entire People's Police, the entire goddamn fucking authority.' The blond lets himself fall into the chair with a crash. 'The cowardly assholes up there are afraid of the press.' He wheezes with indignation. 'And if a single citizen-revolutionary calls "Stasi" in our direction, then we have to duck and run away.'

I don't have anything sensible to say, so I keep quiet.

The blond points to a file on a table, partly turning to me.

'I read your evaluations. They're good. Under normal circumstances, we could slowly train up someone like you.' He shakes his head. 'But now, under these conditions? Nope, you can forget that. Currently we can't do anything, big guy.' He closes the file and seems suddenly tired. 'The assholes are transferring us,' he says quietly.

I'm shocked. I don't understand, I really don't. Now and again, I hear that no one can respond to emergency calls because there are no forces are available. And then something like this. I keep quiet. I have no answers. The blond falls silent too while he scribbles on a piece of paper.

'Were you in the guard in April?' The question just pops out of my mouth, totally unplanned. The blond looks up from his paper.

'Of course I was there! What a giant pile of shit!' He shakes his head. 'How dumb can you be, organising a punk concert on Hitler's birthday? And having it at the damn open air stage . . .'

'And before that, on Alaun Street, were you there too?'

The blond looks across the table, assessing me. Maybe he thinks I'm a press informer or something. But I had to ask. I had to get it off my chest. I've been carrying it around with me this entire time and I had to get it out.

'I was there, too.' I fight back a lump in my throat. 'Thanks!' I can't choke anything else out. The blond visibly relaxes.

'Go to Potsdam,' he says and then he looks down at his scribbles. 'Nothing is being done here. Next week we're being sent to the airport. They'll probably let us search for explosives in the underwear of some vacationers.'

He reaches his hand to me to say goodbye. 'I'm Frank Luger.'

Luger. Like a pistol. I'll remember that name.

CHAPTER NINE

'Medic!'

I shout again with all my might. 'Medic!'

Rotschopf is lying on the floor in front of me. We're at the kiosk, the small store on the corner with the gunshot windows. Rotschopf got hit in the abdomen. His field service suit is coloured dark brownish and is dripping wet with blood. The air is filled with thick, biting smoke. I have no idea where to look for cover. Maybe over there near the bank? Everything looks blurred in this damn smoke. Near, yet somehow not. The bank is probably much too far away and I won't get Rotschopf over there. Rotschopf is bleeding and whimpering. I hold my handkerchief on his stomach, my jittery hands can't get anything else out of my combat pack.

Rotschopf is getting increasingly worse. Fuck. We're taking fire from the right. I think. I grab Rotschopf under the arms, I'm too worried to carry him away on the stretcher. Not in his condition. His guts would probably fall out of his stomach. Walking backwards, I crash into the door of the nearest apartment building. Outside I can hear stomping. Very close. I put Rotschopf onto the stretcher after all and pull him up the stairs, onto the next floor. I have to act fast. Upstairs, I collapse to the floor. My breath rattles like that of an old grandpa.

'You wanker,' Rotschopf whispers. 'I'll get you back for those stairs.'

'What do you want, asshole? I saved your life!'

Downstairs, someone enters the hallway. Boots are creaking and scraping on the stones, pieces of glass and dirt. I kneel, half hidden by the corner, and take out my weapon for the attack. The boot noises get closer. I check the safety. It's on single fire. Better leave it that way. Ammunition means survival. Ammunition is precious. So single fire. I can't miss.

Tack. Tack. Tack. It fires. Three times quickly one after the other. I've been hit. From behind, in the back. Shit. I'm dying.

Rotschopf sits up and looks suddenly upwards. I turn my head and follow his gaze. Up above, Uffz is standing above us and is smirking down at us. A ceiling panel is missing. Us idiots are standing in the exact same house where Uffz had been hiding.

'Are we dead?' I ask.

Rotschopf doesn't look happy. He takes his hands from his stomach. 'Probably.'

End of the simulation. It's over. Oh man, was that embarrassing. My first day in the SKO, the city battle object, not far from Potsdam. I actually managed to get myself transferred from Dresden to Potsdam, and then during the first exercise I nearly grind my partner half to death. And I overlook a hole the size of a football pitch in the ceiling and let myself get shot. From behind. What a disaster.

We've been practising the bloody chaos here for hours. We're practising the rapid advance in the West. In a serious case, during a war, they would drop us off near our destinations. They would load us onto a helicopter and let us fly into the West under cover of night, to avoid anti-aircraft. They would drop us off at city hall. At the airport. Or at the radio station. Officially this is an anti-terror police exercise, but someone forgot to change the script. And the setting. We're simply practising the good old Blitzkrieg. And urban guerrilla warfare. How weird.

I lean against the wall and slowly unscrew the cap on my canteen. Just a few hours of practice in the summer sunshine and I'm already as thirsty as a donkey. And sweating like one, too. Thank God this unit won't fly to West Berlin any more. This unit has already been sentenced to death, just like the entire republic. I finish my water and don't think about anything else.

We return to the barracks late. The Ninth Company building is fancy, but it smells like harsh cleaning products and body odour. It's the typical smell of a men's changing room. And for me, it smells like home. Gymnasiums. Weight rooms. Barracks. Good places. And this place even has excellent bunk beds too. After crazy full days, I sleep like a baby. Running. Marching. Lifting dumbbells. Gjogsul. Handling weapons. Without a sharpshooter. Everything is repeated. And repeated again. And repeated again, in endless sequences. Until it's coming out of your ears. Until it's sticking in every fibre of your being. And in every movement. Elite? That's just another word for a continuous loop. You always do the same things in the same way. Again and again. Numb, that's what they call it here. Elite means being numb, beyond any imaginable level. Numb, that's the best method. At least for what's awaiting us; us poor crazies. Numb is a recipe for surviving. Tired. Hurt. Mangled.

They're flying these guys somewhere. And no film music accompanies them. No trite commentary from off screen.

Everything here is to prepare for the ultimate of all tests: urban warfare. The fight in apartment buildings. War in its ugliest forms. After a long day, I lie on my bed on my floor and don't have to think any more about fighting. I don't have to think about home any more. And not about the river or about Neustadt. I glide into the merciful darkness of the dream magic forest. I don't miss anything there. I don't miss anyone there. Not even Fee. There, I'm safe from her.

I'm standing at the window of our room and looking across the sports grounds to the pines. Bare, high trunks. With juicy green needles up top. Last night was only a respite from homesickness. I long for home. To be near the river and in the mansard. I miss how my grandfather's back towered above me. But I especially miss Fee. She's like a familiar body part that's now missing. That damned woman removed my heart from my chest and left a gaping hole behind. I curse her. Her closeness. Her smell. Her laugh and her embrace. I'm standing at the window of my room and staring at the pines, over there, behind the sporting grounds. I stare at the pines and cry.

The Ninth Company building is a highly secure breezeblock full of weapons. But none of these weapons mean anything any more. The republic is over. The company will be dissolved, everything will be over with reunification. Many won't be kept on. 'Too close to the system.' It's once again this beautiful, convenient killer phrase. And this unit is plenty 'too close to the system.' On the old red wax seal of the armoury you can see the stamp 'Ministry of National Security' very clearly embossed. But there are no agents working here, all these guys are policemen. More accurately, they're professional athletes in uniforms. I've met neither Stalinists nor spies in the company, but these apparently easily provable details don't matter to those making the decisions. And public opinion doesn't care either. This unit is subordinate to a myopic kangaroo court. No witnesses will be heard. No files are seen. No lawyer files a petition for a new witness. Everything happens without practical reason. And without justice. That's how cheap the betrayal of heroes is. The end is coming. We run, march and crawl as usual. And we laugh about our stupid jokes and grin like Honigkuchenpferde in our bowls, to deflect from the filthy grins on our faces. Free of any nutrition or taste. We're crazy. We must be crazy. We run, march and crawl. And eat this stuff. And act as if it were nothing. Whoever comes here, wanting to join the ninth, will get lost in something greater than normal life. And get lost in the community that's born in pain and rises from there. Soon that will all be forgotten history.

Uffz tears open the door to the room.

'Meffire?'

I jump out of bed and to attention. His gaze is hard, as usual. Shit, what have I done wrong? What did my little pea-brain forget this time? Thank God my ass is attached, otherwise I'd forget that and leave it somewhere.

'Someone is at the station.' After a short, icy pause he adds, 'For you.' For me? Why for me? The situation is becoming more cryptic. 'Meffire, we're not a hotel. That's not what we're running here, understood?'

'Yes, sir.'

Now I'm really in trouble. And apparently no clue what this is about. Bloody hell.

'The lady is asking if you could come down briefly. We don't want to make her wait, do we?'

A lady? What kind of lady? I want to sink into the floor.

Uffz has barely left the room before I start running to the station.

It's as if a cornflower has been lit up by a torch. I'd totally forgotten how blue Fee's eyes can be. Fee. Fee in the barracks. I think I must be seeing things. Fee. Living and in colour. She seems small next to the washhouse and the tall fence, absolutely tiny.

Yesterday I lost a canine tooth, during training. Bam. Hit. Out. My lips are really swollen. And the debris is still hanging in my mouth. I'm embarrassed. Fee has travelled halfway through the GDR and I look like a beaten up clown.

'Come home,' she says.

She doesn't say any more. I reach my hand out. I know that now three guys have their faces glued to the window of the wax houses. And I don't care. Whatever. It doesn't matter. Fee takes my hand. I'm lost. I'm rescued.

'Forget all of this. You belong at home,' she reiterates.

A tear forms in my eye. It rolls down my cheek and leaves a long, wet trace behind it. Fee raises her hand and rescues the small, salty expression of my feelings.

And for an unreal, impossible, unlikely moment, time stands still. The earth hardens in the middle of its revolution, and the birds freeze as if they're glued to the sky. The trains stop rolling. The patter of small talk finally shuts up. So does the collective of eternal nagging voices in my head. And for a moment it seems like everything could turn out well.

CHAPTER TEN

Adolf Hitler lives. I know it, I can hear him. He's standing next door in the kitchen and clamours. 'On 30 January, 1933,' he shouts with a lukewarm voice, 'when I moved to Wilhelmina Street, I became deeply worried about the future of the Volk!' The Führer is getting warm. 'Truly,' the man rages. 'Truly, we may be able to do more than any other generation to appreciate the pious meaning of the saying "What a twist by God's providence!"'

Then a door squeaks. Footsteps creak on the hardwood floors. The Führer appears. Under his arm, the uninvited guest is carrying a cassette player, East German, SKR 700, Star Radio brand, nationally built by happy indigenous people and lovingly called 'Star'. The Führer's hair is hanging tired and disorderly; it hangs down from his head, parted on one side, in keeping with the style. He's only wearing a bathrobe and the front is regrettably open.

Fee sleepily rubs her eyes. The first thing she gets to see this morning is the Führer's private parts framed in blond hair. Poor Fee. Before the guy can raise his right arm for a Hitler greeting, I fling a pair of my underwear in his face. Fee tries to hide under the blanket. Too late; the Führer sees her grin. He gives her a hurt, yet also lustful glance, but then he laughs dirtily and shuffles off.

I can't make sense of him. Is he just an upper-class kid gone astray? Or simply a well-educated person who hates people? And if so, what would this fact make me? A tolerated pet? Either way, I don't deserve any compassion. It's my fault. No person in their right mind with my background would get the idea to ask the Führer for asylum. But I look for refuge among familiar evil so often. I returned home from Potsdam broke. My small amount of pay was quickly gone. So I turned to the Führer; after all he used to be my old bricklayer buddy. He's now living in the ruinous, damp rooms of the attic in which Fee also has an apartment.

Since our stint on the construction site, the Führer hasn't become any less eccentric. His taste for interior design is bizarre. Tattered black fabric serves as makeshift curtains, and he painted the walls the same colour. Every square centimetre of this room seems like the waiting room of the undead. The Führer is the Führer, after all. Full of hate and garbage and a spirit of innovation. That's why the Führer needs a bespoke door. All day, he saws and drills and screws. The result is impressive, in a weird way. The door has been reinforced by thick boards and sheets of steel and anchored in the masonry. It can be locked from the inside, too, with metal bars several inches thick. The entire building would collapse before anyone could gain access to the Führer's abode uninvited. And no, I will never find out what our universally beloved Führer is so afraid of. Maybe his paranoia is more alarming than the modified door. We know all too well how the paranoia of the original cost the lives of millions of Jews.

Well, what am I supposed to do? The closeness to Fee is perfect. And I can be happy that I don't have to camp down in much worse circumstances. With my mother, for example. The Führer and I, we've got what you could call a normal flat share between guys. Tidying up and cleaning? No way. In the kitchen, the garbage is piling up between dirty dishes. And the overcharged compressor of the ancient refrigerator rumbles the most. It hums desperately to maintain a set temperature. But perhaps its despair also relates to the yawning emptiness within.

Autumn 1990. November is cold. The Führer and I stray through the neighbourhood, searching for some briquettes. Without fuel, we're going to freeze our asses off this winter. We're unemployed. Most businesses in the city have problems. Many of them are closing different departments or closing altogether. It appears to be the ugly, extremely real effects of the hurried monetary union from the summer. First, I didn't understand the connection, but the Führer explained it to me.

'So, I'll limit myself to a strong simplification,' the Führer lectures, graciously and condescendingly. 'The target market of East German production, and this shouldn't come as a surprise even to a dim-witted Black guy like you, was the East. So Poland, the Czech Republic, Bulgaria, Romania, Russia, etc.' While he says that, the Führer gestures to an invisible map on the kitchen wall. I nod obediently. I can follow him so far. 'That's over now,' he explains. With a dramatic movement of his hand, he makes a vast sweep over the non-existent map.

Now I no longer understand. Do they no longer need our stuff in the East? No machine tools? No trucks? No computers?

'Why is it over?' I dare to ask.

'The problem is obvious,' the Führer determines. 'In the East, they were suddenly supposed to pay for our goods in German Marks overnight. They couldn't do that. So they stopped the trade.'

'Huh?' My response is as mindless as it is unnecessary. 'Why?' I just don't understand it.

'What do you mean "Why"? Those are very poor bastards. They need our stuff, but don't have any hard cash. And it just won't work for them to keep exchanging wares for wares. Our new fat cats have made sure of that.' The Führer grins, sure of victory. 'It's called capitalism, my little brown bunny.' Aha, that's why no one in this fucking city wants to hire anyone. That's why there's an endless line at the unemployment office, as if they were giving out bananas and Western chocolate for free.

I stare at the invisible map flabbergasted. The Führer likes my facial expression. He conjures a small, round piece of cheese from his jacket pocket and lets it disappear in his mouth. 'Bon appetit,' he says smacking and grinning and marches away somewhere.

After a few weeks of little food and much cold, I find a job after all in a home for the disabled. Fee approves of my small achievement. It's Easter Saturday and I've sneaked across the landing to her place from the Führer's apartment. Fee smells like sleep and Nivea cream, and of what we shared with each other last night. How did I deserve this? She's avowedly into the type of guy who's a permanent student, androgynous and with long hair. I, on the other hand, look like weightlifting orc, and I prefer to read Soviet fantasy, instead of Hesse. Or Kant.

'Today,' the Führer screams over there, suddenly and ecstatically, 'today I can speak to the first parliament of Greater Germany!'

Lord in heaven. Will this poor nut never get tired of this number? And yes, his Greater Germany is now reality. Already, months ago, planes set course for the city. But instead of bringing firebombs and death, they brought German Marks. In tons. Dresden longed for the raid. It has spent the last several months in feverish anticipation. The revolution is over. Our utopia of a renewed country, of a refurbished, real socialism is dead. And people like Fee and I, who gave themselves over to such hopes, have become anachronistic remnants. We've disappeared together with our dreams. Aged in a time lapse. And we're foreign in our own city, among all of these people, who wanted something completely different than we did. The country of my birth has been erased from the map.

Who am I? Or what could I be? And for what? The People's Police has been dissolved together with the GDR. I could have tried to join the new West German police, but somehow I no longer have a reason for it. Day after day I experience something that proves Laurence J. Peter to be a prophet: 'In a hierarchy, every employee tends to rise to his level of incompetence.' Some resurrected former comrades give examples of this in their words. In their posts, they cause maximum damage with their inactivity caused by being overwhelmed. You could have just sat blow-up dolls or trained monkeys at their desks and no one would have known the difference.

For weeks, the vampires have been organising their witch hunts in the city for people like me. Nevertheless, the comrades in the ministry responsible for this stand in front of the cameras and deny that there's any problem at all. I probably don't fulfil their definition of a full human being. Why make a big to-do over us? For a few 'barbarians'? And so one dark day turns into another. One awful day follows the next. How gladly I would drag these apparatchiks from their air-conditioned bureaucratic palaces and light them up.

Outside it's getting serious, outside it's the endgame. Dresden had become the pilgrimage site for sociopaths. The hate-filled beings of the underworld rush at the command of their dark master. It's as if Sauron stood on the castle walls of Barad-dûr and called for his Orcs. Scar-faced guys flood the city and it is impossible to confuse them with my roommate, because they're the complete opposite of a harmless Führer clown. These are organised in groups, brigades and districts. They even have their own intelligence service, named 'defence'. And they've long been buying Kalashnikovs from the retreating Russians. And grenades. And explosives. The ministry guards are enthroned in their palace with a view of the Elbe but do nothing, except deny that there's even a problem.

Earlier, the skinhead thugs trained in the gym of the district authority of the secret police and they got their assignments from there too. They were told exactly whom they could beat up and whom they couldn't – and when they could do it. Punks. Goths. Peace apostles from church groups. Vampires got their official assignments and marched off. Admittedly, they were free agents of the state security. Now no authority keeps them in check. They only listen to their dark, hate-filled leaders and the lowest of their depositions. In this new end-time these killers move through the streets and neighbourhoods without restriction, as if the city were their own personal safari park.

Despite my fear, I head to a giant school gym several times a week. There, I train karate, dressed in stiff snow-white pyjamas.

Together with many other people, I indulge in Far Eastern martial arts, sweating and wheezing. It involves of a lot of things that I already know. It's about speed, endurance, and pain. The training leaves a trace of dark blue bloodshot bruises on me. And I love it. Just like I love the dull musty smell of the gym. And all the shouted commands. It's a world of discipline. A world of clear, irrefutable rules and certainties. And it's a world where I can pay with pain in order to belong. And while I am soon rising to be a secretly admired world champion, every night I sneak out of the gym to the bus and the little boy inside me hopes desperately that he doesn't encounter a mass of monsters. Karate is a perfect antidote to boredom, but it only partly helps control my fear.

I turn off the Main Street towards the fire station. Training has completely destroyed me and spat me back out on to the street. I look forward to a cup of tea with honey and my bed. It's another 200 metres to my house, when alarms are set off in my head. There's something up ahead, in the street. I immediately slow my speed down to zero. It's another 150 metres to my apartment building. But I estimate about sixty, maybe eighty metres before I reach the crowd. Up ahead, in the street and on the pavement, there's a lot of people. People who shouldn't be there at this hour. And among these people, a figure staggers around, it's briefly visible before it disappears in the crowd again. In the twilight of the streetlights the scene seems shadowy, blurred. I stand frozen to the spot. My stomach gets lumpy, turning into a round stone. And the sports bag is hanging from my shaky body like a half-full sack of coal. Shit. Shit. Shit! That's a mob up front. A mob and its victim. I recognise her. It's the punk girl with the fiery red hair that I met on the street on my way home from the Junge Garde. That's her, isn't it? It would be hard to confuse that fiery red hair, even in this light. I'm almost tempted to raise my hand and wave at her. The girl falls to the floor, suddenly there's a hail of hits and kicks. She screams, she's just a small lump on the street, with a fiery red tuft of hair just above the asphalt.

Seven or eight shaved heads move back and forth as if in a wild pogo dance and around the girl. They're jostling and pushing each other and they're competing in bloodlust. There's another girl too. She's not lying on the street, rather she's dancing around the redhead like the other vampires. She has this typical peroxide coloured, feathery cut hair. The vampire girl pulls the victim by her red hair to the edge of the street, towards the kerb.

No. No. No. I have to get away from here. I know what is coming next. I have to get away. There's a wall that runs along the building where I've stopped. I stagger over there. Then I vault across two metres of stone into a dark courtyard. There's a wall on the outside. And a wall on the inside. Cross. Shimmy and run. They taught me that in the barracks. How to overcome obstacles through movement, taking fortified positions. I can do that. But it's not enough to help those poor creatures out there. For that, I'm too cowardly. My pulse is beating wildly. I lean against the wall. Choke. I throw up whitish froth onto my trainers. Then I steel myself. Keep hurrying. Up. Up. Up. Keep going up the stairs. Close the door.

The Führer isn't here. I don't turn on the light. I listen in the darkness. Kerb biting. That's what they taught me. The head is dragged to the pavement. Then the teeth are kicked out. And I left her to the monsters. Guilty, that's what the accusers in my head cry. Guilty. Guilty. Guilty. My cowardice is exposed. The accusers celebrate. They won their case. And only a few metres down, there's more cheering and back-slapping. Until the voices recede. Joking. Bawling. Happy.

It's quiet. I should go and look for the girl. But I can't. I want to, but I can't. I should help the girl, but I'm just crouching there, in the dark, dirty kitchen. And no power in the world could bring me to go back onto the street.

Next morning, it's hard to believe what happened. I risk going to the street corner, but the girl is obviously no longer lying there. There was a girl, but she's gone now. I suck in some air. Cry for a bit. And then I go to the baker, who's a block away. That's life. It keeps going. I keep going. Because that's what you do. Even in the leftist-anarchist dwarf state CRN, the Colourful Republic of Neustadt. One questions this basic principle whereby the CRN is some kind of progress. There must be progress, for all our sakes.

Half-smeared chalk lines on the street mark the borders of the new republic. One can hear Beethoven and ska roaring from the residents' open windows. And without further ado, an old lady repurposes her ground floor apartment into a sex shop. Playing children romp around. Barefoot students in colourful skirts swaying to the beat down Alaun Street. There are cryptic performances and theatre in the courtyard, and bars in cellars and illegal cafés. The smell of barbecues and marijuana wafts over everything. The republic of four streetcars has written FREEDOM on its flag. Liberation from a dreary atmosphere. Liberation from bans over what to think and what to do.

We all repress what's in store for us, what's coming. We don't allow any thoughts about a new age of slavery. An age of slavery and the rule of the few. And what last night taught me was that in the new, improvised republic, the vampires will still hunt their prey and tear them apart. What kind of a new, just freedom is that? Freedom without security? Without peace? Without protection? To me that seems to be another worthless fiction.

These four streets of self-empowerment will soon cease to exist. This limited freedom of the communards will be short. This light will soon go out, we all know that. And that's why everyone contributes so the remaining time is filled with life, up to the pain threshold, up to the edge of what's bearable. Fee is even wearing makeup, contrary to her usual habit. And she dances playfully with her friends down Alaun Street.

They dance until the next morning. And naturally without me. Fee only comes home after the day has ended. She smells like smoke and alcohol and strangers' sweat. While I, the fearful one who doesn't dance, wait around here in the mansard room, leaning against the oven. Jealous. Fallen out of the world. No one cares. Not even Fee. And why should she? It's my fault, my fear, the collective of accusers has turned my head into a giant party boat without a helmsman. Fee dances and dances, and I brood while life outside raves. I sit in our flat-share and cry from impotent anger, and torture Fee with my silly jealousy, if she ever shows up.

I read. I devour books and their stories, intoxicated. Fee's bookcase in the living room is full of them: Dostoyevsky, Düster, Bukowski and Miller. Crazy. Hans-Joachim Maaz. Sobering. Sometimes I think I understand everything. And more often than not, I don't understand anything.

Yesterday it burned
Brighter than ever before.
This city has become a rampage
For everything human,
And the mob is dancing in a fever of cheap pills.
The mob is dancing and thirsts for
Revenge.
For everything. For something.
For anyone.

I scribble it on a piece of paper and lay it at Fee's feet. She'll find it at some point. At some point, she'll float across drunk and throw up at me, into our small mansard paradise. This piece of paper is my confession for her. A confusing confession about loneliness, jealousy and world-weariness. In my imagination, Fee is smiling. And she understands.

I'm back. I fall out of my time travel back into Easter Saturday. It's late and I'm still lying in bed. Lying next to Fee. The world appears to be in perfect order. Over there, across the hallway, the door is rattling. The Führer is going somewhere. Breakfast? A fuck? Or on one of his aimless forays? I don't care. I have everything I need. And as Fee sleepily stretches under the covers, which is what a lot of young people do when they share a narrow bed. The Führer has gone out. So now, freed from the eternal listener, it's going to be a really busy, sweaty morning. Who could want anything more?

I think about it for a minute and don't know how to answer. Post-coital satisfaction pushes away everything else. Why can't my life always be this simple?

*

The tiled stove roars to itself. I'm awakened by some random noise. Once again, something is breaking out on this fucking street. Someone is running down there. Someone is screaming. Sometimes it seems is if it's always like that here. I pull loose from Fee and tug a shirt over my head. Stiff-legged, I climb down from the mattress and go see what's going on. I shuffle past the oven to the window and stick my head outside.

There's a lot of people down there. It's not a collection of the usual, drunk vulgar people. No, that's a mob. It is very clearly a mob. A jolly hate brigade has lined up on the pavement. Further back, a long-haired figure frantically stumbles down Louise Street, the troops gathered don't even bother to follow them.

I look down. And one of them looks up. Our gazes meet. For a while, we watch each other surprised. The guy with the shaven head pokes his neighbour in the side with his elbow and gestures upward. The second skinhead is already staring up at me with amazement. It takes me much too long to realise that someone like me should know better than to be staring down on people like them. I quickly hide behind the sloping roof. My pulse is surging. Maybe I have more luck than good sense. For a few minutes, I can hear mumbling from down below. But unfortunately it doesn't stay that way, that's the thing with luck . . .

I run to Fee in the bedroom. I half carry her and half drag her behind me, ignoring her confusion. I pull Fee across the hallway into the Führer's apartment. It's a last-minute thought. In the stairway, the trampling of heavy boots thunders. And as Fee and I stumble through the Führer's apartment door, the first vampire pops up on the stairs. He certainly gets the shock of his life. He probably anticipated just about anything, but not the sight of a half-naked Black man and his fully naked girlfriend. The vampire stops, dumbfounded, and I slam the door. The first lock gets stuck. Naturally. Panicked, I rattle the little lever. It feels like it takes an eternity, then the thing finally snaps into the holder with a scrape. I quickly pull down the thick crossbars.

'Come out, you cunts!' Someone slams down the latch and shakes it.

Fee and I stand in the tiny hallway as if we were rooted to the ground.

'Come on, come out of there!' Bam! A kick against the door.

My heart races. Fee squeezes my hand in hers. No, no, no! Bloody hell! I squeeze Fee's hand back.

'I said, come out of there!'

Yeah, right. They can forget it.

'You fucking Jewish cunts!' Bam.

For a second I consider leaning out the window and calling for help. But what's the point of that? No one is coming to deal with a mob like that, that's for sure.

Bam! Bam! Bam! The door shakes. The doorframe vibrates. Mortar crumbles from the wall. Bam! The upper part of the door bends inward from the kick and then snaps back into position.

I take a deep breath. Then I finally come to my senses. I'm finally awake. And here. I take three steps into the tiny kitchen corner. As always, the sink is full of dirty dishes. Next to that is the equally dirty stove. And next to that is a dented aluminium box with remnants of coals and one frayed book of matches. I grab the rusty, slightly bent poker Then I jump back into the hallway and pull Fee away from the door, behind me. Bam! The mob wants to use all its power to get to us. But they didn't reckon with the Führer. 'Come out here, you cunts!' Bam! 'You fucking n——, we'll get you anyway!' The mortar crumbles. The door quakes in its anchoring. But it holds.

'And we're gonna fuck your cunt to death. Do you hear? We're gonna fuck her to death!'

Fee and I pull the steel bed frame out of the Führer's room, into the tiny hallway and wedge it with the coal box on one side and an ancient chair on the other. Then Fee cowers on the kitchen floor. She is visibly shaking. I clutch the poker.

I stare at the small, naked shape in front of me. Bam! Bam! Bam! The door is holding. And the more the thing lasts, the more likely my fear will turn into something else. Something ugly. Something necessary. Bam! Bam! Bam! Yes, I'm sure. All of a sudden, I'm sure. I'm going to kill whoever makes it through this door. In the worst-case scenario, one can only open the door a narrow crack, thanks to the steel bed frame behind it. They'd have to come in through there, one after the other. And that's where I'll kill them. One after the other. I've never done anything like that, but suddenly I know that I'm capable of it. I know how it will feel, when the metal poker tears through flesh, bones and skin.

Fee says something, but I only hear it as a distant mumbling. I'm somewhere in my deepest thoughts. Until now, I didn't know that this place existed. This cold, murderous feeling. Now I downright wish the door would open. Bam! Bam! Bam! I'm coming father. I'm coming.

'Are you finally listening to me?' Fee screams into my ear. 'They're gone! Do you understand? They're gone.'

I hear Fee. And I'm not there at all. I look through Fee into the past. I run on the dilapidated pavement in front of the bikes, somewhere in the tower block paradise. I run. Until I can't any more. I bend over to a stone. I pick the stone up. I want to hit the spokesman for the guys on bikes right in the mouth. But I'm not allowed to. My mother said, I'm not allowed to behave badly, regardless of what the others are doing. I have to be an exemplary boy. I stand in the Führer's hallway and look through his armoured door into the past.

And the past looks inside me. If the vampires come through the door and I hack at them, then my mother will be annoyed. You don't do things like that. 'What would people think?' Yes, what would people think? They're always going to think something, but for the first time ever, I don't care. For the first time in my life, their opinions are meaningless. The horde out there wants to wipe me out. They want to wipe out Fee. They're vampires. Orcs. They're murders. My mother is wrong. You can kill murderers. You can hack them in the head.

'Goddamit, are you deaf?' Fee shakes me. Fee doesn't scream any more. Fee is standing in the hallway, naked and shivering. And crying.

Later the mob will get their prey after all. By then it will be evening. It's the same troupe. The same hatred. Only a few hundred metres away, almost within sight of our window in the mansard, these guys chase a man to death. He's on the way home. He is his parents' beloved son. His brothers like him. And his friends. And his colleagues at work. He's a quiet, calm guy who does his job and looks forward to his vacation. While on vacation, he wants to visit his parents. But he won't be able to. The vampires beat him to death. A brother. A friend. A colleague. The murderers murder a man.

The man is Jorge Gomondai. He was born in 1962 in

Mozambique, about the time when my father came to the GDR. And ten years after my father died, Gomondai came to Dresden. Today, again ten years after that, and after the GDR has been banished to the history books, no one bothers to use poison if he wants to kill a Black man. They just throw him off the streetcar. At full speed. Badly beaten. Fee and I were lucky. We were saved by the Führer's door. But now they know where we live. They could come at any time. We have to leave. Quickly.

Fee silently broods over her worry, her shock. With tears in her eyes. She loves her apartment and now her apartment is no longer safe. The appearance of the mob soiled her with something. Fee could colour her hair. She could start wearing glasses and hide her face under a hat. I am, and will always remain, a walking target. The big Black guy from Alaun Street. I can see in Fee's eyes that she has long understood. Her brain is more mathematics most of the time anyway. And three times as fast as mine. Maybe Fee can disappear somewhere in Neustadt. But I have to get away.

CHAPTER ELEVEN

'Who peed standing up?'

Barely two weeks later. Radebeul, a suburb of Dresden. A flat-share's kitchen table. Everyone is silent. With the utmost concentration, I study the pattern of the tablecloth. It's a wax tablecloth with flowers. My grandparents had something similar. My hands lie on the table. Folded. Well-behaved. Still. Whoever can lay their hands on the table like this is innocent. I hope that everyone present can understand this signal, that they can translate body language into presumption of innocence. Maybe this time I can get off scot-free. In doubt, in favour of the accused. Or something.

'It's quite simple. Someone peed standing up. And it would be nice if that person admitted it was them, so we can talk about it.'

Peeing standing up. A heavy accusation. And, of course, everyone knows who the guilty party likely is. At the kitchen table are Anke, Kathrin, Regina, Nadine and I – their new roommate for a time. That's everyone who lives in the apartment. And only one has a body part that would allow them to commit such a crime. Denying it is senseless. I submit to my fate and raise my hand.

'I did it. I'm sorry.'

How could I have known? No one told me that men who pee standing up are a problem. Problem pissers. And peeing isn't the only thing people should've taught me. For example, something about women like these. I knew that women sometimes like women. However, I only knew it from schoolbooks. That proved to be a problem. Because schoolbooks are schoolbooks after all. And usually, they have little to do with reality. *Non vitae sed scholae discimus.* 'We learn for school, not for life.' The Führer had that tattooed on his lower arm. He must have really hated school. Women sometimes like women. But that women sometimes did 'it' with other women was a surprise for me. They didn't tell us about that in school.

'I'm sorry,' I repeat. 'I'll never do it again. I promise. Can I still stay?'

The women exchange surprised, slightly exasperated glances. Then they begin to laugh.

'We didn't offer you asylum only to throw you out on the street over such a minor thing,' Kathrin states, the spokeswoman for the group.

'Exactly,' Anke agrees.

'Otherwise you'd be beaten to death by a pair of crazies. And then all of our trouble would be for nothing.'

That takes a load off my mind. I could cry from relief. If I had had to leave again, it would have been more than I could handle. That shit in Neustadt still sat deep in my bones. Leaden and terrifying.

I didn't have a large selection of places to sleep when I hastily left the Führer's flat share. First, I stayed with various acquaintances, always just for one night. I even stayed with my mother, under the pretence of a visit.

'What are you doing here in the middle of the week?' She seems surprised, almost annoyed. She's reacted as though I had come to rob her.

'I just wanted to see how you're doing,' I claim innocently. It couldn't be further from the truth. Of course, my mother suspects I'm lying, but still reluctantly lets me in. She's busy, she tells me. There's a job application lying on the kitchen table. The GDR may be dead, but even the new authority needs worker drones in their administration. Especially in IT. I read on the application: 'That's why I'd like the responsibly of contributing to the task of protecting personal data.' Neatly written. Aha. I understand. So people in administration don't die as quickly as in George Orwell's books.

Early in the evening, I retreat to my old room; my mother doesn't have anything against that. The application she began is still lying on the table.

Next day, I get up early. I head to Nancy, whom we call Nan. She and I share the same skin colour. We also share the same love for books by Asimov and Lem, and long walks along the Elbe. Together with Nan, I founded the multicultural club, but it became too much for her. Nan has to be careful with her strength, and she's almost blind. We haven't seen or heard from each other in a few weeks. She cautiously gropes my face, then she takes her hands away and listens to something that only she can hear. Finally, she turns her head in my direction: 'You seem pretty broken. Tired.'

I am. Broken. And tired. Still. Or once again. I feel restless. Uprooted. And this condition affects me more than I'd like to admit.

Once more I go to my old flat share on Alaun Street. The Führer has disappeared. No one in the building knows where he's gone. The apartment is empty. And the old refrigerator is still buzzing away. In the meantime, something green has grown in its innards. I quickly slam the refrigerator door closed again. There was definitely cheese in there at some point. And now the cheese has become some other life form. I stare at the closed refrigerator door. In my head I hear the boots rumbling up the stairs. I see Fee naked, crouching on the wood floor. Bam! Bam! Bam! I flinch from the fridge. Did I hear footsteps in the hallway? I listen out. Only silence permeates though the Führer's open door. I turn once more back to the refrigerator. Then I leave.

A few days later I buy a train ticket. I travel in one direction first. Then I change trains and randomly travel a few stops in another direction. But regardless of how much I keep an eye out, no one is following me. No one is too tactical. No one avoids eye contact. Or behaves in a manner that would be too conspicuous. I buy a new ticket and get on another train. The people probably think I look like someone. Some office type. Someone in administration. Dress shirt. Varsity jacket. Bag. But the harmless appearance has a purpose.

Under my jacket I'm wearing a lot of tools and equipment, neatly concealed. When that mob attacked us in the mansard apartment, something broke inside me. Some border collapsed. I know now with absolute certainty how the whole thing will turn out. History runs in loops, time and time again. Those who are like me should flee. And everyone who doesn't flee, can't or doesn't want to flee, will die, I'm convinced of that. And naturally, everyone who simply can't afford to flee will be picked up. The vampires are no longer making a secret of this plan.

'We'll get you all!' They scream it when they see me in the middle of the day. They scream it out in the open. And not one of the good citizens, who are all in such a hurry, dares to even shake their heads. Nobody takes my side.

The girl on the street.

Naked, crying Fee.

The poker in my hand.

Something has broken in me. One of the few things that was healthy and still intact in me.

The train takes me out of the city. I pretend to read, but I look past the little book in every direction. There are no safe places any more. There are no safe times any more. The Canadians have issued official warnings. None of their Black citizens should travel to East Germany. And the Americans have made similar recommendations. So I'm not crazy. Or I am crazy, but at least the danger is real.

I buy a ticket to travel somewhere far up north. To safety. I get out halfway. Train stations are equally desolate everywhere. Long platforms. Graffitied benches. Defective vending machines. Overpriced vending machines. Glorious vending machines. Pigeon shit. I go to the bar in the train station. Way in the back, not far from the bathrooms, a small gathering is already waiting for me. A short, heartfelt welcome, a hug and a handshake, then we get started. All the ones who are gathered here have the same skin tone. And thus we have the same destiny.

This isn't a friendly visit. We're talking about the end. The citizens have evidently decided that our death is acceptable. The few core democrats and leftist activists who speak up for us won't turn things around again. We're alone. Spread out across the east. And we're in no way a match for the enemy who's prepared to do anything. There are facts. Irrefutable facts. And one of those is admitting our inferiority. People like us are hunted. They're mutilated and murdered. And no one seems to care about that. Or seems bothered by it. Those are the facts. And this is our homeland. We don't know any other. And when all that's been said, there's a long pause. Everyone at the table stares into his lemonade and is lost in his own thoughts. Who will be the first?

Who's willing to say what's going through everyone's head and the reason why've come? Which one of us will be the first to speak about the final resistance, the last fury? After the server has taken our orders and sneaks away, everyone puts their cards on the table. A few people in the group have studied the contents of some helpful books. And pieced one or two things together from it. And tested it. On telephone booths and garbage cans. And in one abandoned apartment complex or another. The scope for these actions is limited to a few metres, but it will have to be enough. So far so good. While we eat schnitzel and fried potatoes, we come to an agreement about a list of priorities and establish a red line.

'Now, we should do it now. What are we waiting for?' says one of the falcons at the table. The guys advocating violence.

Other falcons nod. 'We should at least warn the citizens,' says a dove.

'A kind of ultimatum. Maybe they'll react to it. At least some-one in Bonn,' another dove agrees with her.

'They should pay. For them, we're just animals,' a falcon says.

'And no more waiting. They should finally feel our pain. Especially that,' the other falcon supports his colleague.

We meet in the middle. After the next murder, after the next big chase, we'll step into action. We'll cut an artery to the heart. Something they'll notice more than a little itch. Something that, when well placed, could bring everything to a standstill through pure fear. It's a fine line to overkill. But even the doves agree. Everyone agrees. Everyone raises their hand.

The spokesman for the Easterners nods contently and returns to his schnitzel. 'But if that's not enough? If it still doesn't stop?' I think the plan is good, but today I'm playing devil's advocate. Somebody has to, somebody has to ask the question. 'What then?' I follow up.

The schnitzel murderer looks up from his plate. The silence in the group tells me more about the abyss in us than anything else. I'm relieved. And sad. The end is near. We won't experience it on a ramp at Auschwitz, naked and full of fear. We'll burn. Everything will burn. And even that's better than quietly waiting for the murder commandos to come and pick up our parents. And our siblings. And ourselves. 'Do not go gentle into that good night,' that's what Dylan Thomas has the son say to his father. We're not going to go gently. The night that is falling over the land will not be a good one.

The initial euphoria of my resistance barely survives the trip home. The old mechanisms of obedience flood my brain with doubts. The collective of accusers gathers in my head. The collective of opportunists. Rebellion is bad, they announce. Rebellion is futile. That's something my mother had already burned into my head and my flesh. 'Follow the rules!' Her voice hisses to the choir of others. That's been stamped into me. But maybe all of this talk about my mother is just an excuse. Maybe I'm just too cowardly. Above all I should save my son. And I don't even had a plan for that. And even if I did, we would be strangers everywhere . . . when the train pulls into Dresden, I've lost all courage. All certainty. On my way through the domed hall of the main train station I sense that I can't save a single life. Not even my own.

Cowardly. And homeless. And helpless. Back in Radebeul, I look through the window of the flat share onto the street. People hurry around, from somewhere to somewhere else. I'm hurrying around too, but to nowhere. And how on earth, against all likelihood, have I even ended up in this flat share of women?

It starts after breakfast and tea, with a trick, one morning, in the week after the Orc raid. 'We're going on a little trip,' Fee says. 'You'll like it.' She smiles reassuringly and brushes me softly across my back. This is probably the method people use to reassure confused old women and stubborn children, when you save them from themselves.

Fee and I stroll towards the city centre. And near the old bridge we meet Nan. Just like that, totally 'by accident'.

Nan is pleased to see us. She laughs. Nan has a bag with her. Together, all three of us walk over the bridge. Talking and laughing. And at Haus der Presse we get on the streetcar, route 4, towards Radebeul. Radebeul: a city on the Elbe, 30,000 residents. District town. It's a little like an outsourced organ of a close metropolis, inextricably linked to its much bigger sister, and yet a different world. As soon as we leave the train station, I'm led into the belly of a nineteenth-century villa. In the villa we go up to the first floor. I admire the stairway decorated with stucco trimmings. Being here with Nan and Fee doesn't feel disturbing. It feels like a school field trip. Or drinking coffee with a distant relative. And that's how we end up in the women's flat-share.

When Fee suggests that I should stay here for a while, I first think it's a joke and wait for a sign. We'll probably keep going soon. We'll probably go to a farm. Or to the vineyards. Or something. But I wait in vain. Fee never gives me a sign. I'm going to be put up by the women. You don't need a degree in Sociology to understand that there can't be any appropriate accommodations here, at least not for a twenty-one-year-old, weightlifting, heterosexual man from the tower blocks. Everything here is vegetarian. And half the calories. The gender of all things in this world is female. And last but not least: you have to pee sitting down, of course. I drink three goddamn litres a day. Three litres of tea, lukewarm and unsweetened. That's what they taught us to do in sports school. Three litres, that means peeing fifty times. Pants down. Squat bend down. The ancient toilet lid is cold and hard, but why else did I complete anti-terror training? I'm colder and I'm harder than this fossil under my backside. The command is now 'pee sitting down'. So I pee sitting down, against all of the natural instincts that demand me to swing my reproductive organs while standing and humming.

Rainy, cold months follow. The sky is always grey. The countryside is always grey. And I only go outside if I absolutely have to. Otherwise, I wait. Bent over a book. Bent over the windowsill. Bent over my doubts. And I wait. I listen to the collective accusers, how they negotiate in my head. That's how the afternoon passes. And after training, I fall into bed like a rock. Fee sometimes comes to visit. Then we go into my room and climb over cartons filled with the clothes of the room's actual owner, the person who has embarked on some sort of journey of self-discovery and hasn't been heard from since. During the day, when the women are out, Fee and I catch up, something that the distance between us otherwise makes impossible. We're a little ashamed of ourselves; two meat-eating, heterosexual foreign bodies in a lesbian-vegan smalltown-outpost. But my asylum means that I'm still 'in one piece'. Unharmed. Uncrippled. Living.

Meanwhile, in nearby Dresden, the post-revolutionary sea is making turbulent waves. The city is accelerating to increasingly higher rotational speeds. I hear about huge parties in a gigantic tent, right by the Russian garrison. There are half-naked dancers there. There's cheap hooch in bright polished glasses. And cheap chemistry. Chemistry for fucking. Chemistry for dancing. Chemistry for forgetting. There's 'Polish compote'. There's cheap 'ice'. And there's a lot of inexpensive sex in newer and newer bordellos. The fast money keeps luring more and more new comrades. And the development of the market is carried out with Russian machine guns. And settled with hand grenades. The city is in full swing. I hear about former party functionaries who dangle in front of their dachas with blue faces, hanging from their wooden verandas like May Day flags. And I always hear about new closures in the few factories that remain. And for people who look like me, one bloody day of horror follows another.

I am spared from Dresden, but not from the troubled times. I don't have any reserves.

I don't have any savings. And I'm hungry, hungrier than the few, meatless calories I get in the flat share. And so I hire myself out as a henchman and help at the door in a student club. 'Cobbler, stick to what you can do.' It's simply the smell of the familiar shit that lures me back to such jobs. That's how the days pass. I read. I write. I devote my morning training routine to elastic band exercises, push-ups and running. And in the afternoon, karate. The rest of my time, I watch the goings on at the train station, while I'm halfway hidden behind a curtain.

More and more often, there are young vampires and their underaged followers hanging out in front of the train station. For now, nothing has changed. For now, no one has really taken notice of me. I have no idea why. Are they too young? Too inexperienced for prey that could defend itself? I don't know, but I still move my running laps to the early morning. Then there are only the shift workers around, rushing to their sales stands and to their work benches. And there aren't a lot of them anyway. And when I'm back from running, from the steep, tiny paths that lead into the vineyards, I crawl into my sleeping bag, unspeakably tired and happy. After running I'm almost weightlessly free and float away, relieved, into the enchanted forest.

That's how the days pass. Radebeul is a quiet place with little excitement. Sometimes I can almost forget that I'm a refugee here.

I sit in a hallway with rows of chairs. Is it a large compartment in a train? No, more like a plane. Outside, shreds of clouds float by. I'm taking a long trip. When my bladder cries out to be emptied, I stagger down the swaying aisle. The rows of chairs to the left and right of me become blurry. I rub my eyes and the blurry images become clear again. Now I'm obviously standing in a hallway. The hallway isn't swaying. It's a straight line to nowhere. The same kinds of doors lead to the left and right. I turn my head to look back, but all I see there is a forest of all the same doors. I stagger from door to door. Every door is the same. Every door is closed. I shake and hammer at these goddamn doors. And I have to find my door . . .

Lately when Fee visits she speaks about America a lot. Maybe that's why I always have this same dream. Of this plane. And this vast, dark shimmering water, deep down. Maybe that's why I have panicked, sweaty dreams of the hallway and these doors that won't be opened. Fee wants to get out. She's tired of waiting and just wants to leave, head somewhere. She just wants to get away. There are also mathematicians on the other side of the ocean. And Fee is so fucking clever and so fucking good at what she does. And she probably wants to go to the endless expanses that her eyes always follow, searching for the perfect shot, the perfect image.

She's already bought herself a new sinfully expensive lens. And until now she hasn't said a word about us going away together. No, she hasn't categorically excluded the option. She weighs her words carefully. And I don't know if it's part of her tactic. Or maybe it's sympathy for the one who doesn't want to get on the plane with her.

At some point, Fee's visits become rarer. And her hugs feel somehow strange, as if they're carefully choreographed and planned manoeuvres. Something is changing between the both of us. I often have to think of my dream.

'Whoever does what he already can, always remains what he already is.' I carry my grandfather's saying around with me.

When I read about a project on the pin board at the supermarket, I apply. My potential employer is a tiny social welfare office, crammed together on the equally tiny floor of an old building. They're looking for 'street workers'. That's some kind of West German and doesn't mean anything more than the office needs people who keep an eye on the unwieldy youth in the city. The office is looking for people who can perform that task and that suits me.

I'm done with endless night shifts. And anyway, it's getting increasingly worse at the club. Drunken construction workers who aren't allowed to enter. Recreational thugs looking for adventure. They're not allowed in either. And, of course, the drunk, young vampires. They're never allowed in. And these excluded, violated kids of the night let off steam at the door. With their frustration, and sometimes with beer bottles, belts and fence posts, too. In comparison, the job at the social welfare office sounds harmless, almost like paid vacation.

'Are you sure you want to do this?'

The clerk holds on to her desk when she sees me. In her face, there's a mixture of surprise and fright.

'Yeah, I'd like to try it.'

I try to keep the tone as calm as possible. I feign certainty. Actually, I'm anything but certain. I don't want to be roaming around the streets, regardless of who I'm with. I'd rather be in a nice, warm office. With some files to stamp, and staples.

'In this project, there are, oh, well . . .' the poor woman is struggling for the appropriate formalities. We are in an office here after all.

'The group you'd be caring for are . . . special cases.'

'How special?' I follow-up.

The woman chokes on her next sentence. 'Hmm . . . yeah . . . well . . . very special, I'm afraid.' She pours fizzy water into a glass as if she had travelled through the desert for some days. 'These young people glorify harmful thinking.' The woman quickly pours more water. 'To be more precise, they glorify . . .' the woman hastily drinks from her glass, 'National Socialism. Or at least we see the danger that the city will lose them to such ideas.'

In other words, it's about little vampires. That's what I thought. I would love to laugh about the irony of the situation, but all I can manage is a forced smile. The vampires and me. The eternal song. But maybe that's exactly why it's a good idea. 'The wolf and the lamb will graze together.' I read that in the Bible. Way at the end. Well let's give it a try. Although I'm afraid that I'm not the lion in this story.

'Somehow I'll make it work,' I assure the woman and say goodbye.

On the way home the collective of accusers run amok in my head. They're rioting in the courtroom. They want to have me declared insane. The walk home turns into a hell tour. The first meeting in the social welfare office is soon followed by another, during which I offer hollow explanations for the details about how I will implement my concept. It's nothing more than hot air. I spread an impenetrable mud of empty phrases to detract from the obvious fact that I was the absolute wrong choice for this job. Everyone nods benevolently above their coffee cups. For a moment, at the end of my speech, it occurs to me that I might be the only applicant for this position. But by then it's already too late. I've been hired.

The next day, I enter my new workplace armed with a cracked

key. It's a halfway dilapidated little castle on the edge of the city, the desolate park surrounding it matches the building. Inside, everything smells like ancient sofas and musty humidity. In the corner of the main room, the damp has eaten through the ceiling and the plaster is freely crumbling down from the wall. The old wooden floors squeak under my feet. It's probably been installed by the rats that live here, a kind of alarm system to warn against the human parasites. Despite the cold outside I tear open the veranda door. Then I wait.

The seconds move slowly along the minute circle and pile up into a small mountain. No one comes. I sit alone with a plate of bribery cookies and a few bottles of lemonade. The next day, I quickly decide to leave the building and go over to the group at the train station. It's early in the morning and the three bald heads belong to three slightly sleepy, adolescent faces that turn in my direction looking astonished. With their pale bald heads, the boys look like a gathering of cancer patients taking a break from chemo. One of them is wearing a bomber jacket. All of them have on boots under their jeans. None of them are Dr Martens, but rather cheap, polished worker boots. Boots are part of the 'uniform' and the cheap ones look enough like the beloved originals to lend a feeling of belonging. These aren't some ideologically murderous thugs, but rather dressed-up candidates for the entry-level program.

But they can be dangerous, too, after five cans of cheap beer and a hate speech from their instigator. I grin widely and seemingly relaxed, while deep inside my head the collective of accusers rants and rages about my alleged carelessness.

'A beautiful good morning.' I drop the sports bag I've repurposed for my work onto the path. 'I'm from the social welfare office in Radebeul and I wanted to invite you to come to the park.' I nod towards the street behind the underpass. 'You probably know the house.'

The three guys first stare at me and then at each other. After a few moments of dumbfounded silence, the oldest of the three speaks.

'Where's the other nut?'

I'm perplexed. I can only guess what he might mean.

'Which other one?'

'Well, the long-haired one, like Jesus. He always brought stuff with him,' the boy explains.

'What stuff?' I'm totally confused. What kind of stuff would a Jesus figure have? The gospel?

'Well, sandwiches and stuff.' He grins hungrily when he mentions the bribery. I grin back. I got you!

'I have snacks, too.' For today cookies and lemonade. And tomorrow I'll really go shopping. 'We can cook spaghetti sometime, too, if you want.'

Spaghetti always works. Kids love spaghetti. Adults love spaghetti. I love spaghetti. Everyone loves spaghetti.

The guy thinks for a second and then nods. The other boys see that and don't need any more time to think. They nod immediately. I nod, too, as relaxed as possible, cool. But internally, I'm close to having a heart attack.

I take my bag and stroll towards the park. At the top end of the street I have to cross the road and I notice that the three baby vampires are following me at a distance, just like baby chicks follow a duck. They must like spaghetti more than anything else. Not a bad start.

'This is still a really shitty place.' The disappointed faces. Yes sir. I can only agree with him. I nod and shrug my shoulders apologetically. Why deny the obvious?

'But we're really far away from the office. At least that way, no one will bother us. Or would you prefer daily check-ins?'

The spokesman's gaze doubtfully looks over the official dump.

'So what now? What doesn't fit can be made to fit. You're big boys, aren't you?' That's my last card. Either flattery works or I'll be sitting here alone again soon. Ultimately, the spokesman sits on the rank sofa and grabs a cookie. The others copy him. They don't speak with me for now. To call this a dream start would be a bit presumptuous, but I sell it as a phenomenal win to the collective of accusers.

'This is almost better than the Interhotel. You can at least admit that,' I say, breaking the silence of the boys. The spokesman looks perplexed for a minute, then he laughs and stretches out again toward the plate of cookies. And somehow we still talk. About the teachers at school. Annoying. About girls. Dumb, all of them. And we talk about unemployed fathers who sit at home and constantly annoy them with their shitty mood.

'Well, at least during the day you're at school.' One of the two followers shakes his head in protest.

'Nearly half of the teachers are gone. Our classes are constantly getting cancelled. Sometimes the idiots make us come to school for a single hour.'

'Good teachers don't fall from trees. And an hour is better than nothing,' I try to whitewash things. That's apparently my unofficial work order. Because I have been equipped with neither teachers nor jobs for unemployed fathers. The office didn't even give me a decent couch for these kids.

'But they often just write down exercises for us on the board.'

The boy rolls his eyes, annoyed. 'There's not even someone there who we could ask for help. What kind of school is that?' Maybe it's even a better variation. Not all teachers are the jackpot in the lottery. But, of course, I don't tell them that. Instead, I nod sympathetically. And then we talk a lot about football. And eat and drink the meagre catering. That's my first day. It could probably be worse.

More and more boys come to the 'castle'. I have no idea what I can do with the emotionally needy masses. I'm poorly prepared and even more poorly equipped. So I just let the boys hang around. Complain, if they want, then come to me and talk. 'Teatime' is what I call it. Although the boys' enthusiasm for my tea has its limits. An open door, cookies from Aldi, and a lot of conversations. I'm kind of like a weightlifting priest. That's how the days pass.

I have a job. Fee still wants to go to America. And I still want Fee, maybe more now than ever before. I don't know what to do about that. I no longer feel as hurried, as helpless as I did a few months ago. Before Radebeul and before the flat share. Now I have a real objective. A job. And some of my clients are so fond of me, it's as if I was their long-lost favourite uncle. I dress up and squirm and the committee of accusers thinks my feelings about this job are pathetic, but it just feels good to be needed. And to have an apparent effect.

I open up the 'castle' and distribute cookies on plates and bottles of lemonade on several tables. Soon the audience will trickle in. A normal day 'on the job'. One of the boys wants to talk to me. He pulls me away from the others. We sit down on the damaged stools in the kitchen. The boy seems worried. I put on my 'heartache-face', it conveys a mixture of empathy and understanding, maybe that will help him a little. The boy impatiently slides around on his stool. Without a remark, I pass the boy a saucer with cookies and some room-temperature lemonade. And I wait. I really am the mother of the company.

'I have a problem,' the boy begins.

'Hmm. What's wrong?' I ask, searching for the new package of tea bags. There should be a large package here, I just went shopping after all.

'Something has come up,' the boy hems and haws. 'I'm not really sure how I should say it . . .'

'Just spit it out,' I say. 'Then we can immediately drown your problems in a nice cup of tea.' My joke is an attempt to build a bridge, but the boy doesn't laugh.

'They want to beat you up,' he suddenly says, near tears. I stop searching in the drawers. 'I was over there yesterday. It's a done deal.'

Over there, that's another small backwater of a town, only a few kilometres away. There, the older vampires wrested a building away from the municipal administration, and now they're living there and spreading a whole lot of trouble from there. This approach of leaving people alone with their problems is called a 'low-threshold'. It's about making offers to especially vulnerable populations. Or populations that are especially difficult to access. I think that's bullshit to say the least.

'But why? We don't have anything to do with them.' I try to calm myself down; maybe it's just pompous talk from someone.

'They said you're disrupting the youth work in this district. That's why you've got to go.' It's this choice of words that make my comfortable hopes come crashing to the floor. These aren't this boy's words. They're the newspeak of the radicals.

'Don't worry, this will stay between us.' The boy can use some encouragement now. He's just betrayed the plans of his dark master. He's betrayed them in order to warn me. But still, he's got a guilty conscience.

'You're really cool,' the boy tries to explain himself. 'You do all of this here. And you care.' Tears roll down the boy's cheeks. Now, despite his jackets and boots, he seems more like a desperate elementary school student than anything else.

'Don't worry, everything will be alright.' That is, of course, absolute nonsense. Things will never be this good again. Never. Not in this world. I lay my arm around the boy's shoulder. 'Everything will be fine.' Sometimes we have to believe what we want to believe, otherwise nothing good would ever happen again. That same night there's a crisis meeting in the office.

I tell them about my teatime with the boys. There's nodding all around. My source appears to be credible. Just last week a house occupied by punks was attacked and burned down. That was also in the forest, next to the vineyards. And because when it rains it pours, this week began with a bang. The capo is dead. The self-appointed, supreme commander of the 'neo-something' is dead. The guy and some of his people got into a fight with the red-light scene. And the Gewerbe shot his head off for it, in broad daylight. The vampire prince is dead. Assassinated. And for the most radical of the radicals, his death is a welcomed reason for a blood orgy.

'It was clear,' the authority rep complained, 'that something like this would happen. And now?'

'What can we do anyway?' The representative asks in a similarly worried tone.

After a very brief consultation I'm put on leave and sent home. At the kitchen table in the flat share, the plenum of women is having a meeting. When I sit down, I brush against the porcelain shade of a lamp and now the thing is swaying back and forth and casting alternating shadows, creating a psychedelic atmosphere.

'They have to protect you!' 'The police have to!' 'We'll go to the press!'

Everyone's talking over each other. I shake my head. There's no use. The police? They have other problems than me. When I list them for the women, I finally realise for myself how real everything is. It falls quiet at the flat-share table. I stare out of the window into the courtyard. The only light there is coming from the surrounding apartments and breaks on the branches of the trees. There's nothing more to say. I'm burned. Once again. And it doesn't look much better for the women here. No one outside will come to their aid if someone decides to storm the flat share.

According to the vampires' interpretation, these wonderful, crazy courageous women are nothing more than unworthy life, because they're perverted. 'Folk pests' that should be strung up on the beautiful, old gas lanterns in front of the train station. Every further minute I stay here the risk increases.

I push myself up from the table and distribute air kisses to the group. Time to go. I gather my things in my large sports bag and take the streetcar. Route 4. This time in a different direction.

As far as I know, Fee is at her parents' house, In the middle of her final preparations for America. In her head, she's halfway there. So I can't spend the night with Fee. But I still have the key for the Führer's apartment. I can spend one or two nights there. I probably won't be as safe anywhere in this city as I am behind that door. And then? Go to my mother again? Go to her in Prohlis again? Impossible, just the thought of it makes me shiver. Besides, the neighbourhood is largely vampire territory. Fee is leaving. Prohlis is a contaminated area. And in Neustadt I'm as well-known as a colourful dog. So I can't go anywhere. I crouch on the mattress behind the secure door and thank the Führer for his foresight. Then I let myself be swept away into the enchanted dream forest before panic can take full hold of me.

Late that evening, I'm woken by the sound of footsteps. Fee has come back. When I knock on her door, she opens it just a little and is surprised. Not long after, we're lying in her narrow room under the covers.

'Can I come with you?'

My heart is beating wildly. My question is stuck somewhere in the darkness of the room. I had to ask. I had to at least risk an attempt. And now I don't know how I should live with her answer. I fall. The abyss is giant. And bottomless.

'I'll find something I can do there.' One last try to turn it in my favour.

'What exactly? What are you going to do?' she asks. In just seconds, her mathematical brain demolished my house of cards. I don't have a plan for America. And unlike Fee, I can't do anything special that they would need over there. My attempt has failed. I can tell from the tone in her voice. I won't be able to hang on to the edge of the cliff much longer. The tears are already rushing up like one mighty flood. I quickly fumble with my pant legs. And with my socks. It's so fucking dark. Where are my goddamn socks? I won't make it in time. I can tell. So I leave the socks behind before the tidal wave can catch me.

Just as I go to push myself up from the mattress, Fee grabs my hand and elbow. I don't want any comfort. I definitely don't want any fucking comfort from her right now. What will that get me? I try to shake off her hand. Just no comfort, anything but that. That's as if you stuck a candy bar into a condemned man's mouth on the day of his execution and soothingly stroked his cheeks. The more I try to shake off Fee's hand in the darkness, the stronger her grip is. Then it's two hands. And arms. And finally, I fall into a indissoluble, infinite, redeeming embrace.

III

Rise and Fall

My father in the company of fellow students

My mother, harrowed in the wake
of my father's death, and me

My brother Moise and me

My father with his colleagues at the drilling site, in the north of the GDR

My mother and my brother as a baby

A studio portrait of my father and mother

My father and mother on a pleasure boat

My father and mother, in a solemn moment, at the East German Carnival

My father, my mother, my brother and a young wild cat, at Leipzig Zoo

'Fallen soldier' – the family in Cameroon gathered at my father's coffin

My father, hero of my imagination

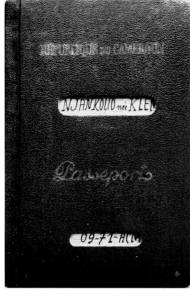

DEUTSCHE DEMOKRATISCHE REPUBLIK

Geburtsurkunde

Standesamt Zwenkau, Kr. Leipzig   Nr. 335/1970

Sam Njankouo Meffire, männlichen Ge-

schlechts,---

ist am 11. Juli 1970---

in Zwenkau---   geboren.

Eltern: Samuel Njankouo Meffire und Marianne

Christine Njankouo Meffire geb. Klemm.---

Vermerke: keine.

Leipzig   den   26. März 1990

                      I.V.

Personenkennzahl: [1][1][0][7][0]-[4]-[2][6][1][1]-[4]

My birth certificate with my already butchered name

My mother's Cameroonian passport

- 2 -

Signalement
Description

Taille :
Height

Couleur des yeux :
Colour of eyes

Couleur des cheveux :
Colour of hair

Signes particuliers :
Spécial marks

Accompagné de _deux_ enfants.
Accompanied by   children

Nom Surname	Prénoms Christian names	Date de naissance Date of birth
NJANKOUO	MOFIRE Moïse	16.10.1963
NJANKOUO	MOFIRE Samuel	11.7.1970

Photographie du titulaire et le cas échéant, photographies des enfants qui accompagnent
Photograph of the bearer and if applying

Signature du titulaire.
Signature of bearer

Inside of my mother's Cameroonian passport, featuring my full name

Mother, young and invincible, before tragedy strikes

My mother and father, so incredibly young and
in love – life is full of possibilities

Studio photo of my mother, my brother (centre) and me

The landscape of barren prefab buildings, the place of my childhood, on the outskirts of Dresden

'The food is finished.' No one stirs in the children's room. 'Curly Whirly, come and eat!' No reaction. Usually just the smell and the banging of pots and pans lures them into the kitchen. Exceptions make the rule. Although today it's Una's favourite dish. Goulash with mashed potatoes. Where could she be? Where is my girl? I really tried. I sautéed onions and paprika. The meat is seared golden brown and then entrusted to the gentle heat for hours. I only cook three meals for the kids: oatmeal; thick vegetable soup with chicken in a big pot; and goulash with mashed potatoes. I can't do anything else. And even that I do only for the girls. So that they can bicker, chatter and happily tuck in. I would be happy to live off white beans day after day, beans out of a can. And beer out of cans.

Feli comes into the kitchen, in one hand she has her Harry Potter book and in the other hand she's got 'piggy', the most tattered stuffed animal from her childhood days. 'Where's Una?' Feli looks worried. She also can't believe that her little sister has rescinded the territory to her without a fight. Together we start walking toward the children's room. 'Sneak,' she whispers. 'Let's sneak like cats! On quiet paws.' With that she puts her finger to her lips. I nod. Understood. We stalk.

There's not a single sound coming from the children's room. Feli and I search all possible corners and levels. We find Una under a purple-coloured canopy, in her robber's cave. She's sleeping. She's sleeping, snoring and drooling.

I look at my little girls. My little peace. And soon they won't be small any more. That's the fate of parents. When in the evening they are finally supposed to sleep, she'll resist. And in the middle of the day, this. While I look down at Una, enraptured, Feli brings her blanket with her. She wraps her sister in it, carefully, almost maternally. And she puts down piggy to keep watch, next to the pillow and head. More love than that isn't possible. My heart skips a happy beat.

'Were you really in America?' Feli suddenly asks, without looking up from her plate. 'Were you in New York?' Feli's eyes twinkle enthusiastically.

'No.' I shake my head. 'I was never in New York, only somewhere in the sticks, way out there.'

'Did you have to sleep in a tent the whole time?' I almost spit out my half-eaten food on the plate. What an idea.

'No, I lived in a kind of village. There were houses there.' And after thinking about it for a moment, I add, 'And people. A lot of people. House parents. Carpenters. Bakers. And, of course, my clients. I helped them. That was my work.' Feli's eyes grow wide.

'You worked in a village as a lawyer?'

I give an involuntary laugh and wave her off. 'No, no. With clients – I mean, the people I took care of.' Feli probably knows the word 'client' from one of her series. She loves *Monk* and his bizarre cases.

'Client is just another word for resident. Some of them had bad difficulties with their emotions, but otherwise regularly went to school or to work. But there were also some with severe brain damage. With arms and legs that grew crooked. And sometimes they just had stumps sticking out of their torso.' Feli has a keen sense for suffering. She looks serious. I can hear how the gears of her thoughts are really rattling behind her forehead.

'Are the people there sad?'

'What do you mean?'

'They probably have a lot of pain. And what can they even do about that, as sick as they are.' True, my clients weren't like the majority of people, and to claim otherwise would be lying. And I don't like to lie to Feli.

'You're right. Many of them were in a lot of pain. Day after day. And a lot of them couldn't do anything without some artificial aid, they relied on hoses and equipment. But underneath all that, they were just people. People who breathe. Who rejoice. And get angry. And are sad. Grown people, of whom some go to the bathroom in nappies and have to be fed. I was the one who rejoiced with them and who got upset with them.'

'And who changed the nappies?'

'I changed the nappies.'

'Would you take care of me like that? If I got to be so badly ill.' Feli has lost interest on her half-full plate. This is now more important than mashed potato and goulash. I get up and walk around the table.

'You're my little girls.' I pull her close to me. 'You. And Una. And Brudi. And Mama. I would do everything for you.'

'Even if we sometimes fight.'

'Yes, that's the way it is in a family. And with siblings. Not everything has to be perfect.' That's not enough for Feli. She keeps drilling and can't hide her smile.

'But for you I'm perfect, right?' Now I'm grinning, too.

'Of course. Absolutely perfect.'

Laughing, Feli rams her little fist into my ribs. And then we embrace each other.

'Did you like it there?' Feli is working on the second half of her plate.

'It's beautiful there. There are green hills. And a river. And nice little farmhouses with a lot of space around them.' I'm searching for the fitting comparison. 'Hobbiton! It actually looks exactly like Hobbiton, like in *Lord of the Rings*, just with streets too. And cars. And a library. And Pizza Hut and McDonald's.'

Feli has to smile. 'Sounds great.'

It *was* great. And no one whispered anything to me when I walked by. And no one chased me or tried to kill me. Over there I was just some guy. And exceptionally, this guy had a completely different kind of problem. A visa problem. As a tourist, I wasn't allowed to work. And besides, in Camphill they were only expecting Fee. But the eldest in the village didn't send me away. Even though I showed up uninvited and delusional and could say as much about anthroposophy as I could about higher particle physics. I was set up in quarters. Given food. And given a single task. And with that I made acquaintance with probably the oldest form of socialism: compassion.

In the country, there's always work to do. You get up early. You bring in the hay for the animals. Or you dig holes, into which many, many posts are sunk. And then the infinitely long pasture fence is nailed to those posts. And you help with all possible tasks, with the clients in the house. The only thing I couldn't do was kill the rats, over in the feed store. The father of the house morosely took the shovel meant for killing from my hand and did it himself. Bam! Bam! Bam! One-hundred-and-sixty-seven deaths. The massacre apparently rescued the farm's accumulated supplies from their sure destruction. And rescued it from the fact that a new, even bigger army of rats could one day use it as food.

The days were long and I hurried from one assignment to the next. I didn't get to rest until after dinner. And then I often walked around aimlessly. Always along the pastures lined with barbed wire. I walked and pondered, and the evening sun sank, glowing red above this remote corner of New York State. For me, this was the 'Land of Milk and Honey' and I so wanted to stay, but the length of my visa inevitably approached its end.

'And Fee?' Feli has finally finished her plate. She's licked it sparkling clean, her eyes light up contentedly. 'Come on, tell me more. Tell me everything! Please. Please. Please.' Feli's zeal for interrogation has been awakened. And in the long run, I'm no match for her devilish, efficient, flattering methods. Every resistance is futile.

'Fee left at some point, for the city. And the university. People like her are sought after everywhere.'

After a brief hesitation I add, 'And there was no other way.' The truth is, it didn't work. What could have kept us together? Youthful hormones gone wild? And our dream of a GDR utopia? What could have kept us together? Probably also the diffuse fear of what would come next. And Dresden. Our postcard-beautiful, bittersweet homeland. But far away, somewhere remote, we simply forgot what kept us together.

'Dad, eat!' Feli admonishes me. I nod and pull my plate closer. But instead of a fork, I have the phone in my hand. My gaze glances at the display. My news addiction doesn't forgive offline breaks.

'No phones at the table, Dad.' Feli raises her finger reproachfully. And grins triumphantly. One point for her.

Suddenly, there is so much flying around my head. It overlaps. It contradicts. I should be able to forget. The time with Fee. And everything with the vampires. I should finally be able to let go. My mother's beatings. And the hard kilometres across the river. And my dying grandfather. How he gasps, how he struggles for air. And then finally suffocates. My telephone goes ding.

'I have to see whether that's Mum,' I say apologetically and check. But no. Nothing from my wife.

'Who is it?'

'It's Jerome.'

'Again?' Feli makes a frighteningly grown-up face. 'Last night, too. Right?'

I nod. That's a real disadvantage from all sleeping in one bed: I sleep squeezed up against the wall. And no trip to the bathroom goes unnoticed. Neither does it go unnoticed when my display briefly lights up in the darkness of the bathroom.

'He's not doing well,' I say apologetically. Feli is worried about me. She's always worried. And since the incident on the street-car, even more so. Sometimes she treats me like an older sister. Lovingly strict and always knowing better. Fuck, I have to work on that. I'm the father here after all.

'Don't worry so much, milk bee. I can look after myself.'

I have to say that now. She has to hear it. But it's not that easy. The boy is finished. The boy is dealing with a really tough phase in his life. It's not even my problem. And somehow it is. I wanted to do a friend a favour. He's a kind of crisis sponsor in a self-help group. And he needs help caring for the boys. I just wanted to support him for a few days. A few weeks max. And that turned into this. I'm dealing with a construction site again.

'What are you thinking about, Dad?'

'I'm thinking about Jerome.'

'Why?'

'Because right now everything is really difficult for him. Things aren't going well. And the news from Afghanistan doesn't make it any better.'

I hold my phone up without a word. The source of all bad news in the world. Feli is working something out in her head, I can see it. Jerome is a parachuter. And a paramedic. He was with his unit in Kundus. And there he got stuck in the grey abyss. Stuck in his head. Between the mutilated, lifeless bodies of his friends, whom he couldn't help any more. Despite the strong pills, he's doing poorly. He no longer has the abyss under control.

His sadness. His anger. He can't play his role any more. He can't go out on stage. He can't be a soldier any more. He can't be a husband any more. Or a father. Or a friend. He's been broken and no one has been able to repair him.

I put the phone away and cover Feli's small hand with mine. I shouldn't talk about something like this. Not during my daughter's lunch. Not during goulash and mashed potatoes. And maybe I shouldn't bother any more with this. But what then? I can't just give up on the guy, that's what others have done.

It's grumbling outside. The rain stopped for a little while. Now it's started up again. Drops splash violently against the panes of the bay window. It's as if Petrus has decided to wash the city off the map.

'But you were still in love with Fee, right?' Feli won't let it go.

I nod. Suddenly I'm back there again, on the return flight.

Alone. In the double-walled type. It's a rickety 747. It's an old, flying tin can. Inside is full of aseptic plastic. The outside is covered with metal. I sit cramped in my economy seat. I've been rejected from the land of my dreams. On the way to Germany. Back to the ordinary folk. People who watch when people like me are chased past their garden gate. I've failed. And everyone who fails has to pay a price. I hate myself. I start to cry from anger. I look out the corner of my eyes to a blonde, older woman next to me. The woman doesn't notice any of my tears. She's completely preoccupied with her mashed potatoes. And her golden-brown meatballs. And all the other things they've brought us on the small, grey plastic tray. Mashed potatoes, that's the smell of my good childhood days. The smell of my grandfather's kitchen.

'So you went home again?'

I nod. Home. Home?

CHAPTER TWELVE

Christmas 1991

I pull on the collar of my jacket. An M60 field jacket isn't appropriate clothing for a Saxon winter. But the jacket reminds me of America, that's why I'd rather freeze than take off this tattered green thing. It's Christmas again. And once again I'm far from the world peace that's been proclaimed. I'm carrying this undead letter around with me. It's the letter from Fee. The letter has been unfolded several times. And it's been balled up many times in a moment of anger. This letter made the trip with me across the Atlantic. And now it's got an oily stain from some leftovers on my kitchen table. This goddamn letter. I found it in the farmhouse. In my room. I took a large piece of paper out the envelope and unfolded it.

Dear Sam ...

There wasn't anything else there. Just that, nothing more. I brooded over the letter and I didn't understand it. And I still don't understand it here. After I stamp the entire way home, I burn the letter, ripped into small pieces, in a tin garbage can in the Führer's kitchen. And after that I go on a rampage.

After I'm finished, the kitchen needs to be renovated. And it doesn't help much that I keep having to cry. And today it's escalated to a panic attack. What did they teach me? What am I supposed to do? I forget most of it. You're sitting in a foxhole. The tank is coming. In the face of over forty tons of steel, you want to climb out of the hole quickly and run away. Fear is good. Only an idiot wouldn't have any fear. Hold your breath, that's what Uffz always said. Hold your breath for a moment. Then just exhale three times slowly. Your upper body will slightly bend forward. Let your head hang. And your shoulders too . . . Don't climb out of the hole, the tank is faster than you anyway, no matter where you are. Breathe. Calm down. And then destroy the fucking thing. I'm breathing. And talking to myself. But calming down isn't working.

Shit. Shit. Shit. I curse you, Fee. You fucking witch.

My country is dead, but the people are still there. Well, at least most of them. There's an absurd, kitschy kiosk on the corner to the tram. Rainbow-coloured fairy lights blink in infinite variations, always in a circle. Football collection cards sparkle in the glow of the fairy lights. And on long metal shelves, Colgate toothpaste, Becks beer and 'fluffy soft' toilet paper rolls are stacked. For a moment, a pink hairdryer called 'Lady Hamilton' and neon green nail polish compete for my attention. There was a really nice XXL flowerpot here once. It was a home for pansies, tulips and ornamental grass. And for the cigarette butts of dumb people. The flowerpot had to make room for the stupid kiosk. The kiosk is like a brightly coloured, blinking Death Star, a glue trap. It announces, *Come here children, look what I have to offer. For your allowance, I'll bring you the glory and the splendour of countless culinary delights. Something like this only exists in capitalism, you losers. Come. Come, children and put your German Marks inside me and buy all the short chain carbohydrates. Just sugar! And the cheap fat!*

I've succumbed to that siren enough times myself. Until a friend had to tell me, laughing and gloating, that in my favourite cookies, the butter Spritzringe from Holland, there's up to twelve per cent processed animal meal inside. Before my eyes, I see a forest of industrial windmills in which soft-furred sheep cadavers disappear. I swear to myself that I'll never again eat my favourite butter cookies, at least none from Holland.

I can hardly believe that I was only gone for a few months. There are so many new things. Milka. Lenor. And Yes-Torty. In Polish that means 'cake', but this damn well isn't cake. I search my tattered lexicon. 'Torty'. That's not a word. At least it isn't in the Oxford edition. Doesn't matter. I buy the stuff and eat it. My flesh wants Torty. I want it so bad, that I stuff three of these poisonous things into my mouth. Well, there's no fighting it.

Actually, I can't afford this addiction. I can't afford to pay good money for garbage. There is a great lull in the city. The earlier conditions have been turned on their head. Where there was once many wanted ads looking for trained workers and assistants, there are now closed factory gates. Nothing is happening behind them. It's the big dying off. The so-called THA, Treuhandanstalt or privatisation agency, is shutting everything down that doesn't look profitable at first sight. And these guys from the THA are also killing a lot of the rest along with it. You can close factories, but not people. Even after they've been let go, they still creep and crawl around, often as life-long, angry pension cases. Except for the ones who are prepared to take a cut and contribute to their permanent 'decommissioning'. They are fathers. Grandfathers. Mothers. Colleagues. A despondent death is making its way around the city. It's a quiet dying, behind closed blinds, under ceilings and in attics. My mother's former department manager threw himself in front of a car during afternoon rush hour, after the end of the workday, a day before Christmas. Wherever hope stops, that's where insanity sets in.

But there are some things that time couldn't break, some don't just give up, despite all of the adversity. I know someone from the GDR authority, from the middle of the middle class, he's Mr W. I was with his son at the sports academy. I meet the former prosecutor on the tattered, crooked, concrete pavement in front of the Neustadt train station. The sixty-year-old lawyer and highly decorated soldier of a lost army is standing in a dirty apron behind a rickety camping table. And selling seasonal vegetables.

Comrade prosecutor is still a sprightly man, with alert eyes and a quiet voice. When Mr W sees me in the hustle and bustle, he smiles and waves. If I were in his position, I would have liked to dissolve in thin air from shame. For a minute I consider whether it would be best for both of us if I just pretend I hadn't see him.

But then I go over to W after all, I owe him at least that. I ask W how his son is doing. And I ask him, how he's managing. Holding on and such. W just grins. Then he bends his arm and balls his hand, dirty from vegetables, into a fist. He says 'No pasarán' in a Berlin accent. I burst out laughing, I can't do much else. W laughs too, before he has to lay some asparagus on the scale for the next customer, as if that was the most natural thing in the world for a former prosecutor to do. No pasarán. I always laughed about that motto during the party trainings. I thought to myself, it was just silly heroic shit, meaningless speech bubbles of communist agitators, from the days of the Spanish Civil War. No pasarán: they will not pass.

I rush home down the poorly lit Alaun Street and wish the socialist creator God had cut me from the same cloth that he had cut comrade W, behind his vegetable stand. If only I had half the backbone he did! Instead, I'm living in the empty apartment of the Führer again and acting like a cry baby because of Fee. The longer the letter affects me, the harder the pain is for me. I feel superfluous and hurt. Without a plan. Helpless. I'm sitting under the roof that's full of holes and each day write a letter. I paint individual letters on paper and fold the pages in envelopes. Daily a letter for Fee. Sometimes even two. I want to affect a miracle with my writing, make her understand, how much I miss her and why it should be like this with us:

> *I wish I could make a bridge*
> *Over the cursed bridge.*
> *I wish*
> *I could bend time, like a giant*
> *Bends a coffee spoon.*

I write. And write. And it has no effect. Time only flows in one direction. And in my case it's the wrong one. I send some letters, but often I simply don't have the money for stamps. Day after day, this overhang towers into a higher mountain of paper. I sit in the empty mansard apartment of the long-lost

Führer, whose armoured door I sit behind, where none of the few things are mine.

I sit behind the door and am powerless against time.

I sit at the pitted kitchen table
With a deserted plate
And a cup with the rest.
I write into the past, for a future that will never
        come . . .
Ich sitze am kerbennarbigen Küchentisch.

'Well, how does it feel to be an American? A capitalist?'
Nan grins. And pulls me with her to the window. To the light. 'You still look like you always do.'

I laugh. I'm so happy to see her. So relieved over her familiarity. And how she bickers with me. Even that feels familiar.

'Of course, I look the same as always, you little owl. Or did you think I wouldn't be ugly any more?'

She brings her face really close to mine. The tip of her nose nearly touches my forehead. I always have to remind myself that Nan can only see as far as a mole. She's not blind, but she's not far from it. She's a paradox for me. How can she stay here? As a nearly blind woman with my skin colour? In a world full of wolves, she is a soft piece of flesh that can't run away. These murderers don't have a code. They don't spare women or children. And Nan is a beautiful woman. I don't know how she manages to survive here day in and day out. I worry. Nan is like the sister I never had. And that makes me worry about her even more.

'What are you guys doing up there?' Nan means the attic. In

the meantime, she's discovered the bloody bump on my head through a mixture of groping and seeing. There's a little bit of annoyance in her voice.

'Training. We're just training a little,' I say innocently.

Nan shakes her head. 'Boys really only have three brain cells. Four max. And you damage those on each other.' Nan dabs a cotton swab with disinfectant on my head. The disinfection burns my wound. I flinch with my head. Nan is happy. And for a second helping she adds a hearty smack.

'It can't be healthy to get hit in the head so much.'

She's right. I know she's right. But what am I supposed to do? I have the choice between the plague and cholera. Between bruises on my ribs or a premature exit in a plastic container. Straight to the Tolkewitzer cemetery, in the flower-lined urn corner. The bloodthirsty boys of the neo-something don't care about neurological subtleties. If I run into them and I'm not ready, then they'll beat the life out of me. And I'll have to involuntarily follow my father prematurely. Meanwhile I'm so lost, so alone, so hopeless and far away from any normality, that I can hardly fear death. But I hate the thought of waste! I have a son after all, a junior. And who knows whether time really does heal all wounds.

I read all of these books – Soviet Fantastic, sci-fi, and German utopias. And French. I've never been able to visit the worlds described. Until now I've only experienced the collective of accusers, that tireless band of assholes in my head. And painful kilometres. And thousands of tons of weights. And the crowning achievement of my painful and equally lacklustre sports career was that I was runner up in the last final of 'strongest apprentice', an East German variation of *Gladiators*, just without bells and whistles and effects. And at some point maybe the little fat messenger of love will shoot an arrow at me, who knows. I won't just let someone take my life, no one. And definitely not some random vampire. At least not without putting up a good fight. We were always taught that nature abhors any kind of waste.

But in this decaying country my existence is a story ending in undeniable meaninglessness. If a sack of cassava flour fell over in my father's village, more people would notice that than would my premature death. If I fall victim to the vampires, I'll be robbed of the last opportunity to put a stamp of 'useful' on my life, this aimless rummaging.

'Suddenly speechless? I don't know you to be like that.' Nan's grinning lights up her face like a Christmas ad on a billboard.

'Excuse me. But I just wondered if you're maybe right.'

'Of course I'm right.' Nan listens to my confusing stuff for hours, bent over a cup of steaming hot cocoa. And in her dark eyes, behind her thick glasses, I think I recognise real understanding. And the all-knowing oracle.

'You need a job,' she determines. Yes, work. Don't think about Fee. Not of the smell of her hair, nor the familiarity of her embrace. Her smile. Work, work somewhere and forget. I get going. There's not a lot to find anyway. This city is a desert in terms of jobs. Going door to door is shit. And the conversations at the unemployment office are as pleasant as an enema. Against all possibilities I actually find a job in a kind of institution. A jail for disabled people. With barred locks and cells. A contradiction to Camphill that's become an institution. A contradiction to everything that the anthroposophists believe. There, the fairy-tale-like scenery with the farmhouse and temple in the middle of green hills. Here, the ashy grey corridors, painted an inch thick with latex colouring, that stink like industrial-grade disinfectant. And like shit. And insanity.

After a few months, I've had enough. I just want to go back to Neustadt. Back to my neighbourhood. I don't want to be a bouncer any more, I am sure about that. But suddenly this job seems indescribably worth striving for.

Working the door in a club, during these troubling times, that's a real Meffire idea. It's a really dumb idea. People party like it's nearing the end of the world. Long parties, hard beats, cheap booze. This city is only held together by grants. And by the anger towards 'the people up there'. And the anger of everyone towards everyone, and especially towards themselves. The only ray of hope is this guy Eggert. He's also an ex-pastor, like Eppelmann or comrade grand inquisitor. This Eggert seems busy. At least his denial stopped, which is quite different than among his predecessors. Will that make a difference?

The formations of the neo-somethings are changing. The new generation of vampires is less uniform. And for that reason less predictable. They're the enthusiastic followers of cheap chemistry. New vampires on speed. Vampires on ecstasy and Polish compote. This army of the hopeless knows no sleep. No hunger. And no fear. And it knows no pain. And their undivided hatred of Neustadt still applies. I know all of that and still want to return. There's no place like home. Although Alaun Street feels diffcrent to me without Fee here, empty, without any life, like a rainbow without any colours.

Dirk is sitting on the second floor of the Barn in the kitchen area on a scuffed stool, bent over the inventory list. It's good that at least the director of this place is still the same. Dirk looks up from his pile of papers. He seems tired and aged. And yet I feel as if I had marched in here for the first time yesterday. Dirk grins at me.

'The Lord graces us with his presence.'

I bow low to the floor. 'Here at your command, your lordship.'

Dirk frowns thoughtfully. He didn't call for me. I still invited myself here, in the hope that my boss would take me back.

'How is the dear wife?'

He means Fee. I want to answer, *shitty*. I hope she's doing shitty. So shitty that she'll finally come home. Because that's all that I want. I'm so goddamn pathetic.

'I understand,' Dirk says. He nods knowingly. 'The Lord giveth, the Lord taketh away,' my boss declaims, from behind his desk, pregnant with meaning. It's something from the Bible. But this has nothing to do with 'the Lord', Fee did it. She ripped my little heart-machine out with all its wires. I would so like to be the loved and cared for dog who trots behind her in America. But I won't tell anyone that.

'Do you have a spot for me?'

Dirk shifts to acting. He rolls his eyes and scratches his chin, in a performance of exaggerated thoughtfulness. This guy is an even bigger child than I am.

'Sure,' he finally says. 'You came at the right moment. Can you get a few people together?' With a few people he probably means guys like me. 'We'll make a few trials with really big bands that can fill up the place. I'll need more people working the door for that.' I raise my eyebrows. That's a whole new tone. Until now he's always talked about 'world peace'. And 'no violence'. Pale faces like to drivel about pacifism, but that's a luxury that people like me can't afford. That makes Dirk's new attitude even more remarkable. It's a real turning point. If I had a calendar, I'd make a cross on the date right away.

'We're gonna drink until the coming of the end of the world. And a lot of people want to riot. We just have to be more careful. Something is changing.' He seems really serious now.

I need good people. And good people are hard to find. And even if I find people, it's not going to work without the men in uniform. So I pay them a visit. The police station is in sight of the Barn in a broken-down, dirty grey building from whose facade the stucco is peeling in chunks. The station has the familiar smell of wax beans and soldiers' boots. Whatever unfortunate ex-comrades of the people's police were allowed to keep working deal with theft here. Bar fights. Sex stuff against female party members. Bloody conflicts between married couples . . . a worn counter, worn benches, grey faces sticking out from uniform collars. This here looks like 'Endstation Longing'.

My request for increased patrol activity is rejected. They reject my request for a few additional rounds on the nights of concerts, without much to-do. I plead. I downright beg. I make an appeal in the name of art. In vain. They tell me, annoyed, the station is understaffed. The area goes up to Bühlau, above the slopes of the Elbe. Too few policemen for too large an area. Not to mention the technology. By now, criminals are driving BMWs and Mercedes, while the station is still equipped with GDR vehi-cles, except for two VWs And anyway, they have more vehicles than cops. The grand inquisitor and his records' authority have also left a trail of destruction here and pillaged the personnel.

My visit to the station ends in frustration. In the end, I'm standing on the street and don't understand the world any more. Will the new authorities allow themselves another joke with the rabble? The guards are run from their offices, while the city drowns in chaos and people like me can barely risk leaving their house. This can all only be a joke.

I run through my list of contacts. Make the rounds, go door to door. Most people wave me off. Most of my friends and family are against this kind of work. It's simply too dangerous. After all, not a week goes by without different incidents filling the local pages of the *Morgenpost* newspaper. I lose other guys to the bordellos of the city. The red-light scene pays better, no question. Should I work there too? And watch city dwellers wanting to mate, watch how they spend the house and farm in these places for a few moments of borrowed intimacy. And overpriced wine with bubbles? The jobs in the bordellos aren't all bad. Sometimes the guys there have to catch runaway women. Women from the East bloc. Black women. Cheap human goods. They're hired to be sold off. To be used. The punishments for deserting are sometimes drastic, they range from beatings to smaller mutilations. Treating women like cattle. That would basically be out of the question, if it weren't for the dear money that tempts me so sweetly.

The first concert with the new crew goes as planned. The house is full. The mood is good. There are only a few excesses. And there's no trouble with the vampires at all, just the usual crap. A blond student with a neat parting comes crashing against the door. He's carrying the insignia of affluence. The shirt of the upper classes, business jeans and brand-new Converse. I don't let him in. We discuss everything nice and calmly until the good lad pukes before my feet. A gush of puke pours out onto the slab path in front of the door. And onto my shoes. I flinch. The youth, half about to stagger away, turns towards me again and throws up the rest of his stomach's contents into the entryway. I'm fully awake. So is he now. He wants to come in. He absolutely wants to come in. I send him away again, this time with adult language and more decibels. The upper-class boy stares at me surprised. And grins like an idiot. And punches me. The punch lands, half meeting my neck and half meeting my ear. I'm more surprised than actually hurt. When the comrade readies himself and starts to swing in slow motion, I'm already on top of him, with my mid-section protected, fists ready to bob and weave. And from there I give him a hook to the lower abdomen. Without stopping. The guy collapses and falls over. I grab him. Using the collar of his surprisingly strong designer shirt, I pull him into the nearby piece of grass. I rattle and shake the guy. And scream, beside myself with anger. I would have liked to urinate on him. Fucking wanker. Within a short time, a group of people gather on the pavement in front of the entrance. I see disapproving faces. Excited chatter.

'You could have dealt with that differently,' someone calls.

I'd like to yell, *How so, you idiot?* But I keep silent.

'All they can do is fight. That's all they can do.' A woman's voice. Would you have preferred if this drunk ape had gone inside and grabbed your tits? That's what I'd like to say to her.

'You don't have to overreact all the time.' That's what some long-haired guy who is standing close to me says. Overreact? At the disco tent, near the highway exit, the guys would have ripped him apart. Talk is cheap. Peace is cheap, if you don't actually have to fight for it. I angrily stomp past the small gathering of people, and don't say anything.

'Leave it alone,' Hannes comments. And I do that, after having a Coke and grinding my teeth. I'll get the kitchen to give me a bucket of boiling water. I'll wash the puke away as much as possible. That's the job. Go around and clean up. And shut up.

During the day the weather has a mild spring temperature. Unfortunately, such days are often followed by sinister nights. A flood of drunks shoves themselves through the streets of Neustadt like an army of roaring undead. And later, a dealer comes up, fidgeting. Despite the punishing cold, he is wearing a sleeveless, holey T-shirt. The drugs set everything about him in restless motion. Eyes. Hands. Skinny stork legs hidden in his baggy pants. The drug sets the pace. And that beat is always murderously high. This guy smells like trouble.

'Hey, boss. Is it worth coming in tonight?' That sounds harmless, but beneath the friendliness there is something else lurking.

'No, it's not at all worth it,' I respond. 'The band is shit and it's too full. We have to let people out first.'

A group of female students heads in, I nod at them while my gaze searches their purses and bags looking for the telltale outlines of bottles or wine or beer and Schnapps. And whatever else people always smuggle in here.

'And what about them?' The dealer gestures with his bony finger to the girls who just disappeared into the building. 'You're letting them in.'

I shrug my shoulders. 'They were here before.'

'Just tell me if you don't like my face, you fucking piece of coal.'

The n-word. That's forbidden language. It's seldom used. At least normal people don't try to say it. 'Coal' is, however, familiar, known from my school days. It's the East German version of the n-word.

The dealer finally spits it out and then turns to go. I take a deep breath and think about a Coke with ice. The dealer is gone, it could have been worse. A large group makes a racket walking up the street and tries to head for the entrance. Keffiyehs. Parkas. Mohawks. Half shaved heads. And a pink ski hat. You know, Neustadt people. And I see how, at the back, the dealer is among them. He holds his head down, but you can't really overlook him in that holey shirt.

'Not you.'

My finger gestures in his direction. He acts like he's deaf and almost gets halfway through the entrance. What a cheeky asshole. Sheer anger burns inside me. I grab him by the elbow and pull him from the stairs with a jerk. The guy's arm is thin. He weighs hardly anything; he's just skin and bones. I think, it's as if he's made of straw. One of those folks who stopped eating, because all of his money is spent on drugs.

The guy spins around. Something in his hand flashes. I let him go immediately, as if I touched a hot stovetop. The guy stops grinning. Now he's just dark, fidgety energy. A knife. A knife. A knife. In my head, I feverishly flip through impossible solutions. It's emergency mathematics on adrenalin. And I'm fucking terrible at maths. My panicked imagination comes to rest on the entrance, on the broom. We use it to sweep the flagstone path, so that everything looks nice when visitors come. That's what the boss wants.

I pull the long broom towards me, hold the handle in the dealer's direction. The world sinks into fog. Sounds disappear behind a wall of cotton. A knife. In close military combat, they repeatedly had us attack dolls. They let people stab at us with practice rifles for ages. Instead of a bayonet, the things had a feather with a rubber sleeve. Clack. Clack. Clack. Every hit presses in the feather with a metallic click. Every hit was a stab. I hated these fucking dolls. Now there's a person standing there.

'Come on! Come on!' the dealer screams. 'Come on.'

I gather up my fear and jump forward. The first poke with the broom stick misses him. He's as fast as a poisonous snake. But then the broom gets him. Without a clack, but with force. The broom hits his stomach. The dealer falls over. And while he's falling, I follow up. This time I use the other side. The broom has fifteen-centimetre-long bristles made of hard plastic. I poke him again and again in the breast, stomach and head. It doesn't matter where. The dealer wriggles and rolls. But it doesn't help him much. He's dazed from the fall and just moves too slowly. In the end, he doesn't move any more. He looks terrible. Bruised and bloody. Shit. A worried crowd starts to form around the scene.

'You're like animals.' 'You should be ashamed!' 'Unnecessary, completely unnecessary!'

Hannes covers me. I can sense that he's upset. Is it because of the people or because of me?

'Back!' he screams. 'Get back I said!'

I don't hear much more. Only distant noises. At some point the sirens and the flashing blue lights. Yet again, the ambulance in front of the door; things are slowly getting out of hand. And besides. I can do this, if I have to. I can do it so well that other people pay me for it. A man needs a job.

Man is nothing more than an ape. And an ape without territory that he can defend is a lost cause. Give a man a piece of wall that he can defend. And he'll be the best version of himself. Or the worst? I was never someone who liked to fight as a kid. Kids seldom knock each other's teeth out. And they almost never beat each other to death in the school yard. There were rules in the school yard. This, here, is different. Here there are no guarantees. This is the abyss. Hurt lurks here. Mutilation. And death.

And fear lurks here. Fear. Fear. But I'm not alone in this abyss. I have Hannes here. I have a brother again. As brave and upright as I wish I was. Being able to stand guard with him is pure soul cocaine for the despondent boy in me. I feel made anew. And for much too short a moment, I feel complete. Except for the thing with Fee. After my shift I write to her with shaky fingers, sitting at the Führer's kitchen table.

> *We were given a different role,*
> *Like the lost pieces of a jigsaw puzzle*
> *But we broke the rules.*
> *And live. And feel. And we're not lost.*

This weather lives up to April. Today it's something between cool and crappy. Another concert is happening in the 'Barn'. A big one. Punk rock. On days like this, the firewater flows by the crate into willing consumers. Praise be to the turnover. But I'm responsible for safety in this circus. The general weather conditions leave a lot to be desired.

I have a little network. And my scouts give me this and that, often they're reports between rumour and presumption. Today, however, many individual parts compress into a big, dark cloud. The vampires are coming. And probably not for the usual riot. I go as fast as possible to the police station and report it. The officer at the visitor counter makes a note. Case resolved. I can't do any more, he explains to me.

'Don't you understand?'

The service group leader with the Berlin accent gestures around him. 'We don't have any people. Look around. Look!'

As a matter of fact, the station seems completely empty.

Somewhere, way in the back, an ancient, limping security guard struggles to get to the coffee shop. And after that he struggles with a pile of forms. Did a zombie apocalypse rage here or a killer virus? Because it could hardly be worse.

'You don't have to have an entire regiment stand in front of the door. Just show up now and again and that would be great.' I try to flatter him. And once more I try pleading and begging.

'Tell me, am I speaking Chinese!' The service group leader points to the station behind him again. In response, I fold my hands as if in prayer. And let that have an effect. Ultimately, the man softens and promises me a call.

Maybe the director has someone they can send. A call can't hurt, the officer says. Then, annoyed, he sends me out the door. I trot away. The makeshift support does not come from the police department or from some other authority, they come from Radebeul. Two good guys and a girl who's truly a karate fighting machine.

I've organised reinforcements for Hannes and me, but I fear that it won't be enough, not by far. Last month the vampires invaded Neustadt with over fifty people. They sought out several cafés and left them in ruins. And when they again are supported by their crazy, West German buddies, we'll be totally lost here. Then we won't even be able to protect ourselves, let alone the house and the guests.

I head to my attic, my musty training paradise is only a block away. The others are already there. We give each other punches, kicks and new bruises. After training, we crouch exhausted over our water bottles. And we're united: we can't handle it today, the 'Barn' has to remain closed. Dirk, our comrade and director, will be beside himself with anger. Around three hundred people already have tickets. Three hundred paying customers. Three hundred potential alcohol drinkers. Regardless. I'm sending the team home. I gather my sweaty clothes and my towel and start heading to Dirk.

On Louisen Street, I sneak past the window displays of the sweet shop with my head bent over. I'm so hungry for chocolate waffles. My stomach is grumbling. Just don't look. Keep going. Someone behind me yells something. I don't turn around and walk quickly down the street. The yelling turns into a concert of screams: 'N——! You fucking n——!'

All of my lights signal red. Keep going, just keep going. Maybe I'll still make it home. Or I'll have to jump over the gate at the school. We'll find out now. Bloody hell. Where did they come from? Where on earth? From the tram? An entire vampire army can fit in a single tram car. I ponder all this for a split second, then it stops. Useless thoughts give way to sheer panic. There are fifteen, maybe twenty men. I cross the street. Try to act cool. But my shaky legs almost fail on the pavement. I follow the movement of the group out of the corner of my eye. They're coming. They're coming. Shit, they're coming . . .

Right after that I hear: 'Shoot!'

'Shoot the fucking n—— already!'

I run. I run. My sports bag full of stinky clothes is idiotically pressed against me, like a treasure. My feet fly across the pavement. Something flies past my head. Sparkling. A flare? . . . What am I still doing with this stupid bag? My ID, my ID is still inside, in the side pocket . . . and somewhere there's dog shit on the path, in front . . . Strange, all of the things that occur to you when you're running away from something. A time paradox.

I move extremely fast, while everything around me appears to be frozen in time. You flee through a slow-motion mush. Past two garbage bins and the Main Street sign and a half-ripped advertisement for toothpaste. I fall into Alaun Street, between the parked cars, into the hallway of my building and up the stairs. There, I slam the Führer's armoured door shut and I lie down the heavy bars. Shit. Again. So history does repeat itself. Only that this time I'm totally alone.

The vampires circled through Neustadt on tangled paths, leaving some bloody faces, rubble and fright behind. And then they disappeared again as quickly as they emerged. I venture across the street to the 'Barn'. I find Dirk in his office, bent over files as always. He reminds me of my mother in her work mania, the way he sits there in the glow of his crooked desk lamp. Well OK, except for the colourful water cup. And the open bags of chips. And all the bruised West German car replicas in miniature.

'Hey. Sit down.' He gestures to a scrawny wooden chair.

And suddenly it pours out of me. I tell him about my visit to the police station and the raid by the vampires.

'Did the station leader report to you?' I ask.

Dirk nods. 'They don't want to help. Or just really can't. And besides, the organiser is responsible for a concert.'

'Then you should close down today!'

He nods his head in thought. A clear yes and no. A yes and no? That's got to be a fucking joke.

'You can't open today! There's only five of us! What could we do against a triple, quadruple, fivefold superior strength? And bats and bike chains and knives? And all of the angry hatred?'

Dirk doesn't seem happy at all. He's staring out of his office window with his lips pressed together into a thin line. In the low light of the desk lamp, he seems tired, he still has dark rings under his eyes and his cheeks seem even more sunken in. Suddenly he slams his hand on the table. The water cup springs into the air and the stack of files wobbles menacingly.

'Fuck! Fuck! Fuck!' I flinch. His eruption comes unexpectedly. I don't know him to be like that. But facts are facts. He can scream and rage as much as he wants.

'Are you going to cancel the concert?' I follow up.

Dirk nods, as if I had given him a mouldy piece of bread. I nod too. And then slink away. To hide behind the Führer's door. That's where I put the rest of this fucking day behind me, with tea, a can of beans and a book.

There's a knock at the door. I'm startled from my Strutgatsky adventure. I love Russians and their epic space fairy tales about a better future. Bumm. Bumm. Bumm. Someone is disturbing my daydreaming. Bumm. Bumm. Bumm. Vampires don't knock and yet, I'm still worried.

'Open up. I know you're there.'

The voice sounds familiar. Hannes? That's Hannes. And suddenly I know what mistake I've made. Shit. My pulse is raging and I'm breaking out in a sweat. I pry the crossbar from its brackets and yank the door open.

'Come in.'

Hannes shakes his head. He's pale with anger.

'Where were you?' He hisses the words. 'Where the fuck were you?'

Suddenly, Hannes slams his fist against the door frame. The

dust trickles like a fine cloud from the cracks. He points his finger in my direction accusingly, he struggles to speak, then he lets his hand fall.

'That's it.'

The sentence is spoken quietly, with cruel firmness. 'That's it with us.'

Hannes stares briefly in my direction, but actually he's no longer there.

The morning is grey. The street is empty and filled with garbage. In the 'Barn', Dirk is sitting at his desk. Again. Or still. In me, bitter soup is spilling over the edge of the plate.

'First, we didn't want to open. But people came anyway. And then I thought it would be better if they were inside. And not somewhere outside.'

'You promised me, you promised me!' Dirk nods. He knows it himself. But there's still something I need to know.

'What happened with Hannes?'

Dirk ducks even deeper behind his pile of papers. 'It didn't go so well.' He pauses for a moment and looks out the window. 'Hannes came and you all weren't there.'

'Because you weren't supposed to open.' This time I'm not the crazy one for a change. Dirk knows that. And I know that I've failed as much as him. 'They … came … storming in … they just pushed themselves through the door.' Of course they did. What were the office ladies going to do? 'And then they ran through the house beating everyone, until they got upstairs to the attic.' Dirk stops. 'That's where Hannes was, in the second kitchen.'

Bloody hell. Upstairs in the attic. There's only a narrow

hallway: just one staircase. It's impossible to flee. And practically impossible to hide, too.

'He couldn't get away. The guys had him.'

'And then?'

'And then, nothing. They beat him up and ran off.'

Hannes in the attic, pinned by the vampires. I can imagine this nightmare all too well. He'll never forgive me. My best friend. My Uffz at the door. My comrade on the wall. I know what will happen now. It makes me choke. Fucking shit. Fee is gone. And now Hannes, too. I'm so angry at Dirk. And I'm even angrier at myself. Thanks to my fucking fear I made a fucking mistake. I forgot to tell Hannes not to come. That's the only reason he came. Of course, the fiasco can easily be outsourced to Dirk. But this has nothing to do with the truth. Hannes was my responsibility. I'm guilty. Basta. This realisation hits me with force. I get up and shuffle off, out of Dirk's office. There's nothing more to discuss.

I lie down behind the armoured door, on the tattered mattress. The old steel springs creak and squeak under my weight. I fall asleep for a few minutes. Dream something crazy. I get up and take a piss. Then I lay back down. What else should I do, everything is pointless now anyway. Later that day, more sombre gossip trickles through the network. The mob that haunted the 'Barn' at night and beat up Hannes, beat two students half to death that night. Because of their long hair. 'Deadbeats!' my mother has the accusers say about them. And the bullying is followed by a stabbing headache. So bad that the world sways back and forth like a derelict boat at sea. Shit, fuck.

*

'You didn't close the door properly!'

Nan finds me the next morning on my mattress, nailed down in self pity. 'What's wrong?'

I try to shoo her away, but it doesn't work. Finally, I get up and make us some tea. We spend the time in silence. We stare out of the mansard window at grey, crumbled streets and people who are just as tattered. Dawn comes early. Too many windows stay dark. The city is becoming increasingly empty.

'You need a real job,' Nan says suddenly.

'What kind? I can't do anything.'

Nan has closed her eyes. For a minute it seems as if she's fallen asleep. 'Go back to the police.' She says it to me. She just said it to herself. 'To the police?' Maybe she meant it as a joke. Is it meant to be a joke? But Nan isn't laughing.

'To the police?' I repeat. To the helpless helpers? The embittered, disarmed and outnumbered servants of a system that no one can really believe in. 'They must have been waiting for someone like me.'

Nan nods. 'Yes. They have.' For a moment that hangs in the air between us. This woman and her cryptic thoughts. She may be nearly blind, but she sees the world much better than many other people, including me.

'Why do you say something like that?'

'You're already a policeman.'

Me, a policeman? I wanted to be one once. Very much so. But that was a different time. In a different world, in a different universe.

'I would certainly feel safer with you out there.'

Nan lays her hand on my forearm. Her touch is warm. And

soft. There's no commanding tone in her voice. Which makes it all the more of a command.

'Nan.' I shake my head and stare embarrassed out of the mansard. 'I'm not a *white knight*. Really, I'm not. I know all the shit in my head.' I should tell Nan, I know what kinds of monsters party there every day. But I don't do it. I'm too afraid of losing her to this little dazzling truth. Usually I'm not friends with women. And definitely not with ones I find attractive. You can be friends or fuck. Somehow you can't do both, I think. Nan is the only exception. She's like Buddha, but much, much prettier.

'I hear so many of us endlessly complaining. But all of that complaining doesn't help. We have to take responsibility for ourselves.' Nan's grip on my forearm no longer feels soft. 'Otherwise they'll kill all of us,' she adds, quietly.

And I know that she's right. But what could we do? I think about the training with the ninth. I think about the winding streets and the urban guerrilla training. We needed half a fucking day in order to get one hundred steps up the street. Fighting in houses in the gorges of tower blocks inhabited by Prohlis or Gorbitz? It's simply impossible. And even if it was possible, no authority would allow that. And at best it would give us time to catch our breath, nothing more. The hatred for us wouldn't disappear from that.

Nan lays a newspaper article that's been folded twice onto the windowsill next to her. 'For you,' she says. I pull the piece of paper over to me. It's a job announcement in the *Saxon Newspaper*. The heading reads: 'Wanted, Trainees in Criminology.'

'I have to go,' Nan says, before she floats away to the hallway smiling.

*

That night, I write Fee another letter.

Stay where you are

I scratch ink onto the paper.

Stay, where you are.
    If you want to listen to my advice: Never return. Don't come home.
    Our dream is dead. Gone. Forever.
    And if you have to dance for a golden calf (and who doesn't have to these days?)
    then at least do it for the original.
    Don't come here.
    Stay where you are, that's my advice, dear.
    Never come back.

I stare at the paper. Something is still missing. Maybe: *And tell me to come, bring me home finally.* Yes, maybe that. But I don't write that, of course. I do, however, leave the rest there. I owe her this warning.

I awake after a mercifully dreamless night. I sit down at the kitchen table, hungry and naked, and stare at the wall. The kitchen wall, across from the stove, is papered with articles, like a kind of strange collage. It's my helpless attempt to understand. The newspaper clippings stand against the chaos. There are no reports that ground-breaking inventions have been made. Or discoveries. Or that some people have come together to form forward-looking political parties. There are exclusively reports about decay and crime. Theft. There is a flood of thefts. And on the margins of Friedrichstadt, in Mickten and even on Stauffenberg Aley, right before the doors of the riot police, there's prostitution. And with that, problems. After a raid, a pimp just casually threw a hand grenade into the station. Prostitution and biker gangs and the war between the Vietnamese groups, a war about illegally obtained cigarettes and the distribution of the earnings. It's an unprecedented brutal murder series like the Saxons have never seen. A true slaughterhouse with a lot of chopped-off heads. Now many are getting revenge.

They brought the Vietnamese to the country to work as contract labourers. As indestructible, hard-working, always-smiling cheap labourers. And yet after the wall fell, they were threatened with deportation. And many of them were loaded onto planes and sent to Hanoi. Now the city has a small, but extremely powerful Vietnamese underground army to deal with. Even the vampires fear them.

I stare at my newspaper clippings and get lost in my thoughts, until hunger forces me out of the house. And in the hallway there are several figures lying around. The front door is ancient and battered, without a lock. And now and again, the party-mob throw their leftovers into our entryway. Or use it as a toilet. Today it's just a horde of strays. They're lying on the bare floor, wrapped up in their holey, grey-black hooded sweatshirts. I can't see much of their faces, just confused, coloured strands of hair. The youth lie densely packed in and they stink and snore. I teeter through the gathering of bodies like a stork. I stumble. Hold on. I step carefully, seeking to avoid anything human.

'Watch out, you old wanker.' I ignore that and have finally reached the door. Then something hard hits me in the neck.

Fluid trickles down my back. I turn around; on the floor in front of me there's a crumpled can of cheap beer. One of the hooded sweatshirts barks a croaky laugh in my direction. In his mouth, there's only a handful of nubs for teeth. It's an ugly laugh.

This fucking laugh. It triggers me. In my head, I briefly see the blinking red light. Before I can complete my thought, I'm in the middle of a tangle. And then the ugly hooded sweatshirt guy is already flying against the wall with a pop. I pull on his jacket, but his upper torso is tangled up in some knot, locked. I pull and pull and just can't get a grip on him.

'You fucking little twat.'

The hooded sweatshirt guy is staring at me with glassy eyes. He's bleeding from his mouth and nose and he stinks like a resurrected corpse. Now it flashes behind my forehead. Stars. Glistening stars swirl around me. For a moment, I feel strangely weightless, like back when the sergeant hit my head, including my helmet, against the windowsill of the Sparkasse building, during urban guerrilla warfare.

I let the hooded sweatshirt guy fall and protect my head with my arms. I stumble. I almost fall. I have to support myself with my hands and give up my cover. Something hits me hard in the ribs. There is a shooting pain, stabbing towards the middle of my body. I kick and kick and finally get free. Half kneeling, I pull the short stick out of my shoulder blade. A worn, sweat-stained, unbreakable hardwood thing. I hit and 'stab' around me. Somewhere.

During the course of the day, I still manage to get some bread. Bread from yesterday. The entire country is from yesterday. Standing still between a past that doesn't want to die and a future that doesn't want to come. Maybe Nan was right. Maybe I don't have any other choice than to stand on the wall and start my watch. And to live in the hope that this will make a difference. I'm not as mature as Fee. I'm not as brave as Hannes. And I'm not as clever as Nan. But I could give my best, however imperfect my best may be. A part of me doesn't want to think about attempts to save the world. I just want to hide behind a book again, as quickly as I can. Or, even better, behind the powerful back of my grandfather. But grandfather is dead. And my brother is gone. And so is Hannes. And I'm on my own.

CHAPTER THIRTEEN

'Human dignity is inviolable.'

That's what he wrote on the blackboard. And then comrade lecturer, with multiple doctorates, strolled out of the lecture hall and left us with this fucking sentence. And a mountain of homework. Giving out homework seems to be the favourite hobby of all lecturers anyway. Homework. And plenty of it please.

Human dignity is inviolable? That doesn't seem to count for police cadets. Our Russian teacher always used to announce, 'домашнее задание', *homework*, at the end of the lesson. And always with a joyful grin.

And even here, the homework is barely disguised as a 'recommendation'. It haunts us at the end of each agonisingly long day of learning, deep into the evening hours. They already warned us, before this crazy pace began, but the reality exceeds all my fears. I wanted to be on this course. Absolutely. Although strictly speaking, this course shouldn't exist. At least not according to career law. This course is nothing more than a fresh meat magic trick for the criminal police. They threw together kindergarten teachers, a field hunter, several office clerks, a few engineers and me, and at high speed they turned us into detectives. With us they hope to fill those holes that the grand inquisitor and his people burned into the ranks of the Saxon police.

This course is unique. And this scholar of law is too. They brought him here from the management academy and now he's supposed to convey to us his finely woven understanding of democracy. This guy is a master brain; a high flyer. His brain doesn't work like others', not like those of mere mortals. And I wonder, why has not a single candidate's head exploded after his courses?

We have to take state law, constitutional law, criminal law, criminal procedural law, police law, criminal tactics and technology. And a former director's secretary teaches us the ten-finger-writing system. And even that presents a challenge for me. Most of the time, I type clumsily on the keys of my typewriter. I probably look like a drunk clown during a late-night show. But without the ten-finger-writing certificate, I can't graduate. So I push extra runs after work. Click, click, click. Then my fingers get stuck between the keys again. Back to work. Start over. Click, click, click.

'*She's homeless, she's homeless*', Crystal Waters repeats again and again, like a mantra. The super hit of last year, 'Gypsy Woman', booms through the old barrack walls. I can feel the beat deep in my chest, that's how strong the floor vibrates. What on earth are they doing up there?

'Man, I hate this song.' Micha grins up from under the dumbbell.

'And you better be careful, you coati,' Micha threatens me with his finger. 'Otherwise I'll flatten you with this thing. So watch out!'

I shrug my shoulders. 'I'm always careful.'

'Yeah, right,' Micha protests.

'You're either thinking about Russian spaceships or you're thinking about that Coco,' he winks at me.

'Probably in a bathrobe,' I protest. 'Blasphemy. Awful slander. Rumour.' I lift the barbell off the brackets and bring it to Micha, so he can do his reps. 'For your information: the comrade is only named Coco in the film. She's really an actress from Austria. Son-ja Kirch-ber-ger.'

Micha has taken the barbell and is groaning. Nevertheless, he can't suppress a grin. 'Have you already identified her licence plate? You could write it out for a search.'

'Asshole.' I grin and leave Micha to his painful fight with the iron.

After a long day of studying, we've made a pilgrimage to the basement. And in precisely these barracks, in precisely this basement, near the boiler room, I used to lift weights for the riot police. And down here it still looks like the dirty hobby corner of a serial killer. It doesn't bother me. And apparently it doesn't bother Micha either. Everything here is repurposed. The bench: a block of planks of sawn pallet parts. The barbell: from Micha. The weights: we 'borrowed' them from the former staff area, where they were just rusting under a mountain of old chairs. For these metal discs, on both ends of our barbell, I am not a being with dignity. Just as little as for the law nerd and his damn homework. For the discs I'm just carbon-based resistance that has to be squeezed mercilessly under gravity. Gravity always wins. That's how it is.

So this is never about a victory. The only thing that's possible is delaying a defeat that has long since been determined. Set for set.

Repetition by repetition. Apparently, Samuel Beckett, the Irish author, once said: 'Try again. Fail again. Fail better.'

Micha and I are crazy about it. We refuse to join the end time cult of the others to booze against the inevitable. The final exam is coming. And it will be merciless. After the final months, the course is eagerly anticipating its end. I've done my best to integrate. But my preference for Soviet fantasy, Bukowski, Hesse and maximum physical exercise haven't really brought me far. People tolerate me in a friendly way. There are crazy people everywhere. Bass booms above us. We have to numb ourselves, everyone in his own way. Some with iron, like Micha and I. And the others with youthful dance music and alcohol.

No one on this course bet on a sure thing. It's completely uncertain how long this so-called 'free state' will survive. At least outside of the general plans of some technocrats in Bonn. They pressurise us with expertise like the French fattening geese before the slaughter. No one really knows, what could help us out there in the 'area'. Outside, chaos is raging. In the media, in *Der Spiegel* and the *Süddeutsche Zeitung*, I read again and again about the 'wild East' and West German worry that the newly patched country will soon break apart again.

Maybe the oppositions are too big? For the criminals in the city, I suspect they couldn't be big enough. Chaos always means full coffers for the usual suspects. For the Apparatchiks. And in the red-light scene as well. That's why, after the test, us fresh meat are sent directly to the front. No one on our course knows where he'll end up. But there will definitely be no more hiding behind law books or typewriters. Part of me wishes I could stay here for ever, in the tolerable, orderly world of the basement.

*

Micha raises the weight one last time with a grunt. Then I pull the barbell to me. Doing that, I nearly miss setting it down on the stand. Bloody hell. Of course I had to think of Fee again. I only ever think about her – and sometimes about Sonja Kirchberger's body, which is out of this world. Fee. My freckled professor. The thorn in my flesh. I quickly find my balance on the bench, under the barbell. Don't think. Don't worry. Just act. Let the pain do its thing. And heal.

Weeks later. We have a criminal patrol. That's one of the new minister's new strategies. The people should know the police on their street. They should see the police on their street. And it's a signal to the criminal elements, *Look here, the time of chaos is over. The state is back.* Well, at least the few of us who aren't too busy with our typewriters and files.

Today, on Ascension Day, the thin personnel cover is especially painful. Ascension Day is another harmless holiday that some crazy people have taken hostage. They get drunk and get into fights. And there are especially a lot of vampires around. For us and in the emergency rooms, Ascension Day ensures full employment. A lot of things will be urgent tonight. And all we have is this ridiculous piece of junk for a car. Back in the day, our red patrol car, a Lada, would have been high-quality equipment. Today it's just an annoyance. Other units are already driving comfortable VW Passats or Golfs. We, on the other hand, are creaking and swaying and rocking in a vehicle whose absurd robustness was originally conceived for Siberian moguls. Anyway, no mixing business with pleasure. An order is an order. At slow speed, we sneak across the cobblestones and past the edge of Nordstadt. When we go slowly, the Lada doesn't make as much noise. Contrary to our hopes, they didn't assign us to back up in the city centre. Instead, we cruise side streets, looking for potential thieves.

The night is warm and still. It's a pleasing contrast to the crowds of the day. The city's streets aren't prepared for the increased traffic. Traffic jams, that's also something you have to get used to. Back in the GDR, most people took the tram or the bus. Now it's the other way around. The bridges are the worst bottlenecks, at least during the day. Even using the siren wouldn't help. And getting somewhere in the city quickly to provide backup is practically impossible. Unless you have a flying carpet. Micha and I drive at a walking pace towards the north. To the left and right of us, dark window cavities eye us from behind closed curtains. Shortly after 2 a.m. we've seen everything – 'without special occurrences'. Except for the weather.

Once again, the weather doesn't comply to any official instructions. A storm is coming. And soon the rain is pattering with a dense staccato on the metal roof. There's a sound coming from somewhere, it rudely cuts through the still of the night. It sounds like broken glass and as if a giant has stepped on a giant piece of hard plastic that has cracked under his shoe. Micha switches our light to 'drive'.

We turn our heads in every direction, but we can't find anything besides the outer wall of the former District Authority of the Secret Police, which is smeared with colourful paint. We bounce down Angelika Street.

There's something near the former main entrance. It appears a large black sedan has driven into a lamppost, apparently without braking. Steel and concrete against a 7 Series BMW. The lamppost won. It cut through the engine-block and right up to the windscreen. We block part of the roadway, so that another night-time driver can't drive into the scene of the accident. The sight of the wreck makes me feel sick, even before I can climb out of our car. I've never seen a car that destroyed. The steps walking toward the BMW are difficult, my knees shake. But I have to do what I have to do. Something is moving on the left side. The driver appears to be alive. His airbag was activated and is now hanging on the steering wheel like a limp balloon. A woman is sitting next to it. Middle-aged. A well-groomed appearance. Remarkably lush hair. Her head seems unnaturally angled and twisted.

'Bloody hell! Goddamit.' I can't get anything else out. 'Call dispatch. They have to send someone, immediately!'

My head understands it, but my legs don't want to go to make the call, I'm frozen. Micha shakes my shoulder. And then we hear the rapidly approaching cry of the sirens. Someone else had already called for help. Flashing blue lights outshine the lantern. The guys from the fire department sit up straight in their truck and they rush to work. 'Have you done anything yet?' the operations manager asks. I just shake my head.

'We didn't feel comfortable moving them.' In contrast to me, Micha hasn't lost his voice. The operation manager waves to us.

'It's better that way.' With that, he's already stormed past toward the BMW. A few moments later, the firefighters have laid the woman on the pavement. I feel like a fucking movie extra.

'Do you know who that is?' Micha nudges me.

'Who?'

'The woman, man!' Micha is unbelievably astonished by my cluelessness. 'Are you serious?' Should I know? 'That's that famous woman from TV.'

I look down at the pavement. Actually, it is her. Apparently, panic doesn't just make you stupid, it also makes you blind. Something doesn't appear to be working. They cut open the woman's blouse. And the rest as well, down to the skin. Several electrodes are sticking to her chest. The hectic pace increases.

'Adrenaline! You there, raise this up for me!' A fireman who's kneeling next to the woman points to his ampoule stock. 'You there! Quickly!' He means me. Bloody hell. 'Adrenaline! Faster! What's wrong with you?'

I panic, I have a panic attack. Is that possible? Until then, I didn't know that absolute horror can still be increased.

'I, I, I . . . I can't do it. Not me! Not that.' I stutter in the direction of the fireman. I wag chaotically and defensively with my hands. I can't!

'Goddamit, are you completely useless?'

The fireman is pissed off by my incompetence. And I wish I could dissolve into thin air. There's a woman dying there. And all I can contribute is standing around dumb. Lightning suddenly flashes at me. First, I duck out of instinct. Then I turn around. A big guy in a leather jacket takes a picture of the dying television woman with his camera. The camera is a giant thing with a lens and a flash and the guy handles it calmly, as if he was just taking some wedding photos.

'You must be crazy! Get back!' My numbness finally leaves me. I finally start moving. Just unfortunately with the wrong text. Where are the fucking words from the police law? 'Disrupter.' 'Expulsion.' 'Immediate threat.' 'Force.' everything is swept away by shame and indignation.

'I'm from the press! I'm just taking pictures!' The fucking press-punk tears himself away from me. He's loud. I get even louder.

'Stop that! I'll take your camera! Get back, now!'

The guy is really tall and broad and pissed off. And he has a noticeable Bavarian accent. A wrestler. That's even worse than a Prussian.

'I'm the press! Do you have any idea who I am?' the punk screams.

'I'll file a complaint. With your superiors!'

He storms off, but I jump in his way. We crash into each other roughly. No pasarán, you wanker. I should play it safe and knock the wind from of him before he can knock my teeth out. I've had enough of this morbid parasite making a goddamn scene. I search my pockets for gloves and a mouth guard. But then the fire captain comes and flies into the guy.

'You can see that this woman is dying! What's wrong with you?' The fire department is less squeamish than I am. The comrade from the 'press' rolls back a few metres. And from that distance he immediately starts with the camera again. The flash goes 'snap'. Snap, snap. The next day, photos from the accident site appear in the tabloids. Including pictures of the dying woman from television. Beautiful new world.

Weeks later. I'm lying awake once again and I'm rolling around. Witching hour. Right now there's hardly any partying outside. Whoever is lucky enough to find a job goes to bed early. Whoever still doesn't have one doesn't feel up to partying. Apart from not having the money for getting drunk somewhere other than home. The party is over. I listen to the quiet. The street out there is the middle of my universe. On this street, I held hands deep in love with Fee. And here, the heart of the Colourful Republic beat for a few days. And here the dream also died.

I'm on this street looking for coal and something to eat. I've found work on this street, in the 'Barn'. And it's here that the ninth rescued me from vampires. On this street I also survived another attack by the vampires. Another man, Jorge Gomondai, did not have as much luck and died on that day, in April 91. Three hundred metres of homeland. Three hundred metres of asphalt and cobble stones. And grey building walls. And damaged roofs. And damaged people. I've seen the seasons come and go. This street is grey, yet charming. This constantly littered, broken street is a miniature model of the world. Splendid and fucked up.

I carried my son around on this street. Yes, I have a son who's only a few kilometres away. At this hour he's certainly lying in bed and sleeping peacefully. And fatherless. The split from Silke eats at me. Ultimately there wasn't any fairy tale with the fairy-tale princess. Silke was ready. For everything. For a relationship. For the little one. For a real life. The way adults live. Silke was ready. I wasn't. I messed that up too. And this guilt weighs heavily on me. I feel awful. Like a fool, an idiot, a fucking asshole. I brought a child into this world and then just left him here alone. Guilt. I think about all that in this grey house. In the mansard flat. Behind the Führer's door.

I did what my little son couldn't. I looked for a new 'family'. Life in this police force is no walk in the park, but it's a much better place than a lot of other places in this city of people left behind. Hate-stories and racism? Not towards me. A colleague from the Chemnitz unit once bullied me, in the staircase of the barracks.

'Huh, are n—— allowed to participate now?'

Something like that. Four colleagues had to rip me and the

good fellow apart so we wouldn't tear each other to shreds. Indeed, my comrades made it clear to him that he should immediately get lost, because otherwise they'd report him. And sure, there was also that thing during the mission. I remember a guy with a ribbed undershirt with coffee stains. What was it about back then? About a robbery? Sexual assault? We rang a lot of doorbells looking for witnesses. We also rang the doorbell of this one special case.

'What's a Black guy doing with you guys?' the guy yelled.

My superior who was there immediately restrained the guy, so thoroughly that he eventually apologised to me. The whole thing embarrassed me, in a good way. Rarely has anyone stood up for me. The Saxon police had some internal problems, but bigoted hateful opinions against people who are different wasn't one of them. In contrast, here the world was as it should be. Here the mission still counted for something. And comradeship. That's why I took my oath with the deepest conviction. To the country. And to this strangely new free state. And especially to what this new minister guy has begun.

He was personally at the swearing-in ceremony. That meant something to me. I don't value the rest of the authority figures, this collection of opportunists and problem deniers. But I do value the minister. He's like Ulbricht, in love with cybernetics, just without all the drawers in his head and without the unspeakably incompetent party of professional revolutionaries on his heels. The minister wants more for the new police, a future that is more than a tepid, approximate promise that no one would ever think of redeeming. The minister is planning for us to have desktop computers on every vehicle, instead of ancient Erika brand typewriters on equally ancient desks in dilapidated departments. The minister wants there to be mobile transaction processing, basically an office on wheels that is constantly connected to the service network. And the minister describes organised crime as a kind of Europewide civil war, in which Saxony is just one of many settings. Human trafficking. Weapons trafficking. Money laundering. All of this yields mountains of profits. And these things create almost unlimited possibilities for the other side. The minister has long wanted to establish overdue 'equality of arms'. And he opposes the vampires. He's put the best detectives on them. And special forces.

Now the days of public trivialisation are over. This minister has the stuff to become a 'big star'. He's working on a utopian world that maybe can't be truly just, but it will at least be relatively safe. At some point in the future. Man needs idols. Ideals. He needs a purpose. Have I found mine? Until now, I haven't been a good father to Samuel Jr. But maybe I can settle part of my guilt. Maybe at least I can do my part so that he doesn't have to grow up afraid in this city. Therefore my oath is to the minister and his offensive.

That's what I think about during the witching hour, about that and a lot more. Once again, I can't sleep. Sleeplessness is probably an almost inevitable side effect of youthful idealism. For some time, I toss and turn under the covers, then finally I get up and sit at the kitchen table with a cup of tea. I think about my son and scribble again in ink on paper:

I'm in a rush to save this city. Or a handful of people on some street corner. Or at least you. A life, at least one. I want to save you. This idea is stuck in my head. It's like phantom pain after an amputation. I'm rushing nowhere

*particular. Sun and rain. Day and night. Victim and loss.
All of this is meaningless without you.*

My son is four years old. He probably knows even less what he should do with my guilty conscience than I would know what to do with a toy car. And the fairy-tale princess would probably shake herself with fits of bitter laughter after reading these lines. All of the work of raising our son falls on her shoulders. And I'm writing a bombastic letter of poems to a child. The fairy-tale princess laughs in my head and rightly so. And with her, the collective of accusers laughs. I never mail the letter.

Days later. 4.30 a.m. It's still dark outside. I sneak into the department and walk on tiptoes past the on-call room towards the office. I push myself to do a three-minute run. I do push ups, at my desk, between the files. Three minutes are a fucking eternity. Keep it together for three minutes. If my grains of strength last that long, the probability increases that I'll still be alive in an actual scenario. My triceps are like clumps of concrete. My shoulders burn. I feel a little dizzy. And sick. Yes, that's it. That's the way it has to be. With this dose, I feel armed for the day. The pain is constant, my fortress. I'm its king. Or subject, depending.

The others are waiting in the on-call room. Waiting is the worst. It's this goddamn limbo between adrenalin and boredom.

I sit between my colleagues who are smoking and slurping coffee and I wish with all of my heart I could get away from this smoking hell. My comrades are in a good mood. They chat and joke while the head of the department distributes papers on his desk. I'm the baby chick among all of these veterans.

I sit way in the back, behind my colleague giant Winrich's

broad back, hoping that no one gets the idea to ask me something. We're the permanent criminal service. The fire department. The permanent service takes over whatever happens to be needed. From bigger thefts and cases of sexual assault to robbery and weapons. We take it and we pass it on to the specialist service. And we search for lost children, view bodies, help with arrests, reconnaissance, and observation. We take whatever comes, we help out everywhere, we stick together. There is no other way with so few people; we are what is left. And we're a colourful, thrown-together family. An armed commune. Men and women. Old and young. College graduates and high school dropouts. Athletic and less athletic. Bookworms and readers of the tabloid press. And naturally a few comrade pigs and busybodies.

Where will I fit in? Or better yet: where will me colleagues fit me in? Outwardly it doesn't make a huge difference. For the criminals, we are above all just one thing: 'pigs'. Shit. Worth less than cattle. That's just how the world is divided. It's the eternal game between them and us. We've chosen a side, just like they have. I made my decision. And now I have to learn to live with it. For me this is a well-known and yet also a completely new world. And thus I prefer to sit way in the back at the service meetings, so that no one gets the idea of asking me a question. I listen to the technical jargon and nod cleverly and take notes in my book. Inside, it feels like I'm a little boy who's snuck in with the adults. The boy must grin a lot.

The phone rings. Someone has something for the boss and brings it over the 'wire'. Whenever there's something important, people avoid the radio. Over the radio, everyone outside can overhear. The department leader transfers the call to an extension and storms out of the room. The staff whisper, we indulge in guesswork. After a few minutes, the boss comes back.

'So, colleagues, we've received information from the specialist service that the accused W turned up in his apartment after a few days absence.'

Oh no. W, that's a sickening thing. It's about kids. Really small kids. Someone from the red-light district hung him out to dry, someone spoke out against him. Until now, the specialist service couldn't prove their suspicion, but things seem to be different now. Long live the spy.

'Our dear colleague Winrich will drive. With Thomas. And take the new guy with you.' The boss points in my direction. 'W is the size of a garden gnome. And at least hasn't had any weapons until now. So you three guys should be OK.'

Tall Winrich looks over to me sceptically.

'The three of us? What about the ZEG?'

The ZEG stands for Civil Task Force. The hammer of the criminal police. It's kind of like a slimmed down mobile task force.

The department leader waves him off. 'It's not available. Get going!'

Comrade Winrich isn't convinced, but he gives in. In the hallway, he holds back Thomas and me. 'We're taking everything we have. The hammer. The vest. The shield. I have no idea whether the crazy paedo has got anything. He has to expect that he'll have visitors.'

Thomas and I nod. Let's take as much as possible, of course. We pack everything quickly into our official road cruisers, over to Neustadt, it turns out to be extremely short. W's house is easy to find. We stop one block away.

'So, comrades, this is the plan: I'll break the door open with the hammer. You!' With that, Winrich points to me. 'You have the vest on and the shield. As soon as the door is open, you run in and throw yourself onto him.' I nod obediently and pretend to be brave. Blood shoots painfully into my fingers. They immediately start to shake.

'And you.' Winrich points to Thomas. 'You're the best protection out of all of us. You deal the least amount of damage in a tight space. You have to secure us in case anything goes wrong and he actually has more than the usual kitchen utensils lying around his place, then you're up.'

Thomas nods. I've already felt queasy just from listening. What we're doing is a good thing. It's clearly a good thing, to do what's in our craft to stop him. Even though I don't want to think much about his 'craft'. The neutrality towards the accused that my official job demands has long been thrown overboard. I have to pull myself together. I can't mess this up.

'You know the drill. We'll wait until 6 a.m.'

It's 5.35 a.m. We could get going. But then everything would be for nought. Whatever we might find in the apartment, whether it's a letter of confession, bloody knives or fucking babies, they would fall under the evidence, because we would have obtained it unlawfully. In the summer, between 9 p.m. and 4 a.m., in the winter until 6 a.m., the so-called night-time limit of the Code of Criminal Procedure applies. That's one of these 'door locks', so that certain Nazi atrocities can never be repeated. The Gestapo liked to drag people from their beds in the middle of the night. The nightly invasions in the workers' neighbourhoods were a targeted variation of state-organised terror. That can't ever happen again. The night-time barrier makes sense. And yet, today it's really fucking tiresome.

We wait. I've already put on the bulletproof vest. It's the monstrous, chunky, blue sewn-up thing that I already had to carry around in Potsdam. I sweat under 20 kilograms of ceramic plates.

Finally, five minutes to six. We cross the ragged street and the pavement, which is no less in need of repair, and squeeze into the house entrance. It smells like piss. The walls are a faded, crumbling yellow. W lives in one of these half-dilapidated Neustadt buildings, in a real shithole. And I live in the exact same thing, just a few streets away.

I follow Winrich and Thomas up the stairs in slow motion. To the third floor. We step quietly. But the old stairs crunch and crack and grunt. We barely reach the door and Winrich swings and strikes with the giant hammer against the door. Bam! Bam! Bam! The door remains shut. It's like a failed magic trick. Giant Winrich with the giant hammer, against this decrepit joke of a door. Winrich looks puzzled, then he swings again. Bam! The whole house shakes.

Thomas suddenly screams next to me like crazy: 'Police!' He thrashes his fist against the door board.

'Open up, police!' I yell. Winrich swings the hammer again like an angry blacksmith. Thomas and I jump away from the door. The hammer strikes it. Again. And again. And again. He punches deep dents in the door, but the door holds up.

Winrich must take a break. The hammer is gigantic and heavy. My supervisor struggles to breathe. Suddenly there's a scratching at the door. The scraping sound of locks. Then the demolished door board swings open. A man in an undershirt and pants stands in front of us. I don't wait for anything else. I jump in front and with maximum strength, I smack into him. He flies backward. And I on top of him. With the shield and the vest and the backpack. And fear. I'm on the floor, underneath me and the shield there's just the guy. My cheek is burning. And my forehead. I smacked against the inside of the shield with my face. Half of my profile feels like it's numb. Underneath me nothing is moving. Not yet? I hide myself. Pull in my legs and arms as good as I can, with all the stuff.

I fidget and struggle, and nevertheless it takes what feels like an eternity until I can get off the guy.

'Everything's good! Everything good. Calm down.'

Winrich pulls me up by my backpack. And then Thomas has already turned the guy onto his side and put him in handcuffs. 'Where are the pictures? Where are the films?'

The guy looks woozy. He's bleeding lightly from his nose and his mouth. A doughy face. The face of a bank branch manager. Someone you wouldn't remember if you were to pass them on the street.

'Last chance, good man. You can hand over the photos and the films voluntarily.' Winrich rips the covers from the man's crumpled night camp and uses it to hide his sparsely covered nudity.

'Or what?' the restrained one growls. Something flashes in his eyes. Anger? Amusement? Great Manitou, what kind of nerve does a guy have to have for something like this, under these circumstances? Freshly flattened and with the police in your apartment. Either this guy is innocent or he's a phenomenal actor.

'Good.' Winrich's voice is now just dripping with poorly controlled anger. 'I hereby inform you of the District Court of Dresden's decision to order a search of your apartment. We are looking for possible evidence that can be used to support the allegation made against you of sexual assault on children in a particularly serious case according to Section 177 of the German Criminal Code.'

In the meantime, Thomas has found a neighbour, who, with great dismay, is standing in the demolished doorway of the apartment wearing an apron. Silent. Pale as a ghost. Her apron is solid grey, made of Dederon, the notorious GDR synthetic fibre. She can't be older than her mid-sixties, but she seems ancient.

'Your neighbour Mrs W is friendly enough to act as a witness during the search.'

The specialist service has told us where to search. But in order to protect the source, we walk a few rounds through the tiny apartment. It's just a single room, with a toilet and a kitchen. There are some cupboards close by, a table, a stove and a shower. This tiny room houses an entire fucking life. I shudder when I think of this guy here crawling away and fleeing. And what kinds of ideas have entered his brain.

Winrich waves me over. We pull the bed out of a corner. There are just dust motes underneath, nothing else. One of the wooden boards in the floor starts to squeak under Winrich's weight. Perfect. Our cue.

'What's that?' Winrich asks sternly. As if he had never before in his life stepped on a creaking floorboard.

'What's what?' The guy acts dumb. He doesn't know what we know.

Winrich lightly jumps up and down on the floorboard. 'This here. And that there.' The adjacent floorboard creaks, too.

Like we agreed, I take the crowbar out of the backpack. I start to work where the board is most loose. Knack. It doesn't take long. There is a rectangular hole in the ground. Inside there's a dented, scraped ammo box with pale Cyrillic characters. A square box, twice as big as a shoe box.

'What's that?' Winrich asks in a hard tone.

The guy contorts his neck theatrically, as if he's hearing for the first time that there's something in this hole. But in his eyes, I see something of the spirit of Gollum, the gnome-like being from Tolkien's masterpiece. Gollum and his treasure.

'No idea! That's not mine. I don't know what that is.'

With cold composure, Winrich turns toward me.

'Before we take this out, take photos and brush the thing off. Use the fingerprint method.' I suddenly feel warm. I'm really not a master of the Pentacon camera. I've only saved fingerprint-related traces this way during my training, on an experimental setup.

'Don't make a face like that. We're not talking about your funeral.' Comrade Winrich bends himself over me. 'We just need a single print that we can assign. You can manage that.'

I nod, yes sir, execution. I'll do it. I'll manage. No idea how, but I'll manage. I hurry back to the car and get the suitcase with the evidence stuff. I first take pictures of the hole in the floor from all sides. Then I brush sooty powder on the cover of the box with a paintbrush. Thomas grabs me by the arm and pulls me out of the apartment into the short hallway.

'Comrade Fred, what are you doing?' Fred, that's the internal expression for an idiotic freshman.

'Winrich said I should do it.'

'Yeah, yeah I know.' Thomas seems annoyed. 'I mean, didn't anyone teach you? What are you doing?' He points towards the box. I don't know what he means. 'You just covered the box with soot. How are we now supposed to make the fingerprints visible on this dark box with dark soot?'

Fuck. I don't feel warm any more. I feel cold. 'You first have to turn on your brain and then get started. The daktyloskopic is important if we want to put that guy away.' Thomas is obviously pissed off. He takes over. I watch a real criminal policeman at work. Within a few minutes, Thomas has brushed a different substance onto the locks of the box. There he pulls the fingerprints off with foil. With backlight, you can see the perfectly preserved impressions.

Evil is waiting for us in the interrogation room of the district court. Dr Plocher. I was looking forward to the display by the magistrate. Finally, being able to finish something. At least staying with it until the arrest warrant. But my happiness is gone as soon as I see the doctor. That's not a person, it's an attack dog who studied law. And considering that his client was caught by us with a box full of damning evidence, he looks shockingly confident to greet us.

'Good day, gentlemen.'

We mumble a greeting and sit down. Then we have to wait again. We sit around with the devious lawyer in the hallway for what feels like an eternity. After two-and-a-half hours it's finally time and we have an audience with the judge. The great theatre, with everything included. The judge. His assistant. The prosecutor. The defence lawyer. The accused, and in this case us too. The judge requested it for whatever reason. Everyone is gathered there. And at first, everything seems to go well. Everyone knows his script. Until the evil doctor stands up.

'Your Honour, I hereby request that the prosecution's application for remission of pre-trial detention be rejected.'

The judge calmly looks up from his files. 'With what reason?'

His tone sounds factual, almost already bored, exactly as if he had already expected something like this. 'Dr Plocher, the evidence in this case seems almost overwhelming to me, and I'm honestly exceedingly inclined to follow the prosecution's application.'

The doctor nods at the judge's every word and smiles.

'I can understand that well.' Then he says, almost sympathetically, 'But unfortunately, you aren't yet in possession of all the relevant information.'

A vertical wrinkle appears on the judge's forehead. He had probably bet on a smoother course.

'The search happened unlawfully. Therefore, all of the evidence obtained is subject to the evidence ban.'

The judge's wrinkle has now become as deep as the Mariana Trench. And his patience seems exhausted. 'With all due respect, Dr Plocher, please leave the legal assessment of the matter to me.'

It's all Greek to me. What are we discussing? The special service has the testimony of the other paedo. And we have a fucking box full of disgusting photos, that document the most severe abuse. Even against an infant. What else does the judge need? Does the guy have to stand in the town square holding up a cardboard sign with the word 'guilty' on it?

Plocher starts. 'The accused isn't the owner of the apartment, rather it belongs to a certain Ramona E, she's the life partner of the accused and lives one floor up, directly above the apartment that was searched.' The doctor takes an effective pause.

'Ms E called me at 5.57 a.m., because she heard noise and cries from her second apartment. I've printed out the call log from my phone.'

The doctor triumphantly waves around a few sheets of paper

in the air. '5.57 a.m. That's a breach of the night-time barrier. Without any apparent imminent danger.'

The judge's expression turns to ice. 'Three minutes?'

Plocher waves it off. 'Of course, three minutes. It's a small thing. However, we are on the territory of the former GDR, an undeniable dictatorship. Special sensitivity is required here. We have before our eyes the terrible acts of the GDR's secret service, the despotism and the violence. Also in relation to nightly searches. What will we tolerate next? Ten minutes? An hour?'

A half hour later, the theatre is over. We stumble into the hallway and begin to compose ourselves. Plocher marches past us. His face is an unbearable grimace of contentment. He briefly stops at Winrich. Whispers something to him and keeps going. Thomas and I want to know what the doctor said.

Winrich shakes his head.

'Come on, what did the guy say?'

Winrich pauses briefly. Then with a stony expression, he explains: 'You had the right guy. That's what he said.'

Winrich leaves us and walks down the hallway of the interrogation cellar towards the exit. Halfway there he turns towards us. 'Sometimes I can't eat half of what I want to throw up.'

The day starts shitty and just doesn't get any better. We make it to a McDonald's car park. To fight our frustration, we get a mountain of worthless calories. We chew on our burgers and talk very little. The radio blares into the silence. The voice of authority. New instructions.

The rest of our meal flies out the window and we race to the southside of the city, up in the hills. There, a few run–down old buildings are crouching in the shadows of concrete castles. The

Vietnamese are apparently operating an interim storage facility for cigarettes. Their 'warehouse boss' isn't just keeping watch over the precious goods, rather he also makes good use of them. And today he's got a visitor.

We roll up to the trash-filled yard at high speed and our siren flashing. An ambulance with a garish blinking light is already waiting there. Winrich and Thomas jump directly into the ambulance. I go into the house. The apartment is on the ground floor. I walk on tiptoes, in order to touch as little as possible for the forensics.

In the warehouse boss's bedroom it looks as if someone has just butchered a big mammal. With a chainsaw. The blood has soaked through the pillow and the mattress, down to the frayed, wavy plastic flooring under the bed. And it flows up to the hallway, stopping shortly before my feet. The curtains were at some point greyish white. Now they've greedily soaked themselves with blood. Bits of tissue are lying around everywhere.

The flashing police light shines through the red-coloured curtains. I see my colleague's legs through the open cargo hatch of the ambulance. So, someone really did hack the head off the warehouse boss, in his bed. Bloody hell. Forensics is going to be livid. I have to hold on to the doorframe. My legs feel like two liquorice sticks in a hot car in the summer.

We can't stay in the apartment of the warehouse boss. The radio blares again. And again, it's serious. Our car races from the yard with sirens and flashing lights, leaving a cloud of dust behind us. We're flying. Vampires have attacked a tourist bus full of Danish scouts and guides at a rest stop. They went at the bus with stones and sticks. Thomas drives the Passat up so quickly that the wind tears the magnetic siren off the roof. Every available woman and man from the police find a way to get there and rush to the scene. But we're still not many. Nevertheless, we hurry. They're just children, goddammit. Innocent children.

After the raid, the vampires have fortified themselves in one of their many clubhouses. And we're too few to get them out of there. At least, not without a bloodbath. The duty officer, down in the control centre, tells us over the radio to cancel the action. Retreat. Fuck. Fuck. Cluster fuck. I could puke.

CHAPTER FOURTEEN

'Dude, that can't continue!'

Thomas stares at me anxiously. In the meantime, he's become something of a big brother to me. And in the way of big brothers, he knows better than me. 'You have to socialise again! Otherwise you're going to go crazy.'

I look flabbergasted. I'm not aware of any mental disturbance worth mentioning.

'Why?' I act innocent and try to give Thomas doe-eyes. Blink. Blink. Thomas is apparently immune to something like that. Or I just have to practise my Bambi imitation.

'Forget it! You're too old and too ugly for that kindergarten trick.' Thomas grins. 'You're coming with us tonight to play Doppelkopf.'

'Huh, what?' What on earth is that, for God's sake? Doppelkopf? With horror, I think of the cow's brain that I once encountered in a classmate's refrigerator. His father was a cook. Does 'play Doppelkopf' mean cook brains? Breaded? Eaten in a group? Probably with tons of mine workers' schnapps . . .

'Where have you been all this time? Beyond the seven mountains?'

With my mother, that's the correct answer. I lived far too long with my mother.

'Doppelkopf is a card game, Comrade Stupid.'

A card game, oh. I'm relieved. I still am not in the mood.

Off-duty mobs of pale faces are anathema to me. They all have grown-up conversations. No one is allowed to pick their nose. And you definitely can't eat the bogey you've laboriously dug out in front of everyone. And people smoke and drink. Boring shit.

'I can't. I really can't.' I try to give him an excuse.

I've put him off so many times, maybe it will work this time.

'Is that a suggestion or a directive?' I barely get the words out before I realise my mistake.

'Directive.' Thomas grins at me. Checkmate.

The evening gathering goes exactly as I feared. Way too many people have gathered in a typical, tiny Neustadt apartment. Feasting. Drinking. Playing. You could cut the foggy air into little pieces with scissors and eat them. I try to make myself as invisible as possible. From my 'hiding place', in the back corner, next to a bookcase, I observe the group sitting at the living room table. They pick up and lay down cards and throw snippets of words at each other. I don't understand what is fun about that. It doesn't interest me. Not in the least.

In the middle of the players, a fräulein is crouching. Even when sitting, she appears unusually big. Her shoulders, arms and back seem like the result of demanding training. Fräulein must have lifted a lot of weights. A shaven head bulges over her perfectly symmetrical face. Not a bald head, but her hair could only be one or two millimetres long. In her hand, the young lady is holding a fat, smoking cigar. She looks like an Amazon warrior out of a comic book. At the sight of her, my mouth becomes dry and I have to swallow. Fuck. I've never been someone who finds it easy to approach a girl. The fear of being rejected was always too great. And this woman looks like she's three steps out of my league anyway.

No stare that lasts minutes long can go unnoticed. The Amazon glances up from her cards and looks over at me through the smoke. That hits me directly in the stomach. Caught. The Amazon looks at me like a giant carnivore who sees a passing animal scurrying in the forest and estimates the effort it will take to hunt the bundle of food to death. After a terrifyingly long second, she looks back down at her cards.

I sweat. This damn party. Fucking Thomas. As far as I can see, the guy is joking around happily and snacking on sandwiches and slurping out of glasses. He can go to hell. I'm still crouching, for some time, protected by the bookcase. At some point I've fulfilled a socially acceptable length of stay. I place my empty teacup carefully on the windowsill and stand up as inconspicuously as possible. I take my jacket from the hook in the wardrobe and I'm almost out the door when someone touches my shoulder. The gesture goes through me as if I had touched a live socket. The Amazon is standing behind me.

'Thomas said that you're getting out of here.' That little sack of shit. With a friend like that, who needs enemies? 'How come you're leaving?'

The Amazon is almost as tall as me. And standing up, her iron power shines even more than when she's sitting down. Her voice. Fuck, that voice. Deep and full, like the buzzing of a beehive in my grandparents' neighbour's garden.

'I came here just for you.' She smiles opaquely. 'I think Thomas wants to set us up.' Clusterfuck.

'Ah, ah ... ah.' I'm rarely that stupid, but I can't get anything else out.

'We don't have to go to bed right away. Right?'

'Ah, ah ... Of course not. No,' I answer obediently.

'No? Why "no"? Do you think I'm ugly?'

Then she bursts out laughing, right in my stupid face.

Why did I become a policeman and not a fucking magician? Then I could have at least disappeared in thin air. She gives me her number. And she mercifully dismisses me.

I go home and sleep alone. Even if my love affair with Fee has slowly healed, it's left a scar. My head is full of file folders. Containing grim faces. Bitter, shattered existences. The next morning it feels as if the day has overcome the night much too soon. I shuffle into the office like a zombie. I make it until lunch and then I save myself by running to the nearest telephone booth. The coin falls into the slot with a loud click. I dial the number. It rings twice, three times.

'Yes?' A low voice. Is that her? Or did her fucking lover pick up the phone?

'It's Sam. Do you remember? From the Doppelkopf night.' So far, so bad.

'Of course I remember. You ran away from me yesterday.' The Amazon laughs.

'I didn't run away. I ... OK, yes, I ran away.' This is going swell. 'Card games just aren't my thing.'

'Am I your thing?' While I desperately search for a response, she once again gives her deep laugh.

'I would love to see your face right now.' Go ahead, it's worth it. I probably look like the 'idiot' Thomas likes to call me.

'Come on, let's meet,' she suddenly says.

'When?'

'Now. At the Elbe meadows, by the rose garden. Can you?'

'Uh, sure. No problem.' Click. She's hung up. No problem? Bullshit. My desk is full of files and I won't be done with work for a while. Whatever.

I lie to the department head and tell him I have a doctor's appointment that can't be rescheduled and I get going. It's quite far away and when I arrive breathing heavily, the Amazon is nowhere to be seen. Has she made a fool out of me? Panting, I support myself by folding down on my knees. My heartbeat drowns out the noise of the birds. Then there's suddenly a hand on my back. I spin around.

'You must have been in a hurry. You were even faster than me on my bike.'

This woman has actually come. I can't believe my luck. She's wearing white broad overalls made of something like cotton, and a sleeveless white shirt. Before I can say something stupid, she sticks out her hand, grabs the sweaty collar of my shirt and pulls me to her. Her kiss is surprising. And wonderful. A kiss. Just like that. Without any rush. Soft.

She could probably pick me up, stick me under her arm, and carry me home without much effort. She doesn't carry me. And no force is necessary.

The Amazon lives in a small apartment, in one of those Neustadt buildings that hasn't decided yet if it wants to continue existing or maybe it would rather quickly dissolve in ruins and debris.

While we're lying together, afterwards, mutual sympathy has become something else. It's an inexplicable, serious closeness. How can that be? But it feels like this woman is an important, missing puzzle piece that has finally fallen into place.

The light of the afternoon sun penetrates the dusty windowpanes of her bedroom. It makes the stubble on top of the Amazon's head sparkle like golden fluff. This woman, with her nearly shaven head and all the muscles and scars looks like someone from a group of medieval spear throwers. But she's speaking enthusiastically about a book of poems by Gertrude Stein. And she smells like summer and blue sky. When I lie on her chest, I suddenly don't long for anything else.

'What kind of scars are those?'

She hesitates. 'I was in the sports academy. I did judo,' she says. Aha, judo. They train very athletically as well. That's where the muscles are from. But the scars?

'Did you guys train on razor blades? Or on beds of nails?' This is supposed to be a joke, but suddenly she gets a look on her face. And the detective in me immediately senses that I hit the mark.

'Where'd you get that idea?' she asks in a tense undertone. Her body has stiffened at my side. All the post-coital ease has been wiped away.

'Evidence,' I say as quickly and as neutrally as possible. I can't make a mistake. Please, Sam, please, don't mess this up. Not this too.

'Evidence?' She turns away from my embrace and creates some distance between us, leans her back against the wall.

'Don't be angry. I didn't mean it like that. It's none of my business anyway. That's just an occupational hazard of mine. You quickly get weird ideas. You've always got an air of suspicion.' And after a short pause I add, 'Some would also call it paranoia.'

Her gaze is inscrutable. My smart-ass speech has changed the atmosphere between us. A poisonous cloud hangs in the room. It smells like familiar fear. And like doubt. It's the smell of my childhood. The demons rise up out of the intermediate world. The Amazon doesn't say anything. And her silence is a weighty indication. I've uncovered something, unplanned and unwillingly. I still don't know what, but it has to do with the abyss, I'm sure about that. Clusterfuck.

'You don't have to talk about it.'

She waves me off. She knows that I know. 'I was already a bully in kindergarten,' she begins. 'In their helplessness, my parents sent me to judo, so that my energy could be directed into reasonably orderly directions.' She takes a deep breath. Her gaze is directed somewhere in the distance, out of the window. 'I was more like a boy. In my age group I defeated everyone. And soon after, kids two grades above me. So at some point I was sent to the sports academy. I was supposed to be encouraged, become an absolute judo *wunderkind*, but kids of my age weren't meant to do that yet, so they sent me to gymnastics.' I don't have my face completely under control. 'Why are you grinning in such a dumb way?' she asks and pinches me hard in the leg. I get a blue bruise. Or a black one. She just has so much power in her hands. I still can't resist a saying.

'You're unusually big for rhythmic gymnastics.'

'Don't you start with that, too. They always just called me little giraffe.'

Little giraffe. I have to laugh. She kicks at me. 'Don't laugh.' She points her finger at me. '"Idiot" also isn't any better.'

Thomas must have told her that was my nickname. 'I even went to competitions with the gymnasts.'

'Really, you did gymnastics at competition level?'

'No, idiot. I was the coach's assistant. I took care of the bandages. The hairstyles. The bags. And tea and snacks.'

'Gymnast-assistant-giraffe, then.' I laugh. And she kicks me again.

'Yes, I was the coach's assistant,' she says. Then she silently looks out the window. Somehow this doesn't make any sense. Where are the demons in her story?

'I tried everything. I told my parents before the away competitions that I didn't want to go, because I always got sick on the bus. But my mother thought I just didn't want to go. And then when I finally told her everything, she didn't believe me.' She swallows. 'And I was strictly forbidden from talking to anyone about it. My parents were probably scared that I would get expelled from the sports school and then they'd have to deal with me themselves again.' She takes a deep breath. And a tear rolls down her cheek.

I hurriedly put together the pieces in my head. My Amazon has scars. These scars aren't from an accident. So they must be from injuries. And the injuries apparently have something to do with the competitions on the weekends. The gymnast girls? No, they were most certainly terrified of her. What have I missed? I ponder for a moment, then suddenly becomes clear to me.

'The coach,' I say quietly. And I search for her hand. 'It was the coach, right?'

Her eyes flood with tears. And her story leaves me stunned. I've heard hardcore shit before, but this breaks the horror scale. In the end, my response falls conceivably short. 'I'll make him disappear.' I mean what I've said. And outside, a ridiculously beautiful day awaits us. What a crazy world. 'One day he just won't come home, without any noise or fuss,' I say. 'And in the end he'll get a taste of that.' I point to the gallery of scars. 'You don't have to do anything. You just have to nod. And then it'll be done.'

She shakes her head. She doesn't want that. She cries. A lot. Without end. No. Why 'No'? It wouldn't be any problem to find that piece of shit. The guy's out in public. Someone like him can't make themselves invisible. I'll find him. I don't care that he turns little people into somersaulting world champs or Olympic winners. Him and his sick assistant coach manipulated a nine-year-old girl. They drove her halfway crazy and humiliated her. And ultimately, they tortured her and fucked her with an absurd intensity. For years on end. Just for the fun and joy of it. Drunk with power. Sociopathic. They only stopped when the Amazon got so big and hard, that they themselves had to fear that one of their sex-torture sessions would get out of hand. For some reason, they pushed the girl into a class for speed skaters and they soon got new jobs in other corners of the republic. A mutilated child was left behind whose body and soul were destroyed.

'Your fault. It's your fault,' that's what the demons whispered to her. 'You slept in the coaches' room voluntarily because you were afraid of the dark. You adored them both. Why didn't you go to the police if you didn't like it?'

These voices are her accusers. She fled halfway around the world. She swallowed nearly every kind of alcohol and drug. Stoned, she staggered through Neustadt. She slept in doorways and in her own vomit. She started fights. She beat some people to a pulp. And she locked herself in her apartment for days at a time, unable to even go to the baker on the corner. The voices in her head stayed. They're like an unpredictable occupying power raging and crying: 'Slut', 'Loser', and 'It's your own fault, you fucking whore.'

The Amazon and I are like two quantum particles of one soul that belong together but were separated for a long time. And we are no longer trapped in our childhood bodies. We've grown into freaks who can defend themselves.

Despite her 'no', I still do some research. The assistant coach died during a motorcycle accident. But the other one is still around. The Amazon doesn't want revenge, just peace in her head. She's like me. And at the same time she's not, thank God. She wants to heal, but not at any cost. She's bright and just in her own way, despite everything.

And yet, years later, without my doing, the entire depravity was uncovered and made public. His death followed a few months later. Someone found him hanging in his cell. Thus, my karma won't be tarnished any further. I escape an even greater guilt, but barely.

The Amazon has opened up to me. I reciprocate with the same frankness. I tell her everything. Even about the therapy.

I started therapy and then stopped it. But Madame Therapies was an adorable hard-cookie psychologist. And maybe with her support I would have been able to penetrate my innermost core and could have possibly recovered some bodies. Maybe it would have been worth the effort. Or I could've found the boy that my mother had ripped out of my grandparents' house. Woulda, coulda, shoulda. An old, beige telephone stood on the table of the therapy room. The same GDR model that the speech therapist from my childhood days had. I always had to stare at that plastic thing. And meanwhile I talked about how I am hounded almost daily in my dreams. That I wake up ten or fifteen times a night. The open window and the great heights whisper to me. And a lot of things from working the door at the club won't leave my mind. All the blood and the carnage are looping endlessly. I experience disturbances to my short-term memory. I experience disturbances to my long-term memory. I momentarily experience losses of my fine motor skills. When jogging, eating and also weapons training. If I were a Volkswagen Golf, brand new from the factory, and had rolled onto the street in such poor condition, someone would have brought me back to the factory a long time ago, under warranty, and scrapped me. But luckily broken people are not subjected to the efficient logic of capitalism. At least not completely. The health insurance paid for my repairs. And Mrs Dr Freud bored deeper and deeper into my head. I resisted. I cried. I remained silent. Finally, I ran away. It was a hasty decision. A cowardly one. A weighty, wrong decision, I knew, even before I left through her door.

'And that's why you write?'

Did I tell her that I write? Goddamit, I have no idea all of the things I've said.

'I write because it must get out. Somewhere.' And because God didn't make an astronaut out of me. Nor a nuclear physicist. I should have added that. Writing is my way of speaking; that's just me. Just like a carpenter is part of the table he builds. And a butcher is part of the pig he sells. We are what we do. We do what we can do well. My mother and my German teacher vehemently insisted that socialism didn't need any more writers, but rather engineers, bricklayers and soldiers. With a little encouragement I could have maybe written an entire mountain of papers. But this encouragement never came.

'Can you read me something?'

I grumble something. I give a half nod. It might also be a shake of the head.

'Promise?' the Amazon interprets my movement correctly. 'Promise me.'

How could I deny this woman? 'Promise,' I say.

I lie because I don't have the intention to follow my words up with any action.

The Amazon and I enjoy the sight of our undressed bodies in the coming weeks. We make good use of this enjoyment. Nights. During our lunch break. Somewhere. Everywhere. And after sex we already have common routines. The Amazon reads a book while she smokes. I don't read, but I sleep rolled over onto her arm. But today I'm not sleeping, I'm stuck in my thoughts.

'My love, what's wrong?' she asks, looking up from her book.

'It's not working,' I growl.

'What's not working?'

'At work. It's just not working. It's senseless,' I choke out.

'What does that mean?'

I shrug my shoulders. I feel tired. It's difficult in the police department. Nothing works without resistance in the jungle of bureaucracy. They want me to box, but their rules also want me to do it on my back with my hands bound together. And hopping on one leg. What the hell? The rules are important. Otherwise everyone does whatever they want. But don't we also have to bend the rules a little? Customise our battles? Our enemy? That's human nature. Making mistakes; making intentional mistakes. Breaking the rules. The borders are often fluid anyway. Yes,

during arrests we've been tough. We lack the appropriate opponent for sensitive persuasion. You can never be sure if someone
potentially has a devastating device or if he will use it. And
these days there is all kinds of horrible stuff. Stuff that destitute
Russians turned into money before their departure now circu-
lates on dark markets for Assassins & Co.

I try to explain everything. But spoken out loud it somehow
sounds wrong. Confused. In some instances petty.

'What do you want?' She doesn't giftwrap her questions, she
comes directly to the point. 'What do you really want?'

What do I want? If only I knew. 'Justice,' I say at some
point, after a long pause. 'I want justice.' The Amazon wrinkles her brow.

'For whom?'

'For everyone. For everyone.' The wrinkles in her brow
became little graves. 'A life without security is worthless,' I try to
explain. 'I'd like to put a policeman on every street corner. He'd
have to give a friendly smile and wave. And he'd have to have a
large gun with him.'

'On every corner? A life without security may be worthless.
But a life without freedom is as well.' I know that. She's right. I'm
talking nonsense and I know it. It sounds like a bunch of Nazi
shit. Like George Orwell.

'The bosses at the precinct have long given up. Or they simply
don't care. I don't know.'

'And Eggert?'

Yes, he's still the minister. But in the meantime, I have sig-
nificant doubts about whether an individual person can do much
against the undying, all-powerful bureaucracy. The minister is
a kind of messiah for me. And a messiah can head into battle

against vampires and fight their dangerous accomplices. But against bureaucracy? I worry no one can win that war.

I pull myself out of bed and drag myself into the bathroom. I have to pee. In the mirror I don't see a policeman. I see a clown. A hamster in a wheel. Some kind of obsessed life form. That can't achieve anything. And can't rescuc anyone. I stare at myself for minutes. Then I hear soles of naked feet behind me on the wooden floor.

'What's with this ad campaign?' the Amazon asks. Her hand is lying pleasantly cool on my back.

The ad campaign. Yes, there was something about that. 'I don't know,' I say. This fucking ad. Another decision I'm supposed to make, but I keep putting it off for days.

'Just go there. Take a look. What do you have to lose?' It's easy for her to say, this fearless wench. 'At least call them.'

She pushes me. She's holding the wrinkled business card before me, the one I've been carrying around in my trouser pocket for days. And I'd wanted to forget. But I got the thing from Simone. And Simone is a veteran free spirit, a real Neustadt authority. A really old friend according to my standards. And I owe this friend something.

'Why should I go? I'm not doing any ad. Ads are shit.'

Ads, the darlings of capitalists. The master plan against the mob. First a desire is awoken for things that you don't need. Then you have to earn a lot, just to afford the useless junk. You can hardly catch your breath. You sleep a little. You live for machines. And at some point you don't think about rebellion against this dullness.

'I thought it's for a good thing?' Yeah, yeah, a good thing. Of course she's right. I still don't want to do it. 'This is important,' the Amazon says. And with her hand on my back, all the complaining somehow doesn't make any sense. This hand on my back is unfair.

'I don't feel like it.' My last form of defence. A final attempt.

'You're talking as if it's for a global pharmacy group.' Yeah sure. It's the *Saxon Newspaper*. And they're doing something against the hate philosophers. But maybe it's just too much fun for me to say no. And maybe I also hope that the Amazon's hand can do a little more to convince me.

'Do it, you coward.' She grins. And her hands slip around my body. That's so bad, so sneaky, so mean. The next day I call.

CHAPTER FIFTEEN

'All of this was created in Saxony,' the photographer explains to me. His studio is a tiny room. The ground floor. A studio apartment. A narrow hallway. The colour on the walls has been painted thinly. It looks like a real Neustadt room. That calms me somehow.

The rest of the campaign lies before me. Porcelain comes from Saxony. OK. Everyone knows that. But coffee filters? I didn't know that. Filter cigarettes too. And toothpaste tubes. The campaign appeals to people's patriotism, which I like. For once, there's no bullying of the lower classes. That's a clever approach. But now my face is added too. Me, a Saxon? It will definitely stick in the memory – when people see that they're going to have a meltdown. The ordinary people have to feel mocked by this campaign. Meanwhile, their market value here has fallen into a bottomless pit. After the fall of the wall, so many people are standing before merciless nothingness. And now people want to go and declare someone like me an indigenous person.

'Just relax,' the photographer guy says to me. 'It won't hurt.' He pushes me with a soft touch towards the background. 'What do you do for a living?'

'Policeman,' I mumble.

'Maybe you can look a little friendlier? Not so serious.'

I try to smile. I can't do it. Now we have to make ads telling people not to beat folks like me to death.

'A little friendlier?' The photographer begs me with a little bit of doubt.

The PR team behind the campaign must really be unworldly idiots. What are they hoping to change this way? After forty years of attempts at socialism, every aspect of East German reality is under suspicion of wrongdoing. All our hard-fought-for biographies have become worthless overnight. Now everyone in the East is an idiot. Work-shy. Or 'red pigs'. The Saxons, with their history, their former greatness and their comical dialect, are being hit by a lot of malice. They are hit often, and they are hit hard. Didn't any of the new bigwigs think about what this would do to all the people here?

Or are they too busy with their meetings in this glorious new self-service store? And that's how things like Rostock. Hoyerswerda. Thiendorf. Yeah, pogroms against foreigners – the hate Olympics. And yet I can understand the frustration. Those are my people, despite everything.

'Maybe smile for a change?'

The photographer finally gives up and snaps a few photos, without a smile and without recognisable hope for a usable result.

Sometimes a tiny pebble gets rolling on the mountainside and triggers an avalanche. The photographer submitted his pictures. And the agency thought I was good, for whatever reason. And the crazies at the newspaper even printed that shit. God in heaven! My concrete face over the black turtleneck sweater flaunted on countless billboards in the city. Not long after, the magazines

Der Spiegel and *Der Stern* print a double-page ad with the same images. It's weird. Now everyone knows I'm a policeman. And now everyone in the republic knows my goddamn face. I didn't think this through. The lead agency of the campaign immediately invites me in to talk. Scholz & Friends. That sounds American. And it somehow suits these ad jerks.

'Hello! Great to see you!' Sebastian Turner, the boss himself, greets me in the doorway. A pleasant guy. This isn't too bad. He doesn't fit my preconceptions. I thought I was paying a home visit to the class enemy. Instead, I'm being greeted by a person. There's tea and biscuits for me. I fall into this bear trap, filled with treats, defencelessly. I can't get around liking the place.

'Why did you choose me?' I ask.

'We didn't.' I'm confused. Turner smiles about my confused expression. 'Not directly. During the first round, you were excluded.' I can sense why. That was my plan. I wanted to be excluded. 'You were too hard looking. That facial expression. The shaved head. We wanted someone who evoked sympathy. And your face was a declaration of war.'

'And then you changed your mind?'

Turner nods. 'We went through all of the photos again. We sieved and sifted. We went back and forth. In the end, everything was too tame. Too obedient. It's an extreme time. Maybe in these times we need an extreme message. Do you understand what I mean?'

I like this guy more and more. I was expecting an unworldly, overpaid know-it-all. And a lot of condescension. But this man has clearly thought about the real conditions. Encouraged, I reach inside the tin of biscuits. Maybe this isn't a fight I have to wage alone? Maybe there are even more? The guy works for an agency with offices in New York and Milan. But he took time for me, a little nutcase from the province. For a freak from the margins. Maybe there will be more ventilation here than hot air. And maybe someone will rescue the fucking world.

'Good day, Mr Meffire.'

An eye-catching Mercedes sedan, model series 126, is parked to the side of the garage door and our staff entrance. This car is a thing of immortal beauty. And unfortunately, this car has become a beloved piece of high art among the relevant bigwigs in the red-light district. Aside from the few nouveau riche businessmen, they're the only ones who roll around the city in these Benzes. And, of course, such a face belongs in such a car. From the back window, the Bavarian prince of Dresden's red-light district grins back at me. His trademark: the unmissable Franz-Ferdinand moustache. So far, I've never personally met the man, I only know him from stories told by Thomas and Winrich. The guy has more of the charisma of a scheming petty lawyer than that of a career criminal. And unfortunately, his wide Bavarian grin is alluring and draws people in.

'Good day, sir.' Short answers. Factual. Detached. Like it says in the textbook. And yet I twist the corners of my mouth into something positive. Goddammit, what if someone sees that.

'Yeah so, how does it look?' I don't react and instead turn towards the staff entrance before the grinning erodes my objectivity into something like trust.

'Hey!' he calls to me in his Bavarian dialect. 'If you don't like it and you're tired of all the slander, you can come to me, pay me a visit.' I freeze. My brain tries feverishly to translate. Did that guy just offer me a job? That's so brazen that it's actually cool. I turn back around and return to the shit-brown Benz.

'Good day! And thank you for the offer.' I put on an exaggerated regretful face on. 'But unfortunately, first we have to talk about something else: where you're parked is a violation of the roadside regulations on stopping. We have to take care of that.' Franz-Ferdinand's grin gets even wider.

'Yes, of course. As long as I'm here too.' He gives me a harmless schoolboy expression and hands me a brochure from the windscreen. The thing is as big as one of those books they give mothers whose children just started school.

On the first pages there are columns for one to enter the place, department, date, time and a signature. Apparently, Franz Ferdinand has a court-ordered reporting requirement. Funny. It's an 'I-haven't-taken-off-yet' notebook for criminals. I hand Franz Ferdinand back his notebook. 'But you still can't park here. Over there,' I point across the street, 'we have a car park for visitors and selected guests.' The bad guy grins and now I grin too. Understanding without an agreement. That's how it's explained in the textbook. Thank you very much.

I leave. A single curiosity rarely comes alone. I've just made myself comfortable in my office behind a pile of files when the phone rings. That fucking thing only rings for work. I hate it. No one ever calls because they're taking an early break. Or a company excursion to the swimming pool. Or something.

'Yes, Meffire here.'

'It's the Saxon State Ministry of the Interior. The office of the minister.' Dear comrades, April may already be over, but it's apparently never too late for a joke. 'Hello, are you still there?' That's a woman. Definitely a woman.

We don't have a woman in the department, so who is that? And who got her to do this? Winrich? Thomas? Micha? Those miserable jokers.

'Yes, sure. I'm here.' I actually want to say something funny, but in the face of my much-too-full desk I am slightly stressed and so nothing comes of it.

'My name is Krämer. Antechamber of the minister. The minister would like to see you. Can you make 3.30 p.m.?'

I want to answer, no, not really. I have a full desk. But at the last second I refrain from that. I play along. I hear myself say, 'Yes sure.' I'm just too tired for any nonsense. Idiots.

'Wonderful, Mr Meffire! Then see you soon.' Click. I hang up. I stare astonished at the receiver in my hand. Who goes through that much trouble to trick me? The list of the possible suspects is short. I'd prefer to just go down the hallway and rip open some office doors. But instead my own door flies open.

'Meffire!' The department head storms in without knocking. Of course he doesn't knock. Thank God I'm sitting behind my files and not doing push-ups at my desk. Or using my resistance bands.

'Meffire! Do you have a suit here?'

'No!' I answer truthfully. I only have a single suit. And I look like a clown in that.

'Do you have one at home?'

'No. I mean, yes. But . . .' Suit is hardly the right word for that. I once bought something for a funeral. It was cheap. And you can tell.

'You need to go home immediately and get changed. And report to the ministry at 3.30 p.m. In your suit. You're off duty.'

Bang. The department leader turns around and slams the

door shut. I'm alone and, panicking, look for all my mistakes. What have I screwed up so much that I have to report to the minister? I can't think of anything. Nothing at all. There may have been minor infractions, but the minister doesn't care about things like that. Or does he?

I hurry home and change my clothes like I was ordered to. I have the suit, but not the dress shirt to go with it. At the funeral I'd just worn a black turtleneck sweater under the jacket. My only one. The one from the ad campaign. It's going to have to do for the minister. Within minutes the sweater is sticking to me.

I'm sweating like in a sauna while I hurry up the stairs to the ministry. Inside, the venerable parquet squeaks with my every step, like it's cackling at me. I'm making enough noise for an entire group of cleaners, bloody hell. And whose idea was it for these kilometre-long hallways anyway? In the anteroom, an older, friendly woman keeps watch.

'The minister will be with you shortly, Mr Meffire. Please take a seat.'

I'd rather stand. Standing is better in case I decide to run away after all. To Siberia or somewhere. The hands of the wall clock twitch by, second by second. Click clack. The anteroom is as big as a helicopter landing pad. It has a stuccoed ceiling and huge windows. I stand around like a child who's lost his parents. 'Little Sam would like to be picked up from the toy department.' The anteroom attendant looks up and smiles compassionately. No thanks, I'd really prefer not to sit. I'd rather stand and sweat while waiting. And sweat. And then I'm suddenly shoved through a door.

The minister's refuge is more of an assembly hall than an office. One could play soccer in this room with two youth teams, that's how big it is. In the far-left corner, next to the window, there's an absurdly large desk. Behind that sits a bald man. Bloody hell. This is serious. The guy could play a field marshal in any history film, undisguised. Or Caesar. Apparently, I'm totally fucked.

The Field Marshall gets up. He strolls across the soccer field. I want to click my heels together, as a reflex, to report, 'Comrade Minister, Detective Meffire reporting for duty!' That's what the voice in my head yells. But before I can put my hands on my trouser seam, and before I can start to speak, the minister holds his hand out to me: 'Good day, Mr Meffire. Nice that you could come.' He points to a chair. So this is how it begins. This is the overture to the end of my short police career.

'I actually just wanted to find out how you're doing.'

Excuse me? The field marshal likes to joke. I hastily wipe the sweat from my brow. 'But it seems as if this has caused you stress.'

What can I say to that that doesn't sound completely dumb? Denying it is useless.

'What do you think of this idea? I'll take care of a few urgent things here, then we can meet in Neustadt at 8 p.m. in Raskolnikoff. Does that work for you?'

I nod, at least that halfway works. I don't quite understand what's happening, but apparently, it's not about firing me. Not yet. I nod and grin stupidly.

The minister points to my suit. 'You don't need that. We're not going to the presidential inauguration.' And with that I'm excused. Like a zombie, I shuffle my way back. Past the anteroom lady. Through the endless hallway and the squeaky parquet. It's still incomprehensible to me what is happening here but apparently at least I still have a job.

I sit down in the grass on the Elbe and look at the brownish green water. I've just met the pale-faced version of Mandela. Or more like Gandhi? For me the man is definitely a rock star. And in a time when all the other political bosses in the republic shine with their stout smugness, Eggert is different. He seems to be a quick thinker and driven. He lives together with other ministers in a flat share. A flat share? For God's sake, how cool is that?

For me the man is, above all, a messiah of peace. For me he's hope on the frontlines. And not for nothing. He was invited to Israel as a guest of state. Him, the little minister from the East German province. The ancestors of Jewish survivors instinctively know what this is about. This is the German endgame. Maybe, even if I leave my naive enthusiasm aside, this minister guy is really more than a gust of hot air in a tailored suit. Maybe he's the hoped-for saviour? And if not? What if he's just better than the other idiots at presenting himself and lying and giving speeches?

Ultimately, the guy is a pastor and works as a politician. We'll find out soon. No one can live without hope, that would be an unbearable condition. And thus, I have no other choice than to risk hope. And to wait.

I meet the Messiah in Raskolnikoff. The inner life of the café consists of reclaimed and improvised furniture. There is sand spread on the ground and every step feels like a visit to a gravel pit. Usually, the room is packed with partygoers, tourists and Neustadt punks. But today it has a suspiciously high percentage of men in dark suits, middle-aged men who are posted around the Messiah, conspicuously inconspicuous, clutching their coffee cups. They might as well stick colourful notes to their foreheads with the label 'Bodyguards'. For these men, the chaotic café must be a living nightmare.

I squeeze myself past the entrance with crunching steps over to the Messiah's table. He's ordering. 'Do you want a coffee too?'

'No thank you, Mr Minister, but chamomile tea would be nice.' The barely legal waitress reacts to my order as if I had asked her to bring me cocaine on a silver platter. She scratches something laboriously onto her notepad and trots off without a word.

'Mr Meffire. Let's start with a formality. Can we address each other by first names?' He indicates around us with an expansive gesture. I understand what he means. In this dump, using formalities would seem as appropriate as if the homeless people outside Aldi spoke to each other in the third person.

The Messiah sticks out his hand, 'I'm Heinz.'

My palms are embarrassingly sweaty. 'Sam. I'm Sam.' The Messiah squeezes my fingers in his paw.

'So, Sam. Now I'd like to know why you ended up with the police.'

Sweat runs down my neck. That might be because I'm wearing my bulletproof vest under my turtleneck sweater. Ultimately, I'm meeting with a man who is the thorn in the side of a lot of people. The Messiah is hated by the anarchists, the Trotskyists, the Maoists and other factions on the Left as much as he is by the vampires and their leaders. In addition to that are the former functionaries of the not-so-secret-any more 'secret ministry', towards whom he has shown little indulgence. That's why I'm equipped like a one-man-army for this visit to the café. What kind of unbearable shit would that be, if the Messiah got chopped up right in front of me? Nothing against his bodyguards, they seem extremely efficient, but I don't know them and anyway I don't trust anyone, except for maybe a few villagers from my daily life. The Messiah seems free of any worry for his safety. He seems relaxed in the middle of the bustle, almost amused in the face of all the chaotic Neustadt liveliness around us. Either he's ignorant or he has much more defiance of death than me.

'Tell me, what motivates you to take a job like this? And how's it been going?'

These simple questions are making me speechless. Never has anyone seriously been interested in me. Most people just see a bailiff when they see a policeman. In the best-case scenario, a necessary evil. And for many, we are barely higher than a dog who is supposed to protect the yard and who you can otherwise shoo or kick at will. And someone who has to keep watch during the night, when the demons roam. No one asks how an officer is doing otherwise. With crushed victims, tormented loved ones, and strangely forgetful witnesses. And, of course, the perpetual stream of delinquents on the social fringes. I hadn't expected something like that. A dam breaks and endless words spill out of me. This will be a long report.

The Messiah takes me to different events. Party events somewhere in the country. Typically, they are endless discussions about endless problems in the area, to which I have nothing to contribute. We're invited to panels together, and to other interview opportunities. It's a safari through the newspaper pages and TV shows, for a public who has little to do with the wild East German machinations, and who are utterly confused by the bloody, unappetising events and the East German frustration. It's an avalanche. And it rolls: land rushes past our convoy like an alternative reality. Behind greenish armoured glass ten centimetres thick, the world seems like a different universe.

If I had the choice, I'd entrench myself forever in one of these rolling fortresses with a mountain of chocolate. Behind the glass, the world isn't a threat any more. No imposition can reach me. Leaning back against the comfortable leather seat of an Audi V8, you can tolerate the world. Unfortunately, the armoured monstrosity never just drives around the area aimlessly. There's always an appointment at the end. Of course, it's always about appointments.

The Messiah always wants to hog the spotlight. He has visions. And he can sell these visions to his audience. He's a speaker you'd want for the cup final. Someone who can shake people awake. Someone people follow. For me, it's incredibly flattering to be sitting in the spotlight as his sidekick. My contributions are extremely small. Often people interpret my sitting there quietly, grinning bashfully, as modesty. And that is a gracious, favourable judgement considering my over-promotion. The guys from the press are turning me into a colourful printed wallpaper that they need for their stories. I'm a welcome olive branch in a time when the Canadian embassy is warning its citizens of colour not to travel to Saxony. In the empire of the acorn, Saxony is becoming a restricted area for tourists.

A private station requests to film a report about me. My battery is empty from the constant stress. I'm no longer interested in this charade. And I mistrust private stations anyway. I tell Winrich and Thomas about the request. They immediately agree.

'Of course you're gonna do that, missy!'

'And at the meeting, tell them how unbelievably photogenic your colleagues are, too.' Thomas is hopping around the office on one leg and is turning around in circles. It is very uncoordinated. While he does it, he clucks like a hen. 'Yeah, look, this is how the movie stars dance.'

Both clap. Haha, how funny, dear comrades. I give them the finger. And then a second one. Thank God the three of us can still laugh together. Not everybody in leadership finds my undeserved fame appropriate. There's gossip. There's ugly talk. And unfortunately all of the press hype about me has actually taken a bizarre turn. Since the disgruntled sideway glances in the cafeteria have increased, I avoid central catering. I eat granola and soup out of Tupperware, at my desk in the office.

'You're doing a good job.' Suddenly Winrich seems serious. 'At least they're listening to you. Tell them what's going on here.' He makes an expansive gesture and I know exactly what he means. Dresden. Saxony. Everything. And with that the brief discussion has been decided.

For three days, a camera team follows me around and films me. At home. Bent over books. At the gun range. Even while I'm shopping. I talk during filming as much as I can. I talk about the chaos in the city. And that people should know what is happening behind their cardboard wall of seeming normality. And above all, why it's happening. I rant about how threatened their carefully guarded civil peace is. And the team films me in desolate streets and in front of empty factory halls with their windows nailed shut.

I talk about how so many people I know are unemployed despite having been trained and having a college degree and having work experience. People who take care of their balcony plants and spend their evenings drinking tons of canned beer. I say, if it weren't for this dullness, there wouldn't be any vampires.

Or at least not as many. And not so determined. I say that no one bothers to connect all of the individual parts. Except for maybe the Messiah. And he's the most threatened creature. Each day I reckon that he'll be blown to pieces, following the murdered magistrates, Borsellino and Falcone. He has simply made too many enemies. And some of them are exceedingly powerful and 'relevant for the system'.

I also tell the camera about my long-lost dream. That Fee and I and many, many others dreamed about a just socialism. And that instead we got the colourful consumer paradise where in 'flourishing landscapes', as Helmut Kohl said, losers can press their noses against the shop windows of stores. The anger transforms into fights and battles. The have-nots wage war against each other. And any police force in the world is powerless against this kind of revolt. I speak into the camera for three days, as if it's about life or death.

When it airs, I'm frozen in horror. Nothing I've said has remained. They portray me like an armed clown. I played the sweet, exotic deer right in front of the hunters' shotguns. And, of course, they fired. That's their job. My job is critical observation. And I failed in that across the board. I'm despicable, naive and vain.

After the shoot and the broadcast, I need a few days to collect myself. I escape to old construction sites, into old patterns. I've long been a pain junkie. I sweat daily, exactly as if the minister-messiah immediately gave command for the final battle. But there is no final battle. There is always a new day, with always new shit. That's the job. Until the day I sit on the edge of my bed and know that I can't do it any longer. That I don't want to do it any longer. The show pony is tired.

*

I'm in some tiny hallway in E1, the staff department. I go around another corner. And another corner. I stand still again, in view of the office I am about to enter. How did I get to this hallway? How could it come to this? Why do I want to get out of here at any cost? Is it just passing anger? Or the long overdue dive into freedom?

Winrich is gone. Winrich was removed from office. They suspended him. Winrich probably overdid it with his 'unofficial employees'. He met with a lot of people in the neighbourhood and possibly saw too many pieces of the puzzle. Too many believable rumours. He profited too much from what alluring female comfort providers, in various designer beds, heard. Puzzle pieces related to those in authority. Puzzle pieces that show which higher ups are in cahoots with which directors in red-light establishments. Or who was in these premium establishments that are disguised as condominiums. Basically, who is in bed with whom and where. Who snorts cocaine, too. Who is holding out their hand and for what. Who drinks with whom and where. Winrich only ever implied anything to me. Thank God. I don't want to know any of that crap. My belief in the new system tends towards zero anyway.

Winrich crossed boundaries. Moral ones? Very likely. Legal ones? Of course. And criminal ones? I don't know. But the frightened authorities don't take any chances. Winrich has to go. They'll uncover some dirt for that. And, naturally, he also has a dark side. We all have one. No one can do this job without having a close personal relationship with the abyss. This isn't just the case for Winrich. We all regularly need an exorcist, a specialist for our daydreams and demons. But the 'oh so righteous' in the office naturally deny these facts. They'd rather indignantly point to Winrich and complain and scream. They're good at that. They're looking for the splinter in the eye of the other, while the plank in their own head doesn't disturb them.

Meanwhile, they're the ones who long ago betrayed their oath and duty, the city and the people. And sold it. For their indifference, their opportunism and their fear. The 'righteous' have long since made deals. They have splendid official titles on their office doors. And they climb the pay grades while the beat cops and the detectives walk their asses off on the street. Winrich is suspended. His investigation success and his hubris have brought him down. I had long feared it and yet the enforcement came surprisingly fast. How could I keep fighting against the idea-eating, ancient walls of undying bureaucracy without Winrich? They swallow everything that you carry in to them. My idealism, my zest for action and my new workgroup concept. Everything gets swallowed up and disappears in the administration's internal digestive organs, never to be seen again.

I loved the idea that my work made a difference. That I could help. But it was like tilting at windmills. Even the incorrigible, optimistic Thomas is increasingly resigned. Micha long ago quit and only gets through the days with schnapps. And Winrich is completely gone. What am I still doing here?

The smokers' area of the hallway lies before me. There are two scuffed chairs encircling a half-dead houseplant and an upright ash tray. I sit down, tilt my head back and stare at the torn ceiling panelling and I hope for some inspiration. I sit and wait. I can't seem to find any inspiration. It only rises from the shallows when it wants to. Completely different from other things in my head.

I remember, unmediated and unsolicited, how the authority

of the bureau requested a conversation with me. On my very first day, even before I could have done anything stupid or cause any damage. Nevertheless, some director screamed and raged while one of his senior subordinates had to witness my senseless humiliation.

'Meffire, you're now in my jurisdiction!' His spit flew across his huge wooden desk.

'Here you're nobody! And you will do exactly what you're told. Understood?'

I hear him, but it's hard to understand how the meaning of his words relate to me. What does he want from me?

'Are you even listening to me?' I hear the scream come from his uniform.

I hate being yelled at. It painfully reminds me of my mother's rule. Screaming people put me back in that base state. Back there, where only survival counts and nothing else. Whoever hesitates will be hurt. Whoever hesitates will be mutilated. Or killed. 'Don't want! Don't hesitate!' At this point, the collective of accusers in my head are exceptionally unified. I prepare to walk around the swanky desk and slap my superior across the face. And keep slapping him until he's silent and his demons retreat. Not to wait. Not to hesitate. 'I'm neither you're fucking n——, nor your slave, nor your dog . . .'

That should be my spiel for him. The company boss in Potsdam was a small, unassuming man in his fifties. And I've never experienced him screaming. Not once. He didn't need to scream, he led by example. Whatever he expected from us, he also expected from himself. Led by example. He sweated. He worked himself to the bone, while crawling, jumping and march-ing. All that at over fifty. Every one of us would have allowed

themselves to be broken for 'the old man'. He was a just king.
He was our father. And we would have followed him into hell.

In contrast, this screaming and uptight headcase of bureaucracy, on the other side of this desk, only has a title. Nothing
more. He is just a sociopath with a rank. I was looking for the
spirit of Potsdam and instead I've found myself at a desk where
a dwarf is showering me with spit, unchecked and unpunished.
Don't hesitate, the accusers yell to me. But I keep sitting on my
chair, like I'm rooted to the spot. In the end I'm just a schoolboy
disguised as an adult, who someone is threatening that he won't
be allowed to play. Just a despondent boy. The screaming director. That was my very first day. Am I going to throw in the towel
because of that? I lift myself off the chair and go to the smokers'
corner in the staff office.

'Good morning, I'm supposed to report to you.' The woman
behind the desk looks up.

'Oh yeah. You wanted to report.'

A friendly face. A smile. In her voice I can find a person. I
had thought I'd have to go into the ring one last time with some
bureaucratic weasel. And once again I'm surprised. This place
is full of people. And most of them are struggling, day after day,
so that this city doesn't go to the dogs. People like Winrich. Or
Thomas. Or this woman here. Then why am I leaving?

'I'll bring the rest of my papers.'

The woman takes my stuff and lays it out on her desk.
She looks at each section of my form thoroughly and opens
some binders. Compares things. Crosses some out. I wait and
watch her. My gaze wanders from her desk over to the oblig-
atory office pinboard. Postcards from distant beaches. Family

photos. Family. Why am I leaving mine? What was I expecting? Bureaucracy is bureaucracy and it's no adventure playground for stubborn children. Bureaucracy means that everything goes miserably slowly. It's life at the pace of a crawl. Signed umpteen times. Stamped umpteen times. For the highly mobile, excellent specialised counterpart, we are always far too slow. You have to be able to breathe. That's the way it is. And in my position, an adult could do that too.

'Mr Meffire?'

The nice office lady brings me back to the here and now. 'You still have to sign here.' Of course. I'll do that. And then we exchange a few friendly sentences about the hot, dry summer. Should I maybe rip all my stuff out of her hands and rush back to my desk? It's too late for that. The über bureaucrat would probably rather get a colonic with sulfuric acid, in the middle of the office, than take me back. It's too late to give in. The nice lady makes a few more notes, then it's over. I let myself be amputated from my family. I tell myself that I'm free now. But right now it just feels shitty.

In the car park, I sit in my car for a few minutes. I realise that my hasty resignation will also really fuck up the Messiah. I didn't just bury a policeman, rather I killed his little 'publicity-pony' too. And in these unquiet, ugly times, that's fucking shit. A promotional disaster from the Messiah's point of view. Maybe I should have avoided the whole public circus. Maybe I had to avoid it. All the trouble. The kissy here and kissy there. Of course that's nice. Very nice even. Very flattering. But it also drains everyone's soul. While I was grinning at cameras and turning letters into sentences, so much that should have gotten done was left undone. Change something? Make a difference? The whole notoriety business only brought me gossip. And lots of jealousy. Or was I just too dumb and clumsy to use my public image for something useful?

What I can't imagine while brooding in my tin box: the Messiah won't survive my departure. He risked criticising the inventor of this flowering landscape. He risked questioning the holy, infallible chancellor of German unity. What hubris. Someone goes after the minister of the province with the concentrated power of backroom dealings. They crush him into an East German lump of aspic. It's like straight out of a goddamn playbook for the secret services, one of disinformation. Someone unearths dirty shit against the Messiah. The Messiah has to resign. And with him, all of his ideas die. It can be that easy. And that dirty. But I don't suspect any of that.

I'm sitting in a sticky car in the visitors' car park of my department, and I think about my mother. She'll be grossly disappointed. All the hype around me has meant something to her. Finally, her offspring has turned into something presentable. After all the wasted years of professional sports. After the insufferable bricklayer apprenticeship. After the nurse training and a chaotic existence in Neustadt, her good-for-nothing failure of a son had finally picked himself up.

On the day after Eggert had ordered me to the ministry for the first time, I drove out to the tower blocks. I had butterflies in my stomach. I almost had to throw up in front of the front door from sheer nausea. I had stayed away for too long. I hadn't stayed away for long enough. It's still the same old iron grip of fear. And it was fear that made me sneak home to my mother. I wanted to present this moment of success so my dark queen could bless it. My mother seemed reconciled. Her son, a hero. It was as if, for the first time in her life, I appeared to her without a glow of worthlessness. To celebrate my short-lived ascent, my mother took me to an Italian restaurant. She was already a little drunk. I still went along with her. An excursion like that was the closest thing to a loving hug in my mother's world. And yet I inexpressibly longed for a little affection from her.

At the restaurant, she ordered a salad, noodle casserole and a chocolate tart. And a bottle of wine. That was typical. And it was bad for her condition. I hated seeing her drunk. Everything reminded me of her terrible eruptions and this fucking age of fear. Respectably drunk was the only state in which my mother would tell me anything about my father, when her walls would begin to crack.

In between the noodle casserole and the dessert, she talked about the 'forbidden' topics. About grandfather. About father. About Cameroon. Even about Moïse. She looked at her hands flat on the table as if they didn't belong to her. She still couldn't say his name. She said 'your brother'. That's how long he'd been gone. I've long since asked myself whether he might be wanted anywhere. But he isn't. And even the search service of the Red Cross can't find him. Forty-five years after the war, they're still finding missing soldiers on battlefields, but they can't find my brother. It's inexplicable, like a dark magic trick, Moïse has disappeared.

I took advantage of this opportunity and flattered and lured as much out of my mother as I could. We never had a discussion. Time doesn't heal all wounds. Some things, once they've happened, remain unspeakable. But this time I want more. I have a right to it. I keep at her, keep asking questions.

'Don't start any trouble.' Mother sipped her wine. She stared off into space. Took another sip. 'Don't cause any trouble. You hear? That's inappropriate.' Even in her drunk state, half responsive, half mumbling, she oozed superiority. This way of talking immediately stabbed through all the layers of my patience. I no longer had it under control. My fist hit the table so hard, that the glasses hopped around and clinked. Mother flinched.

'Bloody fucking hell!' I was beside myself with anger.

'Sit back down. It's embarrassing how you're acting.' Mother whispered the sentence very quietly, but her anger in those words filled the entire room. Only then I noticed I'd jumped up.

'I don't want to speak with you like this. Not like this.' Oh what? Really? I haven't wanted this for a long time, you old witch. I don't want to obey any more. I don't want to be amenable.

'You will sit back down immediately!' I didn't sit down.

'Immediately!' She whispered it furiously. I left.

That was many months ago, the last meeting. Now I'm sitting here, glued to the steering wheel, and stare at this car park, this piece of bureaucratic asphalt on which my car has no business being. I've failed, failed in every respect. I leave the motor on. Failed? We'll see about that, I think. Then I roll away.

CHAPTER SIXTEEN

'We need a name.'

Robby is right. What are we going to call our activity? It's supposed to be a machine that rescues the world – at least, rescues the city. But when it comes to marketing, we're a bunch of duds. At least we have an office. A Seventies desk dominates the room. A big, tasteless accident made of pressed wood and an unspeakably ugly veneer. The previous tenant of this container plant probably extracted it directly from a former GDR authority for next to nothing. Or it came from one of many nationally owned businesses that were condemned to death thanks, to being sold off. The container is made in the GDR. And the table. And the chairs. And the grey, holey plastic covering on the floor. The undigested yesterday is still buried in all of these things. In all of these things, the past is buried. It lies like a thick layer of dust on everything. We're all still young, but we come from a world that's already perished.

'Something with "Security",' Robby says. 'It has to be reflected in the name right away that the firm stands for security.'

Our voices echo: 'Lame!' 'Dumb!' 'Boring!'

Frustrated, Robby throws the marker on the table. I'm sorry

for him, it's our fault. We have no idea, whether we're more than just a random group. And poor Robby has to suffer the consequences.

What connects us exactly? Several of us have completed operational training or were in the special forces of the GDR. Many of us were at the sports academy. Many of us studied at university. We're Russian Germans. And East Germans. And me? I'm something in between worlds. There are also old acquaintances there: Udo is there, the Gjogsul artist from the barracks yard of the riot police. Frank Luger, the giant with the name of a pistol. The flow of time washed us into a place like magic driftwood. All of us together in this old office.

What do we want? To make something better. The opposite of what can be admired every day in this crazy city. What can we do about it? Execute. Endure. Withstand. Be there, where other people give up and run away. And we want to, and have to, earn money with that. The city is full of traumatised people. Angry people. People without prospects. Controlled by opportunists and cockroaches. The locals. And those of West German provenance. And there are the vampires and the orcs. And defeated magicians. So there are enough problems, but there are hardly any successful businesses. There is simply a lack of prospects among the people. Who can afford to go shopping? Who's going to be able to pay us for bringing in brainpower, moving our iron every day and hitting ourselves on the head? Who will be able to pay us for selling our skin at the market?

'Alpha!' someone yells into the general confusion. 'We could call ourselves "Alpha".'

For me personally that sounds too much like KGB Task Force A. With those guys, A stands for 'Alpha'. With them, things take place in a completely different universe. Any name with a resemblance to theirs has a flavour of megalomania.

'Omega,' I respond reflexively. All heads turn in my direction, then silence follows. And a hum of approval follows the silence. 'Omega.' The last letter of the Greek alphabet. The last bastion. We remain, where others retreat. We do what the higher up bureaucrats aren't allowed to do. Or won't. We do what the West German security forces find too minor to do in this city. Or too hard.

Omega. It's pathetic, but after all it's a name. We think our business model is as simple as can be. We acquire neighbourhood after neighbourhood, block after block. Walk from one club owner to the next. We knock on the doors of store owners and building owners.

Our pilot project is Neustadt. There are countless cafés, clubs and stores. That means countless thefts and property damage, wrangling and fights. Freshly renovated buildings are vandalised. Partygoers and tourists are robbed. And again and again drunk busybodies or professional troublemakers start fights. That affects sales and ruins the market value of the area. A lot of time passes until the policemen, who are suffering from a lack of personnel, show up. We know the neighbourhood. We know our foe. And our lookouts wait everywhere and feed us information. We practically invent the concept of the city patrol, long before people called it that in other corners of the republic. We don't make any friends with this idea. It's an unofficial questioning of the overwhelmed central power. But we don't notice any of that. We're sure that it's good. And that it will work.

So every day I get my corduroy jacket out of my cupboard

and iron my jeans and clean my shoes. I try to convince unbe-
lieving and increasingly annoyed business owners about my plan
to rescue the world. With very, very moderate success. They
think the idea is good and really useful, but only a few want
to pay. At night, I stand at the doors of different stores. I can
luckily say that despite many conflicts not one person is beaten
or stabbed to death.

Today is Monday. A lot of stores are closed. Clubs too. The
weekend was hard. There were several violent clashes. We
needed an ambulance at the site several times. Now I'm allowing
myself some luxury and sleeping behind the Führer's door half
the morning. The Amazon had to go to Hong Kong for some
consultant job and has left me alone for a few months.

When I am awakened by the singing of the birds who populate
the gutters of Alaun Street, for a moment everything appears to
be good. And all the shit is finally over. I turn the small chair
toward the sky and put my feet up on the windowsill. Down on
the street, the traffic rolls by with a quiet hum. Now and then I
hear bits of conversation.

Mondays are strange interruptions to the rest of the hustle and
bustle. Mondays are Sundays in my job. No one wants anything
from me then. Usually, I go jogging. After that, I do ten, twelve
long presses with the bar. With a little weight and many repe-
titions. And combinations of push ups and expander exercises.
As soon as my body and spirit have been tortured with enough
resistance and pain and have calmed down, I lay down in bed
with a full plate of something or other and allow myself to enjoy
a book. I love Mondays.

It's a wonderfully mild evening, with a clear sky. I'm running along the other bank of the Elbe. And as always, running feels right. I dream of how it would be to keep following the movement of my feet. Out of the city. Past the autumn fields. Further and further along the old Handel Street until I get to Nürnberg. And further. And at some point, this city would just be a pale memory, far away.

'Well, how's it going? This time you were here before me.'

Franz Ferdinand laughs, booming. His Eminence likes to joke. When last we agreed to meet in the Omega office container, he let me wait a long time until his shit-brown motor carriage finally came rocking up. His tardiness was surely calculated. The clever comrade never does anything without a reason. For today, he's asked me to come to this premium bar. That too is a message. 'We can't not communicate,' is what Watzlawik said. At least that's what they taught us during our training.

'I walked, you're driven around. That's not a fair competition!'

Franz Ferdinand waves and gives the waiter a sign. 'Do you want to drink something?'

I nod and crouch down. The comrade appears to be in good spirits today. Maybe it won't be as hairy as feared.

'Are we eating real meat or fake meat?' Franz Ferdinand grins. I grin quickly, too.

'Is the Pope Catholic?' I try to maintain the relaxed atmosphere. Maybe he's calmed down since our last meeting; we transition to the day's agenda. Unfortunately, my hope doesn't last very long. He suddenly gets started. His voice is quiet, but his gaze is hard.

'I've helped you a lot in the past weeks.' So he still has his issue. And it's still my move, I have to deliver. And I still don't understand how that could happen. How, for heaven's sake, could I get involved with this? Being indebted to the wily Franz Ferdinand? But he is right to ask. And I know it, too. And he knows that I know.

'I've taken you to important meetings. Thanks to me, you have every important contact in the city.'

I nod, what else can I do? He's right, it's exactly that. We didn't notice it, but that's how things have developed in the last weeks. Franz Ferdinand has become something of a mentor. A business coach. A kind of fatherly advisor. And it's slowly becoming clear that a number of things will not work with Omega the way we planned, at least not as soon as planned. So I finally accepted his help.

'I supported you with money!' Now with every word he's slamming his open palm on the table. He's visibly pissed off with my silence. Yes, he's right. And at the same time he's not. I try a slight contradiction.

'Yeah, but for that you're a silent investor in the company, that's what we agreed upon. You wanted to build up something clean, that's what you said.'

Annoyed, he waves away my objection with his hand, as if he was trying to swat a fly. Suddenly, Franz Ferdinand is no longer the helpful uncle from the West.

'That's too little! Much too little, when you consider what I've done for you. And what I'm still supposed to do. Just think about the commercial office and the permit to carry weapons for the company.'

Fuck. Fuck. Fuck. How can I respond? He's right. My concept with the city watch is still stuck between an idea and implementation. And far too few escort contracts and company investigations are coming in. And it's unthinkable to consider the planned expansion with radios, vests and vehicles. And the fucking promotional bank is opposed. From the beginning, Franz Ferdinand was the only one who stood by his promises. At least concerning this special issue.

'What comes of that? Only good excuses. Do you think I'm dumb? You're gonna fix this for me, or I'm out. Did you hear me?'

Yes, yes, I understand. Vaguely, anyway.

'You definitely don't want to upset me.'

That's exactly what I've always wanted to avoid. Upsetting Franz Ferdinand. That's exactly what wasn't supposed to happen. But naturally, this has already happened. Bloody hell. Shit. Shit squared.

I hear myself say, 'I'll do it. I'll take it to the others. I'll take care of it.'

He briefly stares across the table. Then he gets that old, familiar grin on his face and while rubbing his hands together, he turns towards the steaming plates that are floating on the young waiter's arm. My teeth bite into the sinfully expensive steak and in the meantime the wheels are turning in my head.

What could I have done? I had to make a trade-off. Omega isn't doing well. Bullshit, actually Omega is doing *terribly*. I'm practically living from the revenue of bouncer gigs, everything else is being eaten up by the company. I can't go back to the police. Not as long as that circus ringmaster has the final say there. And another German state can't employ me for at least five years, that how the individual states want to prevent the poaching of their trainees. And maybe it won't be half so bad.

Maybe I just have to take care of this one task for him. Maybe then his 'need of support' will be subdued and he'll let me do my actual job. Franz Ferdinand is ultimately the master of a sex emporium that serves the yearning, slightly wet dreams of the lonely. And we don't want to steal or kill for him. We'll just win back one of the glittery lairs he was cheated out of by his former partner. The place lawfully belongs to Franz Ferdinand with everything included. At least that's how he sees it. So I'll have to secure the movement of cocaine, or hunt down the prostitutes who've run off. I will most certainly not do that, I tell the collective of accusers. Or is that just a quickly cobbled-together lie?

Actually, Franz Ferdinand is not the evil arch force that my old bosses sold him to us as. He's more of a well-read gourmand who looks after the women who work for him. I could swear that his is a real, twisted affection. And maybe those things go together – exploitation and affection. I know he once shot up a bar with a shotgun, drunk and incensed because of an argument. During everyday activities he doesn't give me the impression of a violent psychopath. Violence seems to be a necessary evil for him. A useful tool every now and then in a work environment with adverse conditions. In some conversations, I have the impression that I'm sitting with a sociologist and not with a feared boss of the underworld. Franz Ferdinand casts a fishing line with shit and catches people. Women. Bookkeepers. Or people like me. He's chosen a side and he's successful at what he does.

Me however? I thought that in the meantime, I knew who I was. But who am I? I'm leading a double life. A triple life. I'm living multiple frauds. During the day I pursue my idea of rescuing the world, I wear business suits and a civil smile. In the early evening, I climb onto an old roof and train Wing Tsun, my new martial arts religion. My trainer beats the soul out of my body. That's how I learn best. With mistakes and pain. And when it's dark, I'm on a mission to keep watch until the morning. This turbo life is my legal, but not any less toxic drug, from which I can barely find my way back to a normal state of consciousness. Reflect? Why bother reflecting? Everything is already complicated enough. Everyone seems to have conspired against my plan to rescue the world.

'There is no destiny that can't be overcome through contempt.' Fee had this quote from Camus stuck to her mirror, above the sink. For me it becomes complete contempt for reality.

'We have that under control,' I say to the Messiah. The comrade minister and I have agreed to meet in a Neustadt café. He can no longer take me to get coffee in the local party associations. I'm not a police dropout. I'm now an opaque security something, so the Messiah has to keep a certain distance.

'What do you have under control?' he asks me, probing.

Goddammit. I had hoped for advice, fatherly farsightedness. Instead, he's serving me reproaches. Why does everything always have to be so difficult?

'We're on the right path,' I try to placate him.

He doesn't let it go. 'Then stay there. And keep yourself away from certain people!'

This was actually supposed to be a brief, friendly coffee. Tea, in my case. But the Messiah appears genuinely concerned. My contact with the red-light prince is an open secret to well informed circles in the city. It would be stupid to deny it.

'He's not the evil guy they portray him to be.' His behaviour is much more pleasant than that of some other higher ups in the office. That's a fact. And that's what I should tell the Messiah, but I can't get the words out. The Messiah shakes his head imperceptibly but doesn't say anything. This coffee break is a badly disguised departure. Yet another world closes its doors before me. This will be the last time that the Messiah and I will meet. The Messiah gets up from his stool. The bodyguards are behind him.

'Watch out for yourself, OK?' he says and walks away.

I remain sitting for a while with my empty cup. When I get out on the street again, I understand what must happen. That's the signal for the early start of my shift. I rush back to my place at the door. At least I know what I have to do there. I'm a diplomat, intelligence officer, substitute police protection and an executioner in one. As a rule, those in authority are conspicuous by their absence. They lead their own fight, tilting against windmills of paper and words. And against incompetent high-level bureaucrats and their dangerous negligence.

And if they do come and see us, then it's usually far too late. And they're quite happy about the fact that we're rolling around with the crazies. If not for us, they would move up to the front row and would have to take their own risks for the sake of public order and allow their own heads to be warped with bloody bruises, just like us.

It's a relatively quiet night. During the middle of my shift, Franz Ferdinand shows up. It's already his second official visit today. First a minister. Then a king. Franz Ferdinand walks across the street towards me. Not that! The Bordello Prince and the former model policeman deeply engaged in a conversation, that would be a nice picture for the press.

I let one of the guys take over the door and I hurry over to Franz Ferdinand. We sit down in his Benz and slowly drive around through the neighbourhood. The car has tinted windows, so faces are completely invisible behind them.

'It's settled. We'll get started tonight. I'll call you beforehand, let it ring twice and then hang up. Don't actually answer. We don't know who else is listening in on your line.' Franz Ferdinand nods, so far so good. 'As soon as the object is secured, I'll drive over to you, on the side street and give you a vocal signal.' That gets a nod, too.

'Take care of yourself,' he says. Astonished, I notice he said it in standard German. I didn't even know he could speak that. Franz Ferdinand says it very quietly. It's not an instruction, just a gesture. Comrade underworld boss probably can see more clearly than me just what kind of situation I've found myself in. Franz Ferdinand has significantly more experience than me with the dark side.

In the early morning hours I give the order for commence. It's my responsibility alone. I alone am guilty that we are now going over a cliff, in a brotherly embrace, shoulder to shoulder. Maybe we've just arrived in the middle of the labyrinth. And there is a gaping abyss that seems to have escaped our attention. The impact is immediate.

At my command, we start the first round of our violence Olympics. The previous observation of the club was sufficiently accurate. The tactical entrance goes smoothly. We use the element of surprise. And we use the natural fright. Everything only takes a few minutes. Then the club is empty. All the women have left the building. And all of their Johns too. So far, so good. Outside, on the pitch-black street, I pull the balaclava off my face. A moment too early, as soon becomes clear.

*

Three days later, I meet Franz Ferdinand before the gates of the city. They've set up a high-tech disco temple the size of a football pitch there. And a giant pool with a sunroof. Franz Ferdinand has gathered a few people there, they're his executive guys. They are all extremely well built. In addition to that, there's the boys and me from the outside. The mood in the room appears to be relaxed. Everyone is acting like they just got off work. Franz Ferdinand pays for drinks. Most of them take schnapps, I stick with the only tea flavour in the house: mint. The music is boom-ing. Bodies are moving. These are familiar sights.

'Hey, you.'

I recoil. Fee is standing next to me. She looks different. She's applied a generous amount of lip gloss and her eyelashes have been lengthened with mascara. She smiles, slowly walks up to me and leans her arm against me for a second. I can feel her warmth. And I smell this perfume. It smells like lilac and the winter cold. For a split second, the mirage is perfect. Then I've collected myself. That's not Fee. That can't be Fee. Yes, the woman looks like her twin, she's her spitting image. But that doesn't mean she's Fee. Is this all a coincidence? I turn around and look past the table over at Franz Ferdinand. He looks over too and grins. Once again, he's done his homework. The fake Fee and I don't say more than a handful of words to each other. We don't ask each other anything. It is what it is. It's OK.

In the morning, the place empties out. I'm happy to get out of that youth dance hell full of smoke. And the doppelgänger Fee. I climb into my car and drive across the giant, ghostly empty parking lot on the way to the city. In the distance something is blinking in the dawn light. Maybe three hundred, at most four hundred metres away there's a car, in the middle of the country road. The warning lights shine bright orange in the semi-darkness.

Across the road, on the pavement, a figure drags itself over to me. It's one of the guys. He's been shot. The wound is bleeding a lot. As it will transpire in the coming weeks, my mistake outside the club already made an impact. In fact, the abyss has caught up with us. It will swallow us. Devour us. And when a dam has already been broken, the water surges through the gap with tremendous force, and the gap becomes wider and wider. Out of vanity and pride, and from the inability to make a halfway mature, sensible choice, I chose the dark side of power. For five-and-a-half weeks, I plunge down the slippery slope of my lies. Five-and-a-half weeks are enough to destroy my comfortable existence. Or the appearance of it that still existed.

I lead the guys into the deepest darkness. I don't just destroy one life, but many. I commit extortions and robberies disguised as debt collections. My actions destroy the lives of dozens. Among them are a retired married couple and a cashier from the post office bank. In the hallway of a city villa, I'm looking for the wife of a corrupt building magnate and I scare her child half to death; we hadn't factored that in during advanced reconnaissance. We also hadn't factored in that her husband wouldn't be at home during this time. Bloody hell.

We storm the back room of a disco and leave a bloody swathe of desolation behind. We had been tipped off that we would find hundreds of thousands of Marks in black money in the safe, which we wanted to use to secure the company; the tip was wrong.

Our safari of violence ends in pointless failure. But everything that's rational in me has long given way to irrational anger, as the basis of an equally irrational justification for a killing spree. I have so much anger towards myself and my constant failing. Anger towards my mother, by whom I feel betrayed. Anger towards my brother, who left me along with her. Yes, even anger towards my father, who just let himself be killed instead of swinging me on his knees. Instead of living. And to love me.

'There is no destiny, which can't be overcome through contempt.' Camus was right. At least that's what I tell myself. I cause pain to countless lives. Everything, with the excuse that the ends justify the means. The city has to be rescued after all. Of course by Omega. And that's why I have to blackmail and steal. And at the heart of this nonsense, it's naturally about the lies regarding my own value. And it's about the wrong assumption that I could change something.

My heart races through the moments. It beats so painfully fast, that it feels like a single, burning heat in the middle of my chest. My sweat is everywhere, sticky and sour. And there's a feeling of sickness and the loss of balance, until it appears the whole world is wildly and uncontrollably spinning. It becomes a cascade of dots and lines and bubbles before my eyes. And blackness. And then, the impact. Somewhere. Towards somewhere, towards the ground. Whoever has felt that, has pushed themselves over the cliff. Or found themselves in the grips of a demon. All my victims share this feeling with me. Only in this case, I'm the demon. I had a choice, they didn't.

A call reaches me on the car phone on a country road at night. It's not a number I know.

'You were recognised. On the pavement, in front of the club. You have to get away!'

This feels real. 'They want to pick you up early tomorrow morning. They have an arrest warrant!'

The voice is speaking standard German. It's Franz Ferdinand. He doesn't say anything else. Fuck.

CHAPTER SEVENTEEN

When you're on the run, time tends to jump at random. There are cryptic movements from moment to moment, from block to block. Sometimes the seconds pass painfully slowly. And sometimes the hours, days and weeks race by, without you being able to say what happened. You feel everything. The paranoia penetrates your bones and flesh. It's like too much sun during a beach vacation. It leaves behind a constant, vague feeling of restlessness. The enemy is nowhere. And he's everywhere. Excruciating waiting. Nagging impatience. Yawning boredom. A vortex of thoughts and emptiness. Flight is born of fear. The demons are the travel guides. Flight is a hell of a trip.

I climb over the wall in the backyard and sneak up to my apartment. I turn on the light and feel my way forward. I frantically stuff clothes into my duffle bag. What about the weapons? They're lying in the depot well-hidden. But who knows who knows all that. I don't want to take any risks. What for? When you do that in a movie, you get various weapons from olive green boxes, shining with gun oil. But this isn't a movie, it's real. And no person with two cents in their head would pull a weapon in

the middle of the city in the face of a persecutor. You might as
well shoot yourself. Or should I hide in the forest? Live in a shelter, somewhere in the Harz forest on the former border? Hunt
wild boar? Collect fur for a warm winter jacket . . . and shit in a
little hole behind my makeshift hut.

Forget it. I'm not a naturalist. I'm an overbred huge urban
guerrilla. That's why no weapons and no attention. The rest can
be quickly gathered.

Only on the highway do I realise that somewhere behind
the Führer-Tür, I must have left my passport. A careless mistake I made thanks to the goddamn panic. I roll through the
night and curse to myself. How am I supposed flee without my
passport? I curse and rage. There's sparse traffic driving north
around this time, thank God. I drive and curse. And I follow
the speed limit precisely. And keep a safe distance. Just so I
don't stand out. That fucking song is on the radio again, 'She's
homeless, she's homeless.' Crystal Waters again. After that it's
the news. A plane has crashed somewhere. There was an attack
somewhere. And in the Congo, the Mobutu regime is falter-
ing; a civil war seems unavoidable. The usual craziness. And
nothing about me. Reassured, I turn the radio off. I overtake a
midsize car that's driving sluggishly slow. The father is sitting
at the wheel, the mother next to him, in the back two children,
asleep. A family. Normality two metres away from me. And yet
infinitely far away.

Somewhere in Brandenburg I reach the end of a traffic jam. The
lane is blocked by a police car. I roll forward. So, my flight ends
here. A strange feeling of quiet embraces me. I won't risk being
shot and killed. I won't jump around like a pathetic copy of Bruce

Lee, rolling around with my ex-colleagues. I step out of the car slowly. I hold my arms up in the air at my sides with my palms up. Hopefully it helps. Hopefully they aren't any trigger-happy cowboys. I walk over to the patrol car. The driver has his window rolled down.

'Good evening, chief constable.' The comrade has two green stars on his shoulder. And maybe my correct form of address lessens his desire to make use of his service weapon. Who knows what my homeland wrote in the wanted report. 'Wild animal on the run! Armed and dangerous! Save yourselves!' Something like that? If that's the case, I'll be wearing a rather holey jacket. My knees shake.

'Heavy transport. Got stuck. Could take a while.' The officer barely looks at me. He seems bleary-eyed and ready for a vacation. I stare dumbfounded in the direction of traffic. Then back to the officer. I can barely believe my luck. Then I mumble something, turn around and shuffle my jelly legs back to the car. My heart beats faster than a sewing machine can rattle. I close the car door and hold on to the steering wheel. I could cry from relief.

I know someone who knows someone. A gentle person who feels compassion even for someone like me. I can lie down on the couch, hidden in the guts of this giant city. I sleep little. Early in the morning I want to go to the nearby station and ask about train connections. My plan is set. I will distance myself from the location of my defeat as far as possible, from the place of my nonsense and my shame. The house of cards is destroyed. Now I have to worry about my freedom, every rescue attempt comes too late for my bourgeois facade.

Berlin, early in the morning. Grey is the colour of choice. Grey pavements. Grey tenements. The grey faces of those who are rushing to the assembly lines and the construction site in the early morning hours. I just want to quickly go to the car to get my duffle bag. The car is parked far up the street. I chose the farthest parking spot that I could find. The licence plates have been smeared black-brown and are unreadable. There was no time to find a duplicate, a doppelganger licence plate, so I had to get some help from a muddy puddle. Maybe that will give me some extra time. I didn't want to leave any stone unturned.

The car is still where I parked it. From the distance, everything appears to be fine. But this could be wishful thinking. I walk around the road crossing, I take the access passage between two buildings and I make smaller and smaller circles around the car. I put on my hood. I hold the handkerchief pressed to my face, pretending to sniffle. I still feel naked. A year ago, my turtleneck hung larger than life on advertising pillars and billboards. Bloody hell. I scurry past the car, stopping fifteen or twenty steps away.

A VW Passat is parked on the opposite side of the street. Two male occupants are sitting idly in the front seats. Dress code: auditors. Both stare noticeably unobtrusively at my car as they chew on some sandwiches. Or are they staring at the construction site behind? There are two bright yellow safety helmets lying on the parcel shelf, and paper rolls typical for architectural designs. I would do that too. With a credible role, a story that fits my stance.

Bloody hell. Keep going. Don't turn around. Just keep going. The paranoia has me in its grip. I rush to the train station. In line at the counter, I fumble around with the notes in my trouser pocket. I fish out a crumpled 50-Mark bill; in my head, panicked, I search for a destination. The line moves forward in slow motion.

The mechanical numbers on the indicator board above me click over from time to time. They create new patterns, new places, new destinations. No one seems to be in a hurry, except for me. How long is this going to take? And more importantly, where can I still go? The republic suddenly appears ridiculously small. The letters clack. Stuttgart in five minutes. I won't make that; the line is much too long for that. Munich: nine minutes. That's gone too. Cologne in fifteen minutes. Cologne? I'll take what I can get. Cologne, the other corner of the country. The Wild West. Cologne. I get this train.

As we leave the train station swaying and groaning, I breathe freer. I barely got away. Got away? From two construction workers with ham and cheese sandwiches?

I'm floating on a thin thread through the blackness of space. Space is cold and empty. My scream doesn't have a sound. This damn dream. It's eating its way through my nights, again and again. That's causality. I've thrown myself into the abyss. And now I'm fish food in a pond of demons. Something comes from something. My space is the foreign. Far from home, I'm surrounded by strange faces and an equally strange language. That makes my arrival difficult, from a technical point of view. But it makes my camouflage difficult too. Here in Paris, strange faces are a common part of the city landscape, the everyday. That's useful, just like Paris is useful. My own upheaval uprooted me at home. And now I have to be here, but different from the thousands of people who've chosen to be in Paris and the millions of tourists, this city isn't my place of longing, it's an exile. And it's always better than the stay in a Saxon prison.

The train station is full of heavily armed military officials, railway security, and police in uniform and in plain clothes. I quickly get away from there. Paris is as paranoid as I am, and rightly so. There have been bomb attacks. And new terror is expected every hour. This is the city of love. The city of lights. The Gallic spider. The city through which my father travelled, searching for a better future. Maybe he walked past the same fancy shop windows on Hausmann Boulevard. Maybe he took the subway, route 1, out to the Château de Vincennes. Or he sat under the same tree in Jardin des Tuileries.

Paris can be breathtakingly beautiful, if you're not illegal. My father absolutely wanted to go east, I absolutely want to go in the other direction. This is a noticeable overlap, but there isn't a lot of opportunity for nostalgia. After the tower blocks of my childhood, I'm once again living in a concrete block. With the little money I have I couldn't organise anything except this hole of a single room in the north of Paris. It is one of the worst areas. The unit may have been modern in the early Seventies. And an example of social progress. Now there's the smell of trash, excrement and poverty in the hallway.

From here, I start my daily struggle for a few Francs. Paris is unbelievably expensive. I don't know how normal people can survive here. Police officers. Taxi drivers. Nurses. I urgently need money for necessities. For rent and something to eat from the supermarket. When you're illegal, finding a job is like a magic trick. I take what I can get. I work as a removalist. As a coach for bored upper-class customers in a fitness studio. And as a bouncer again. Basically, I'm going round in circles. I do what I've always done. I just wear a different name, and a baseball cap and a beard. And thick horn-rimmed glasses that I found for ten Francs from the junk corner of the drugstore.

I shouldn't go out at all. Behind every path, the danger of an ID inspection and unmasking is hiding. And working at the door of a club is pure insanity. But I have to earn money somehow, otherwise I couldn't even afford this rathole in the northern part of the city. The city of love? It's the city of money. No place for the have-nots like me. This isn't going to last forever.

I decide to travel a few stops along the Metro, away from home and work. There, I find a dirty phone booth and I dial the number of the prosecution. I want to make a deal with the authorities. I claim my innocence, not realising that my hastily cobbled-together plans are already coming apart.

Something awful has happened in my homeland – and I didn't play any part in it for once. A murder for hire. A bloody spectre from the wreckage of Omega. I didn't organise it, nor have any knowledge of it. Yet the homicide cops will be after me. They will have plenty of information from the guys they arrested. They'll find out about my place in Paris. I quickly pack my stuff and flee to another rat hole, even more run down and even further on the outskirts.

My flight from Dresden has allowed me to escape two crises. On the one hand, my arrest. On the other, my participation in something unspeakable. In my hubris, there is a high probability I would have participated in an illegal assassination. A self-righteous contract killer pumped full with the false ideals of an alleged 'resister for the good cause'. A man, a father, a son, a brother and friend, simply wiped out. I didn't take part. This guilt passes me by. And instead of murdering, I barely got away with my life.

So-called friends try to lure me back to Germany. They promise me a safe shelter and with that everything I long for in exile. I'm supposed to meet them in Strasbourg, but at the last minute I get a stomach bug and I can't get on the train. The diarrhoea saves my life. When I'm healthy again, my supposed 'helpers' have already been arrested for something else. That's how I barely escape an early annihilation. Later investigations uncover that my supposed 'friends' had already singled out a piece of forest in Elsass where they wanted to bury my body.

I know from well-informed sources at home that in the meantime, a monstrous, elaborate manhunt has started for me. My mother is being watched. Friends and acquaintances are being spied on. The Saxon Free State is pissed off, and something like that isn't without consequences. They insist on observing telephone booths from which I once called someone. It will be difficult to find me among eleven million people in the convoluted, ancient quarters of the city. But the net is closing in. At least that's what the collective of accusers suggest to me. Is the danger real or is this just the agitating voices in my head? It's summer, and amid the warmth, the flowers and the lush green, Algerian terrorists are following their threats with acts. And with the terror comes a flood of armed military and police units. And their paranoia is at least as great as my own. The paranoia gives the hunters wings. That's how it is in my imagination. And just like months ago in Berlin, now Paris, the metropolis of eleven million people, no longer feels so big. I have to leave. I must get further away. Now.

*

Swenu Alongi Boboto. That's my name now. I threw away anything that could have betrayed my identity. Everything that could
have betrayed my identity. My old self. Why did I even bring those
things with me? Maybe I didn't want to totally and completely
dissolve, maybe that was the reason. But now all that stuff had to
go. With it, I never would have made it through the strict control
at the airport. My past fits in a medium-sized plastic bag from the
supermarket. As such,, it becomes food for the incinerators.

I'm sitting in an aeroplane heading for Zaire. I'm carrying a
fake name in a fake passport. And the false, completely unreal-
istic hope that I will actually find the Amazon. The Amazon has
a job in Namibia, but who knows what will happen if I make it
there. That woman was forged in fire. The term 'surrender' isn't
in her dictionary. And maybe she'll refuse to give me up. Maybe
I haven't lost this part of my life after all. I flee with this vague
hope. This chimera is the only thing that I still have.

I'm hovering in a flying tin can above water, clouds and land
into the heart of a continent, to Kinshasa, to the banks of the
mighty Congo River. Far away from Cameroon, the land of
my father, where the captors of the Free State will look for me
at some time, if I can't be found anywhere else. So I choose
Kinshasa instead of Cameroon for my transit.

In the arrivals hall, the scorching heat already hits me in the face
like a well-aimed slap. Tottering and half-dazed, I make it to the
airport exit, I get stuck in a chaotic crowd of people, carts and
cars. It's an indescribable swarm of pushing.

'Monsieur, taxi au centre-ville?' Someone is tugging on my
softened shirt. I ignore it and keep pushing forward. The voice
rushes after me: 'Monsieur. Monsieur!'

Now I do stop. I must head to the city anyway. I have to get out of here. God in heaven, somewhere, the main thing is away. *'Oui, centre-ville. Combien?'*

The alleged taxi owner is a frighteningly emaciated man. He says something. I give him five of the dollars I've exchanged. He stares at the bill, then takes my bag without comment and drives me to some hotel. More of a barracks, with clearly visible patches in its corrugated iron roof. The room is half as big as my room in Potsdam and twice as decrepit. Regardless, this is the price range I can afford, at least these days.

I'm lying on a musty smelling bed. There's a fan spinning above me that must have existed since the days of the Belgian occupation. Outside, the city is roaring. Africa. This doesn't at all feel like my homeland. Or like a homecoming. I'm a child of the East. An Ossi. A German roll. I like having things regulated, orderly and predictable. This is the opposite of that.

My next flight leaves in a week. That's not a lot of time. I have to hurry and take care of my crap. My passport is good, but it's only counterfeit. That's why I'm here; I could only afford a Zairean passport. And its international value is close to zero. The Zairean named Swenu Alongi Boboto needs a visa for practically every other country in the world. And I can only get the visa for my next trip here, in Kinshasa, the capital city. I need a visa for Namibia. And I need it immediately. So I get going and I wander around sweating, until I have used all the hand gestures I could to ask how to get to the embassy quarter.

After an endless walk past an ocean of huts and few houses, I arrive at streets surrounded by mountains of garbage that lead to the embassy. A mass of people are already waiting there. There are mostly women, plump mamas in colourfully printed wrap skirts. Sweating, I get in the disorderly line behind them. My pulse is beating quickly. I didn't bring any water with me. And in this unbearable heat, the line of people only moves forward centimetre by centimetre.

Despite my expectations, I reach the counter of the embassy by early afternoon. I'm supposed to pay a robust office lady a fee. I look for the bills while the lady flips through my passport, staring at it critically. With shaky fingers I arrange the dollars into piles and shove them across the table. And I try to smile while I do it. They'll probably throw me out of the embassy now. The lady only looks up briefly, doesn't show any expression and stamps my strangely virginal Zairean passport with a business visa.

I have a passport. I have a visa. I've come farther than I thought. Everything seems possible. I buy myself water and drink the small bottle immediately. Then, exhilarated, I take myself down the same stretch of huts, houses and mountains of trash. Not far from the embassy quarter, my shoe gets stuck on something, and I fall to the ground. That's annoying. Dumb. But it's also no wonder, with this goddamn heat and the long paths, I stumble. I pick myself up and nearly get to my knees. Suddenly I have a twitching stabbing pain at the back of my head. It explodes in a flickering red and a sudden wave of pain and panic.

Then, out of the corner of my eye, I see a leg approach and a shoe lands in my ribs with a crash. The pain that follows is even more intense as the one in my head. I struggle for breath. With both of my hands, I grab my burning stomach and my ribs. I roll and writhe, and for a moment I fall out of the world.

When I come to again, everything has passed. I feel around

me. My shoulder bag is gone. Someone has robbed me. My passport is gone. Even my boots have been stolen. And naturally my pride, too. What an ironic turn of events! The violent offender has been beaten up. The cheater has been cheated. In the dirt, on the nameless, littered caricature of a street, at the other end of the world. I laugh. It's not more than a cough, but it has to get out. I laugh. And the laughing becomes a cramp. And afterwards I cry. People walk by. They don't turn to look at me. My plight doesn't appear to be of any interest.

I crouch on the roadside; I wrap my arms around my knees. For years, I've trudged around the human lowlands, but I hadn't expected this. I don't belong here. This isn't my league of chaos. It didn't even take five hours for the locals to show me how the wind blows. I might be a carnivore at home, a predator, but here I'm a pathetic victim. I make it back to the hotel barracks, barefoot and bruised. The woman at the reception stares at me. I'm no longer a welcomed guest.

After the hotel, I stay in a guest room near a church. It's not a guest room; rather it's a storage room full of bulky waste. In my desperation, I knocked on the church door and I was invited in. The church is led by a small, round-faced pastor. Without their charity, I would be part of the army of homeless. But worse. But instead I'm here. I have gathered some tattered cardboard boxes for the night. My sleeping camp is encircled by mice and rats. They're likely hoping for something edible, in vain, just like me.

In the morning I have more luck. The pastor talks little, and from the church's lost and found I get ancient but lightly worn shoes. And I immediately start working as an assistant. I carry rice bags into the parish hall. I sweep the nave and the small, bumpy forecourt made out of stamped clay. I caulk the toilet pit so the smell doesn't become unbearable in the hours long church service. And I do everything that the pastor instructs. I don't moan about it. I'm thankful. Because the pastor doesn't ask questions and I'm spared the street. Life can be so simple.

Days go by. Weeks. I work and eat and sleep. And I'm probably rescued by the fact that I count as a 'pale face' in the Congo region. Le Blanc. The white one. At least the obvious descendant of a white half. Something like that counts as a status symbol in Zaire. It's a kind of social nobility, this thing with my skin. Those are my mother's genes. You don't let someone like that die on the street.

My 'lucky situation' doesn't last all that long. I get a strong fever. From one hour to the next, I'm so weak that I can barely make it to the toilet pit. Fever and the shakes take turns. Sometimes I freeze on my cardboard boxes under a worn Red Cross blanket, sometimes I sweat like I'm in a sauna. It's been going on for days. The pastor explains to me that it's malaria. His worry is carefully hidden behind a smile. I have malaria and no money for medicine. But the pastor doesn't want to just watch a European curiosity die in his storage room. He puts on a jacket and walks through half the city to some nuns. The nuns give him pills. The pastor returns with them. He shakes me awake. I wash the giant pills down laboriously. Then I fall back asleep.

Hours later. Or is it days? I turn myself over on my back. Some of the mice scuttle away without haste. Maybe they are other, bigger rodents? I stare at the cracks in the ceiling. Peeling colours. Crumbling plaster. It's like a menu of my own decay. Dying might be easy, I think. It's almost like just falling asleep. Getting increasingly weaker and then being gone some time. Rubbed out. If only the collective of accusers could finally give me peace. 'What would become of your mother?' 'Your poor mother.' 'She didn't deserve that.'

I think about my mother. I should think about the Amazon. I should grieve for my loved one. She won't know how I died either. But instead I think about my mother, the arch enemy. The tormentor who is eternally dissatisfied with me. That witch won't even let me die in peace. Somehow, she's managed to make me miss her awfully in these final moments. In the corners of the room, the rodents ponder these thoughts along with me. It's like a mixed breed public assembly. It doesn't bother me any more. A child is crying outside. It's screaming and crying bitterly. Then the crying stops. The child's mother probably picked it up comfortingly. A good mother, not like mine. Drink. I have to drink, I think. Then I doze away.

The pastor comes. He gives me water from a crinkly plastic bottle. And even more pills. The pills work. The fever is going down. But my body feels strange and has the colour of a curdled dessert. All of the drudgery of training over the years couldn't have come close to preparing me for this. The tablets work. The fever fog slowly retreats. I drink water from a crumpled bottle and eat small clumps of cassava porridge. I can't tolerate much of either thing.

Almost hourly, I roll out of the cardboard box and at the toilet hole, a watery, almost clear fluid comes out of me. The pastor I referred to before is not amused. Hastily, he puts on his jacket again and rushes with worry lines to the city, to the nuns. Before he goes, he gives me a badly worn, spotted block of paper. Thin paper that is held together at a single point by the binding. This collection of pages makes a terribly wretched impression on me. I open them up. It's a Luther Bible. In German. I can barely hold the small, mottled thing, my fingers shake so much. I actually have to go back to the toilet hole, but I don't have the strength.

'Read. Pray,' the pastor says to me. 'You might go to your father. Soon.' With these words, he leaves the storage room.

My English is broken, and my brain feels like it's been shaken too often, but I can't misunderstand the man that much.

'Lord, teach me that my life must have an end and my life has a goal and I have to get away from it.' Psalm 39.

At this page, a piece of cardboard is inserted into the damn book. I let both fall beside my cardboard mat on the floor and turn onto my side. At some point the pastor comes back and stuffs new pills in my mouth. Then I sleep. I'm so tired. Dying is somehow very easy.

Outside there's a noise. And the noise tells me that I haven't arrived in the afterlife yet. It's the unmistakeable, ugly metal rattle of a Kalashnikov machine gun. A shot goes off, then the gas pressure drives the breech with a mighty backwards jerk, so that the empty shell is thrown out and the new bullet is pressed into the magazine. Clack. Clack. Clack. Nothing sounds like a Kalashnikov. And between that, now and again there's screaming. The desperate screams behind the wall. I roll myself into a ball out of fear. Clack. Clack. Clack.

Where is the pastor? How much time has passed? I must have fallen asleep. I feel thirsty, but the plastic bottle is empty. The pastor is gone. When I knock on the back door of the main hut, no one opens it. I stagger past the toilet pit to the outer wall, in which gapes a giant hole. Behind the wall, there's a wall of garbage, waist high.

I climb over the wall. My legs give way several times. I'm weak, but I make it over the wall. That's where the street is. That's where the quarter is. That's where a battlefield is. Already on the other side of the street, a ruin juts out above a row of intact huts. It's rusty black and still smoking. And not far away there's the burned-out skeleton of a car. And between that there are bodies. Some in large pieces. Others in small parts. The dead flesh probably belongs to five people. Maybe six or seven. The body that's closest to me is lying in a bizarre contortion. Arms and legs demonstrate giant, gaping wounds that are being swarmed by a cloud of flies.

There's a body behind me that's just a torso. The limbs and head are gone. Only from the frayed remains can you see that something was once there. The torso is small. Too small for an adult. I see some things but only understand very little of it, in my dehydrated condition my brain needs a long time for everything. But not long enough. This is like a horror film. And I definitely don't want to take part in its production. I walk down the street to the left, past the ruins of more huts. I don't walk far. My head wants to but my legs can't. At some point, I crouch at the edge of the street. Where should I go? I crouch there and wait for nothing.

'Come!' It's the pastor. He's collecting his little flock. The pastor isn't dead. 'Come with me!'

I shuffle with him, back to the hut.

'Sit down.' He pushes me softly onto the cardboard boxes and I lean my back against the really cool wall of the storage room. He looks at me seriously. 'You have to go to your embassy. This is going to be worse, believe me.' There's no joy any more in the man's round face. 'Much, much worse.'

After the scene on the street, I understand what he means. 'I have to go to Namibia. I must try!'

The pastor glowers and shakes his head. 'You cannot. You will never pass the check-in on the airport. Not like this. And you know that.'

'Still, I have to try.'

He shakes his head again. 'You can only take the ship. But ships only go out from Matadi. And the route is full of check-points.' He thinks for a minute.

'You could also try the river and then the land, but that's thirteen hundred kilometres. Maybe fifteen hundred. You would have to go to Lubumbashi. There is no drivable road, even with a good 4×4 it would be difficult to get there. And from there you would have to continue via Zambia.' He shakes his head again. 'It is impossible, simply impossible. You will die trying. Do you understand?'

I cry. Just like that. I can't do anything else. The pastor waits patiently until my little bout of self-pity is over.

'I'll give you a hundred and fifty dollars,' he says. He says it very quietly.

My head springs up. One hundred and fifty dollars. That's a fortune here. And a new debt. To take so much money from a person in such circumstances is practically another crime. This money means that the pastor and his family can go to the doctor. And eat. And bribe people. You can convert this money to lives. If I take it, I may as well kill them.

'I'm going on a missionary tour next week. My family will accompany me.'

He wants to leave here. 'Why?' I have to ask him. It's a dumb question. I know the answer. I saw the answer outside on the street.

'Because this is the end. It's the end.'

The pastor is leaving. He's leaving and won't come back. What will become of me?

'Can I join?' Even I'm surprised by my question. But how am I supposed to survive this without him?

'No. We have to go to Ghana. And you can never do it without a proper passport. It would be very, very dangerous for all of us.'

He looks down at me. He seems tired. He seems exhausted beyond all limits. 'Go to your embassy! Go home!' I shake my head. I can't. The pastor turns to go. After a short pause he says, slightly annoyed: 'You will die here, do you understand?'

I didn't listen to the pastor. I find myself boarding a barge. The thing is packed with human freight, but it's better than nothing. From Kinshasa I travel via a tributary of the Congo into the jungle. After three days on the river, I become sick again. Intestinal obstruction. I'm suffering, lying on a fucking Congo boat, the postcard beautiful world all around me. Underneath me comforting water rushes by. And my body fat index sinks into the abyss, my flesh just falls away. I look like a big skeleton draped with donations from the church. And then, the goddamn boat gets stranded on a sand bank. And I have to continue my insane tour on foot.

The entourage of passengers sways and crawls sixty kilometres through the jungle, until it reaches the railway line of a former Belgian mine company. I spend the night in a Congolese military base. I pay for a bed. The bed is in the death room of the hospital. How fitting. I don't protest. There's fighting outside. I hear the gunfire in the distance. I'd rather be lying in a dry and safe place among the dying. 'Monster! Monster!' cries the choir of accusers, but I hear them only faintly, in the back of my head, because I am an unspeakably drained, tired candidate for death.

The next morning we continue. And on and on. And somehow I survive the crazy trip. I make it from Kinshasa up to the last corner of Zaire, to Lubumbashi, near the border. Across the country. *Deus vult?* On days with a clear sky I see the mountains in Zambia in the distance. Freedom seems so near. And somehow not at all. I get the stomach problem again, with diarrhoea for days and watery, clear fluids. And the city is full of the half-starved, the crazy and the mutilated.

I wander around and ultimately sleep very far away on the margins in the ruins of a football station. Final destination. I stare at the stands covered in weeds around me. Then at the sky. *Deus vult?* The dusk breaks in like a time lapse. And around this time my stomach always cramps. And life sneaks out of me. 'Go to your embassy,' that's what the pastor said. 'Go home.'

A faint glimmer of brightness hangs in the sky, time for a final reckoning: I will never make it over the border to Zambia without a bribe. And I can't call the Amazon. I don't have her number or any more money. This hell of a country doesn't have anything more for me. The only thing you can get here cheap is death. So I sit in a stadium without football players, in a life without hope.

I go to the German consulate. More precisely, it's her Belgian counterpart. The consul has fallen into disfavour with the reigning dictator because of her unwelcome criticism. She's had to flee to Johannesburg but her husband has stayed and does everything he can for the German sheep entrusted to him. He books two seats in one of the few aeroplanes heading to the capital city for the price of a mid-size car.

The German Deputy Ambassador picks me up from there. After a short trip, I'm dropped off at the domestic intelligence office. This is because the embassy isn't allowed to arrest me. That's what bureaucracy demands. The domestic intelligence in this country is responsible for extraditions, so the ambassador drives me there. The responsible secret service agent is a larger-than-life character in a satin-y tailored suit.

'*Je récupère ce monsieur sain et sauf,*' the Deputy Ambassador addresses the secret service agent. He speaks slowly and quietly, but there's an obvious hardness in his tone. '*Si vous ne le faites pas, le ministre de l'Intérieur m'a assuré que vous auriez de très, très gros ennuis.*' Despite months in Paris, my French is absurdly bad. The Deputy Ambassador takes this from my helpless expression. 'I told the man that he will have great problems, if I don't get you back from him unscathed.' The Ambassador walks away without a word.

The secret service guy looks surprised, then he nods. I guess immediately what the deal is with this preamble. In the backyard of the secret service headquarters there's a nondescript barracks. That's where they take me. But as is often the case with nondescript things, the outward appearance is deceptive. In this barracks there's a fissure that goes to the very depths of hell.

I come to. It's an abrupt shift from sleep to the present. A short, violent ramping up. Did I dream of screaming? Did I scream myself or was I awoken by screaming? It sounded so unbelievably suffering. So imploring. How would you have to torture a human creature for it to make such sounds? Smack. Smack. Smack. The sound echoes through the hallway of the cell wing. It sounds as if a butcher is working with a piece of schnitzel. Smack. Smack. Smack. And then screaming again. Smacking and crying follow each other in a rapid change.

I hold my ears closed, but that doesn't help much. If only I was a noble knight on a beautiful white horse. If only I could be the hero for once. I would throw myself against the cell door and protest. But I'm not like that. My only worry is myself. Will they also come to me and repeat the horror of the neighbouring cell on me? I cower in the farthest corner, and I pee myself. And I'm still shaking long after the screaming has stopped and the torturers leave for the evening, laughing.

Here there are men working in business outfits, with suit trousers and nicely striped lilac shirts and shimmering silver ties. You could mistake them for lawyers, but unfortunately their consultation is of an entirely different nature. And the urgent warning of the Deputy Ambassador is all that stands between me and these men. It's not that they could force any useful information out of me anyway. I don't know anything. But that's not the point. People are tortured here, just so they may suffer. A victim's pain manifests the urgency of the situation for their relatives. The internal secret service is practically operating a department of kidnapping and blackmail. And judging by the employees' clothing, it's had some commercial success.

I crouch in my cell and pray. I say Psalm 39 so often that I have the impression I'm going crazy. I pray and whimper. And mostly crouch on the concrete floor, in the far back of the cell, and I rock back and forth there, wrapped in my own arms and constant panic.

Once again I'm awoken by screams. This time its accompanied by machine gun fire. I stay lying on the brown-spotted mattress and sweat fear. But no one comes into this barracks, no one comes to me, my cell door stays shut. Only much later in the day will all of the prisoners be forced into the courtyard. We have to stand in long rows. Instead of the usual secret service workers dressed in civil clothing, there are men everywhere in uniforms. Big men with hard faces. And MP5 machine guns. The whole scene has the classic appearance of a firing squad in a war film.

Then a fat giant joins them, also wearing a uniform. He's even bigger than the others and he is in control of everything. The giant paces past the row of prisoners, as if he had come to visit the slave market during his lunch break to get a deal. In the background, a bailiff loads his rifle. My fellow prisoners stare at the ground. I stare at the ground. Maybe I'll be chosen as a particularly exotic pet and not executed with the others. There's still a last chance. A final hope, before there's not any more and everything is over.

I suddenly remember a bit of Latin that my comrade from the wall brigade caught me, the ex-seminary student: '*Proficiscere, anima christiana, de hoc mundo, In nomine Dei.*' 'Go, Christian soul, in the name of God.'

I mumble the magic phrase to myself that is supposed to call the soul-taxi to the dying. Next stop: Paradise. But does the taxi still come if you don't believe in anything any more and can't trust anything? Does the taxi also come for robbers? For someone who's stumbled. Someone like me?

'*Proficiscere, anima christiana, de hoc mundo.*' I will soon be with my father. And my grandfather. They are probably already sitting laughing and feasting and smoking a pipe on a cloud and are getting along. I'll soon be with my father. A single tear rolls down my chin and falls into the dirt between my feet.

IV

The Long Way
to Freedom

Bonn, mid-July 2021

Now it's quiet here, while outside apocalyptic rain falls on the city. The girls are with their playmates. No one is calling me. No one sends any news. That's a good sign. And even if there was something to report, I would be the last to find out. Fathers are like dispensable, superfluous appendages in a perfectly organised world of mothers. I've now accepted the fact that my wife is all-powerful and all-knowing on earth. But right now my WhatsApp message to her only has a lonely grey tick, nothing more. The message has been sent, but she hasn't seen it yet.

I stare out of the window at the rain and although it is in the middle of the afternoon, the sky has a dark colour as if dusk has already come. A true end-of-times scene. The girls are still out. My wife appears to be 'lost'. And Jérôme doesn't pick up his phone. And I can only sit here and wait. And keep myself occupied with matcha tea and homemade butter cookies. While the cookies melt away into their buttery, sugary and cinnamon-flavoured pieces, I daydream, travelling beyond the rain and through the years and past the abyss of time.

CHAPTER EIGHTEEN

I crouch deep under the earth, in a windowless, white tiled room. I'm barefoot. And this isn't an experimental, 3-D cinema. It's not a scene in Batman's hidden cave. I crouch in an underground cell, which has been built somewhere, deep under a stronghold of the authorities. I crouch in the corner, my back leaning against the tiled wall. The room is completely empty. And irritatingly hot, almost like the imitation of the hottest summer day imaginable. The air vibrates from heat. Although I can't see a heater anywhere. And in the corner of the room, someone has made a drain hole, for necessities. Four by four wide steps in a square. That's my cell, my bunker. My castle. The entire scene is lit by a luminous panel behind a plastic tank that someone has built into a wall, level and smooth. The panel is filled with a surreal twilight, as if I am sitting in the middle of a crazy art installation.

Someone has stuck me in this cell because it is the safest place they could offer me in a hurry. They know about the former member of the Russian special forces, the Spetsnaz, who had telephone surveillance on me by order of Franz Ferdinand. The comrades from the Spetsnaz are something like an out-of-control combination of parachuters and state-certified assassins. They're human machines, who do nothing more than produce death and destruction. It is entirely within the realms of possibility that I have only survived the craziness in Africa in order to be shot to death and blown to bits in my homeland. Or whatever the super-soldier comes up with, in his destructive creativity.

I don't wear a watch, but I can't have been here longer than an hour. So according to the computational methods of the Upper Franconian maths genius Adam Riese, I have twenty-nine hours, then they'll come and get me. Then the thing will come to an end, one way or another.

The idea of having to wait that long underground makes me feel sick. I wheeze increasingly heavily. I suffer a panic attack and can't breathe; I don't have many moments left. I run and skip on the spot. I pump my legs faster and faster. I choke for the next breath. Legs up. Forward. The balls of my feet tap fleetingly on the ground. Faster. Faster. I run away from the shock. And from possibly passing out. From suffocation. Crazy running on the spot. Pumping with my arms and legs, running without moving forward. A symbol for my life. Sweat runs down my face and my neck, but the uncontrolled gasp for air fades away into a merciful, saving pain that flushes the panic from my cells.

It wipes out the sky, somewhere far above me. It wipes out my fear. It wipes out everything.

Kinshasa. Two years and six months before the tiled cellar.

The turbines cry, the plane rolls, rumbling over the starting line. Faster, always faster, until it frees itself from the ground with a hop. I can barely believe it. In a few moments we'll be gone. And as long as a marooned anti-aircraft battery doesn't bring us back to the ground, I'll finally get away from this horror film of a country.

In the end, it was very close. My retrieval was on a razor's edge. The civil guard, practically the military police, created a coup against the interior secret service. There was unrest in the city centre. What would have been a beautiful twist in a Hollywood movie involved a lot of carnage. The Saxon authorities spared no effort. The target scout who flew in just for my liberation, together with the guys from the special task force who assisted him, are supposed to secure my return to the kingdom. Because of the coup, however, they crouch helplessly in their hotel and are just as stuck there as their precious, dirty-bearded target in the torture barracks.

'Samuel Meffire?'

It is difficult to recognise me under my beard and the month of dirt, but it is me. For sure, a criminal on the run is seldom as happy as I was now to meet my pursuers.

'Don't cause any problems, OK, big guy?' the commando leader tells me.

We've just landed in Tegel, Berlin. We're standing in the doorway of the Boeing in the way of an annoyed stewardess, who wants to get her cargo out of the hold as quickly as possible. I shake my head. And risk a smile. Actually, I want to grin like a Cheshire cat about the sheer improbability of still being alive. I shake my head forcefully. *No*, I won't make any trouble. I'm as innocent as a lamb.

I spend the trip to Dresden stuffing myself with the contents of two food pouches. The Zaire hunger craze sits deep inside me. The special forces guys are looking at me through the protective glass in the car, half astonished, half empathetic. They have apparently picked up a crazy wild one.

We race down the Autobahn to the thundering sounds of Rammstein, towards Saxony. I crouch in an improvised isolation unit, almost airtight. I have been seriously ill and I still might be, even in my new, government-provided clothes. My flight led through the very area where, in 1976, the first ever Ebola outbreak occurred. The Saxon ministerial bureaucrats who organised my return are now afraid that I'm bringing the apocalypse with me. That's why they organised for a police van to be turned into a rolling isolation station with a plastic screen and a lot of tape.

We hurtle towards Dresden. The duty magistrate receives us with a tired face. The pre-trial detention order proceeds quickly. And before the signature on the paper has time to dry, a convoy of armoured BMW limousines disappears into the night. I will be quickly driven somewhere. And will throw up on someone there. I'll be handcuffed and tied up multiple times, moved from one car to another. I see and hear everything and understand nothing. Why all this trouble? What's happening here?

The man points to the car. We're somewhere deep in the West, near the French border.

There are only two more years and three months until the cell in the tiled cellar.

I hesitate. 'I'll shoot you in the back if you run away.' The man's face and stance are full of contempt for me. I've got long weeks of pre-trial detention behind me. I spent them in a high security wing. Hidden in total isolation. That eats through your essence. The first words from the man in the car couldn't have been clearer, or more explicit. No greeting, no small talk, just that. His companion and superior is an otherwise hyper-correct civil servant with a PhD, but that doesn't stop her from allowing this threat to proceed.

'Did you understand that?'

To be threatened by a man who should be rescuing you and protecting your life, that's not without a macabre irony. I get a taste of my own medicine. That's how life goes. What goes around comes around. Yes, of course, the dog on a leash understood. The man didn't for a moment consider that despite the handcuffs in front of my stomach, my mind is still free. My spade hand could wander, long before this official piece of lard has touched his holster or the weapon inside it.

It's simple mathematics. First, the guy has to take in what he's seeing, work out what's happening, then transmit this information through his nervous system to trigger a fine-motor reaction with a shot of adrenalin. In my experience, at this level of stress, that's no walk in the park. The spade-hand movement has been ingrained in me a thousand times. On the training roof in Neustadt. At the doorframe of my kitchen door, high up above Alaun Street. Against the paranoid imagination of an enemy in the shoebox-sized hallway of my concrete box before the gates of Paris.

The spade hand is the last defence in close combat, a defence in the face of potential destruction. It lashes out like a cobra and presses the larynx in. It doesn't need a lot of force for that. Maybe fifteen kilos, hardly more, I once read that in a book about the physiology of martial arts. A few years ago, a freak pushed my larynx out of position, just a little. Nevertheless, for a week I had a nearly black bruise on my neck and I could barely eat anything.

Two-one-thousand. Three-one-thousand. Four-one-thousand.
I breathe out my anger until it dissipates. I say nothing and get
into the vehicle that's waiting.

'We'll bring you to Waldheim,' Ms PhD explains to me without emotion. She flips quietly through a big, red-covered file of
papers in front of her on the desk, as if she didn't have a dangerous, potentially deadly threat in the room. The gunslinger
sits sideways behind her and grins contentedly. My pre-trial and
criminal trial must be carried out according to the so-called 'Law
of First Process'. The judges will come together in Dresden in
order to pass judgement over me. The institutions closest to the
Saxon capital city are in Waldheim and Bautzen. And those are
both institutions with dubious reputations. In Waldheim they've
been maintaining this reputation for almost three hundred years.
Waldheim is the oldest jail hole in Germany. And one of the worst.

'All you can do is confess.'

This sentence confuses me. 'I already confessed. I admitted
everything to the investigating judge. Everything!'

Ms PhD isn't satisfied. She shakes her head.

'That's not what I mean. You shouldn't testify to your crimes,
rather to being given the weapons and the raid on the club.'

In a fraction of a second, I freeze inside. How dumb can you
be? How naive? The entire time I've not guessed why I've been
hidden away in one of the secret detention houses. And why
they're keeping me in the high security wing, in complete isolation, so far away from Dresden that it might as well be the other
end of the world.

'The others have long testified.' I try to be evasive. 'Everything
has been uncovered. Why do you need me, too?'

Ms PhD closes the folder with a flourish. That's probably supposed to seem dashing, but it appears accidental and funny. Even so, I don't feel like laughing.

'Don't worry your head about that.'

She points at the closed file in front of her.

'All of your paperwork is in here. And if you don't want to testify, then you'll go directly onto the transport.'

My tongue is stuck in my mouth. Waldheim, that won't work. That would surely be my end. And a painful one at that. I would like to put forward something in my defence, but I can't choke it out.

'And there's something else I want you to think about,' she says, as she stands up from her chair. 'He ... wants to see you dead.'

Her tone leaves little doubt who she could mean. The words echo as if someone has superimposed a clever sound effect on reality, once the lawyer and her trigger-happy helper have already long left the room. They let me stew. I sit chained to the radiator near the window. I have time to absorb the ugly facts as they begin to sink in.

He wants to see me dead. I look out of the window and try to work out how hopeless my situation is. A little hopeless? Very hopeless? Or absolutely and completely hopeless? Is it now time for an act of desperation? There's a park on the other side of the window. Beige-grey stone paths meander between the winter-bare trees. All my cards are played, all the troops have long been sent to the front. In this battle, neither sticking it out nor running away helps.

If I testify against Franz Ferdinand, I'm as good as dead. The man has a legendary memory, he forgets nothing and he never forgives. If I don't testify, I'll be locked in one of the secret detention houses, with other criminals I've helped bring to justice.

I stare out of the window hard, as if a well-hidden solution is hidden somewhere in the park, between the bare bushes. The paths meander through the winter wasteland. They lead nowhere. And it's the same for my future. My stomach has formed itself into a concrete ball. A cramping pain meanders slowly and quite thoroughly through my intestines. I press my bound hands against my stomach to alleviate the cramping, but it's like trying to put out a forest fire with a carpet beater.

The following day. A new interrogation. A different team. A different approach. There are friendly, familiar faces. A familiar inflection in the voices, a hint of home. For a start, there are two cheeseburgers for me, and a small Coke. The unusually tasty food leads to a fit of euphoria. Eight weeks of prison food. Eight weeks of culinary mishaps from the dented warming tubs of the central kitchen. Thus, the burgers appear to me like manna in the desert. I chew happily on bread, cheese and meat.

'Listen. We know everything,' one of the officers interjects. 'It was the interrogations about the assassination. There was so much accidental evidence, that it also solved our cases.' I shrug my shoulders, I have my hands full. And I had nothing to do with the contract murder. Thank God.

'The murder wasn't my task. Not my decision. I was in Paris hiding myself away. I didn't know anything.'

My interlocutor waves me happily off. 'We know, we know everything.' What comes now must be the crux of the matter. 'After the murder, we quickly investigated backers and shooters.

And most of those involved tried to avoid getting sent down for life. That's why they testified.'

'Excuse me – then why do you need me?' I ask, still chewing and smacking.

'After a while, we made it clear to your former comrades-in-arms that they should think about their future.'

That sounds obvious. Yes, but Franz Ferdinand's arm has a far reach, even to the Saxon detention houses.

'There's supposed to be a trial at some time.'

Now it comes.

'We may have confessions, but no one wants to repeat them in front of the court.' The man points to me, in order to avoid any confusion. 'And that's where you come in.' The mouthfuls of burger get stuck in my throat. I swallow desperately.

'Me?'

'Yes, exactly. You,' he says.

'Especially since you have to make sure that you get out of the line of fire,' his colleague adds, in a friendly manner as if he's giving me a helpful tip while I'm looking for the Northern train station in Paris. His explanation clarifies the situation in my mind: under no circumstances can Franz Ferdinand risk the disclosure of my testimony. That's why he wants my 'preventative disposal'. He was also involved in the plan to let me disappear in a patch of forest near Strasbourg. The plan failed. Now there is a second attempt, with the rentcd Russian super-soldiers.

'And that's why he's making all this fuss?'

The officer nods seriously. 'He has to – at least to his thinking. He has cancer really badly. Advanced.'

All at once I see the bigger picture. The authorities want to scrape together everything against Franz Ferdinand. They want to put together a complete criminal case, in order to put him away for so long that he rots in jail. Then his empire will become prey to hyenas and he will be too weak to fight. His time is running out. It's his final battle.

'If you want some advice, then you should make a statement. The weapons bag, with all that crap, ultimately was not yours. And the club wasn't your idea. That's all that they want to hear.'

What choice do I have? I've made deliveries to almost all of the prisons in Saxony. Therefore, some of the cons I've ratted out are still there. And a former policeman is on the lowest rung of every prison hierarchy. In every prison I'm practically free game. And to top it all off, I still have the problem with Franz Ferdinand, who's currently fighting with time, the most implacable and single almighty enemy of them all. Franz Ferdinand, who soon will stand before his creator. Who has nothing to lose. In this combination of scenarios, I'm as good as dead. In every Saxon prison. This certainty makes me shake, as I continue to hold the half-eaten burger. It's gone cold.

As I decide, everything goes very quickly. The deal is set. Testimony for protection. As night breaks, other men come, release me from the radiator and put me in another armoured car. Then we head north, this time without the fanfare of Rammstein.

CHAPTER NINETEEN

Grandmother wakes me up. Her hair has been glued into a blue ball with tons of hairspray. She takes the construction off her head and, turning it upside down, puts it onto my small side table with the little cupboard. It's a hairy bowl, filled to the brim with plum jam. Warm and tasty.

'Dig in,' the wolf says. 'You have to grow big and strong. Come, let's eat.'

I point to grandmother's toes that have become black. 'Are you even allowed to eat something like that?' Grandmother has diabetes.

'What?' She takes a pair of scissors and cuts her black big toe off. 'Now it's OK!' Grandmother points to the bowl: 'Take plenty of gravy too. Then it will go down better.'

There's blood soup in the hairy bowl. I spoon blood into my cupped hand. Whatever spills, the greedy wolf licks off the floor. The carpet is dyed the colour of milky ice. At the end of the ice is a jetty. There, my coach is angrily hacking at the frozen water. Further out on the river, ice floes the size of a living room table are swimming, and on each and every single one is Franz Ferdinand. He's wearing a shiny black penguin suit with a red bow tie. And slippers. And all of these countless copies of the man are floating down the Elbe. And in the process, they're hopping from one leg to the other. Someone is playing the beautiful melody of the GDR national anthem on the troika. Singing loudly, Franz Ferdinand floats by me a thousand times and rushes down a huge waterfall just below the bridge. I pick myself up and help my coach with the hacking. Today we want to go out on the water.

I sing full-throated: 'A boat trip is fun; a boat trip is nice!' The ice is a living room door leading to Neustadt. Now I sing a different song: 'Sam Meffire, Sam Meffire, strong as the jungle animals, our Saxon police officer, if that's not awesome.'

'Is the moon already shining?' Thomas turns to Winrich while I hack. 'We have to wait until the moon shines, then the vampires will be fast asleep.'

In the staircase it smells like baby's vomit. Baby shit. And alcohol. Behind the door there's a child's room that's been painted pink. Silke is sitting on the floor, she is rocking our sleeping son softly in her arms. She waves her hand at me, I should get lost. She seems rather annoyed.

'That's the wrong door,' I say to Thomas. He shrugs his shoulders.

'What we're doing here is meaningless anyway,' he says, resigned.

'Why?' I wonder. 'We're going to the right door and arresting the guy. We're saving children.'

At that moment, a greasy little man walks past us and goes down the stairs, as if he has waited for his cue in order to make his appearance. With a felt tip pen, someone has written 'child molester' on his discoloured yellow spotted undershirt. Thomas turns to the greasy one.

'Do you know if the moon has already gone up?'

'I can't help you with that,' the greasy one says smiling. 'I'm unfortunately in a hurry, I have to go into the basement, I've got my little nephew chained to the radiator there.'

'Oh, then I don't want to keep you any longer. Have a nice day,' Thomas says.

'Don't we want to follow him?' I ask, confused.

'Oh, little one!' Thomas waves over. He steps very near to me and whispers: 'It's always the same story. We catch them and Santa Claus lets them go, the drunk pig.' We go through the door to my childhood bedroom. My mother is sitting on the bed. She is pointing accusingly to the still newly wet pee stain in the middle of the mattress.

'You're in kindergarten now.' With one sentence she jumps up and comes closer. I try to pull out my weapon, but something gets stuck. My mother steps up to me grinning. Out of the corner of my eye I see how Thomas is using the crime scene camera to take pictures of my pee stain from all sides.

Click, goes the camera.

Click. Click. Click.

Mother is tattooed from head to toe and smells strongly like a German Shepherd. I got it wrong. It's my judge. He's laughing.

'I just hid the West Marks in the underwear. Take it already!'

The judge is holding out a large fold of notes. I raise my hands defensively. I don't want that damn money.

'Just take it and buy something useful for the company, my boy,' the judge says. It's my great-grandmother. 'Don't you want to know where I got the money?'

Wumm!

The block of money swoops down on me. 'I robbed a bank!' she screams.

Wumm! I try to crawl away on all fours. Through the chopped-up door. 'I robbed old people!' My great-grandmother's voice screams behind me. I make it into the hallway, I make it to the stairs. 'I robbed some prostitutes!' The voice screams, now much closer. In a final, panicked effort, I throw myself down the stairs.

Where am I? In the tiled cell. Fuck. Goddamn dreams. The light is out. Only a tiny emergency sign above the door is lit up and illuminates the white tiles on the wall. My heart beats, frenzied, into the darkness. These cursed dreams. I wipe sticky sweat from my arms and head, I can't do anything about the sweat on my back. I roll onto my side, I sit up clumsily and I pant in the darkness until my panic subsides.

It's astonishing how quickly the absence of daylight can kill any feeling for time. How much time do I have left? I guess six hours. It could also be twenty. I run around, from one wall to the next. Then in a circle. I've done countless push-ups, my arms, shoulders and chest are almost completely dissolved in pain. And still there is this numb feeling of being buried alive.

'Ground your attention in the now,' that's what I read from Dale Carnegie, my kitchen table philosophy psycho guru. That's supposed to make it possible to shut yesterday out. And tomorrow. And the fear. And the death. Easy for Carnegie to say. How is that supposed to work here? I try it nevertheless.

'Count the things you're thankful for,' is some more advice from Carnegie.

And so, I try to glue together both methods into a powerful

spell. What can I be thankful for, here and now? Probably that I'm still alive. That is something, after all. Yet that's not exactly my sole magic trick, I had some help. So many unusual things had to come together to keep me alive, that I can hardly believe in any coincidences any more. The longer I'm here on earth, the clearer it becomes how little I know. How little I've seen! And understood even less.

My father experienced the bloody fights for independence in Cameroon. He clearly had to digest more horror than I did. And yet he was a man of faith. Maybe in my situation he would be on his knees by now and appealing to the soft God of his toothless grandmother. And the longer I think about my father, the more pointless it seems to deny the existence of a power behind the cardboard wall. There's something there. There must be something there, beyond the ordinary. Or in the ordinary? I can't believe in a petty God, not in a bushy beard from a children's book and not in a guy who spies in people's bedrooms and the chamber pots.

Whatever might be behind the cardboard wall, I no longer see myself separated from it, that's how much my bout of running amok against the world taught me. And against reason. And against myself. Whoever or whatever is behind the cardboard wall, I certainly don't have any credit with them. No one there owes me any favours. That's why my survival is even more curious. The only one I know who could make a few requests with the Creator on my behalf is my father. Maybe he passed on his line of credit to me? He couldn't have used them up himself. And if that's the case? How much could still remain from this credit?

I've fallen into the lowest depths, into a bottomless abyss. And now I'm living like a zoo inmate, caught and well-fed. And

I drift day by day, through a toxic soup of thoughts, to nowhere. Franz Ferdinand and his Spetsnaz executors are outside. My two former friends and a nameless few would like to see my hide burn in revenge. And yet God, the universe, or whatever is behind the cardboard wall, decided that I should live. He has summoned an entire army of guardian angels.

So many faces. So much courage. So much unearned empathy. In retrospect it seems as if the bearded God I've suspiciously eyed and doubted has his happy, undaunted agents everywhere. Suddenly the cell underground no longer feels like a coffin. I'm no longer alone. I haven't been left by everyone. As much as I fear the coming hours, as much as I fear the future, it appears to me that someone or something isn't completely finished with me. I lay my head on the hand-warm tiles of the floor and I doze again into a restless half-sleep full of half-digested memories.

Dresden. The trial. The great tribune. Two years before the tiled cell.

The trip from the North once again happens at night. It's heading near the new capital city. In the distance, isolated lights sparkle in the outer districts. Human life. Unreachable, far away. I end up in an ancient, musty, prison castle. The windows are holes barely the size of notebooks in massive walls. When I stand all the way up, my head touches the ceiling. Next to the bed there is barely enough space to stand.

For several days, a young vampire with cabin fever rampages in a neighbouring cell. The prison has dissolved the last of his restraint. He yells and screams and attacks everyone who tries to enter his cell after he flooded it with water. Ultimately, the boy is dragged away with a rumble by a unit of former colleagues.

Then my outing comes. Hooded giants bring me out of the cell and into the prison transport and there I will be quickly shoved into an SK4 vest. The weight of the armour plates feels familiar. All the officials are armed with the stubby MPK, the micro variant of the usual machine guns. Most noticeable are the two-part magazine clips on the weapons. And in each one of their vests there are several thirties magazines stuck in the front pockets. That's a lot of firepower for a minor 'office outing'.

Everyone is clearly tense and nervous. And no one explains anything to me. I press my food bag to myself like a treasure and crawl into the door opening of the BMW. The gate opens and the convoy races away with me across the Autobahn, towards my trial. Tree-covered embankments fly by. And happy families in small tin boxes. And trucks as slow as snails whose brightly printed tarpaulins gleam in the sun, full of advertisements.

The convoy moves in snaking lines through the unsuspecting civil traffic. It's a rapid movement on the verge of what is permitted for a multi-tonne armoured vehicle. Do they always drive like that? Or is there a special Meffire-transport speed assigned by law? I feel like a physics experiment that's out of control. Soon the nausea sloshes up from my stomach and I don't want to look at the embankments any longer, or at the trees and the happy families. And I don't care where the LKW is crawling to.

I keep my head lowered and fall asleep. Two-one-hundred. Three-one-hundred. Four-one-hundred. Breathe in. And slowly out again. Not much helps, but nevertheless I don't throw up all over the guys in their beautiful tank. Think about Carnegie. The here-and-now. Not the judge. Not the judgement. Not the damnation. Being here. And nowhere else. The Autobahn is my purgatory. The armour plates on the torso. The leather of luxurious upholstery beneath me. My feet on the vibrating floor panel. My here. My now. I am.

Then there's a dull crack. The right side of the vehicle sinks. We're moving at an estimated 180 km/h. Four tons of total weight. Tank steel. Tank glass. It feels the same as muscle mass. In addition, several hundred kilos of equipment and weapons and munition. All of that is now rolling across the Autobahn, while the guy in the driver's seat tries to react with unbelievably fast jerks at the steering wheel. I hectically begin to pray.

'Break open Christian soul ...' That's as far as I get, then the BMW that's come out of nowhere rumbles across the hard shoulder and comes to a halt at a nearby rest stop. 'Think about the things in the here and now. Shut everything else out.'

I hold my food rations tightly. I scrutinise the here, and also the now: a hard-boiled egg. A sandwich with a green-greyish piece of meat. A shrivelled apple. What else could be in this goddamn bag? Did I forget something? Outside, the other vehicles of the convoy scurry up to the rest stop. They appear like a swarm of black, shiny locusts. The commandos stop and take their security positions. Heads turn nervously back and forth. Bloody hell, what was that?

'Are you OK?' the commando leader asks me.

I nod silently.

'We have to change vehicles! Can you make it?'

The man's worried look darts over to my hands which are gripping the bag tightly. I nod again, I can do that. Someone rips me out of the car. Not even a stone's throw away from me there is a tourist bus, out of which a small army of retirees flows out. A lot of white-haired heads turn in our direction. There are unbelievable looks from big eyes in the face of a parade of heavily armed men in civilian clothes. I use the opportunity and hop over from the retirees to the open car door unnoticed, as quickly as possible, with a very short ankle bracelet. I'm the most desirable target here and, naturally, I'm in a hurry. I've barely buckled my seat belt, when all the remaining vehicles and the convoy shoot out onto the Autobahn.

'Bloody hell!' the commando leader on the passenger side yells and hits his open hand on the dashboard several times. 'Bloody fucking hell, I'm so sick of this!' I dare to say a word, something that doesn't make any sense in my head.

'How could they have even hit us, at this speed?' I ask in the direction of the angry man. He turns around, still red in his face.

'Hit us?' He shakes his head. 'These assholes. These goddamn assholes.' He takes a deep breath. While he does, his hand makes a circular movement in the vehicle.

'This thing needs special tyres. The administration takes care of buying the tyres. And so that they can brag about their savings, they take the cheapest offer. It's ultimately taxpayers' money.'

I can sense what's coming.

'But you can drive the most affordable tyres up to 130 kilo-metres per hour, and past that only for a few minutes, in an emergency.'

The man catches his breath.

'In practice, that turned out to be a shitty idea. Then they took the cheap tyres out of the rotation. Allegedly.' He wildly rubs his hands around on his face and he struggles for composure. 'We didn't know that some of those tyres were still on there.'

I imagine how the BMW rolls over several times and everyone is crushed into bloody clumps by the tons of special steel, because the free state of Saxony, to whom I've surrendered, wants to save money. It's absurd. What the invisible Russian killer hasn't been able to achieve so far, an anonymous clerk in some procurement office almost managed to do with his pocket calculator. Fuck. Fuck. Fuck.

Our trip finally ends at the giant gate of the district court. There's only one access for vehicles. The trial has been made public and everyone knows that I have been brought here, from wherever. Franz Ferdinand knows that. And, of course, so do the violent hitmen he hires. You could touch the tension of my companions with your hands. The gate remains shut. The BMW is standing across the roadway. It's still missing a painted target. Suddenly I'm very, very warm. No, not warm. I'm cooking in my vest and in this goddamn car, in which far too many people are crouching and breathing quickly. Why isn't the goddamn gate opening?

'Close the door to the burdened past,' Carnegie advises. I'd like to close the fucking door to the burdened present, I'd like to just be unconscious until everything is over and I can rot alone in some cell. The commando leader jumps out of the vehicle and thrashes with his fist on a wooden door. And he screams in righteous fury. Ultimately, he has to lead the fucking suicide machine.

'Open up! Open up, goddammit!'

First nothing happens. Two or three endless seconds go by. Then the door swings open creaking and the confused face of an aged judicial sergeant appears.

'Open the goddamn door!' the commando leader screams at the overwhelmed man.

'The door! Now!'

The justice officer eagerly pulls open the second door while the commando leader signals to the driver that he can move. The

BMW jumps off the road through the opening gate. The lock is dark and the fairways are narrow, but it fits.

There's no surprise waiting for me: the courtroom is full. The gallery consists of brave and less brave citizens who all hope for a gripping spectacle. There are housewives. Bored pensioners. A smirking delegation of vampires – in company lies strength, of course – and in their own uniforms of green flight jackets and shaved heads. There are still countless journalists. And just two arms' lengths away from me, my former comrades are sitting.

The crew. Technically they're my ex-colleagues, but in truth they're much more than that. I looked up to them as role models. And I loved them as older siblings. Omega, that was also an attempt at a family. Something that I ruined; I ruined it and it spat me out, just like all other families before. In the courtroom there's also the judge. Several judges. The gaunt prosecutor. Everything else is lost in a white noise of stress, particularly evident in the appearance of my tormented victims, who also have to appear in court to testify.

My memories of the trial are blurred and colourless, like a pair of jeans you've worn for years and often washed. The sentencing has almost completely disappeared, been repressed. I do know that afterwards I sat frozen still in an office, somewhere in the courthouse.

Nine years and nine months. They might as well have said ninety-nine years. I'm twenty-six years old and for me it's as good as a death sentence. Nine years and nine months is nothing that my mammal brain can understand even to a limited extent. And actually, I don't need protection from Franz Ferdinand's plans any more, because I'm destroyed anyway. Comprehensively and completely.

Nevertheless, they try to accommodate what is left of me somewhere. 'Protection' is always just relative. And you have to contribute to a lot of little puzzle pieces in order for it to work. Indeed, I can barely find the strength for this cooperation. They have a new arrest warrant for me, with my invented Zaire-name, that only very few people know. And there's a carefully compiled fake CV that I have to learn by heart, like the text of a drama for a school performance. They drive me to a football club where I've never played. I walk through a street where I've never lived. They show me a school where I've never been. Then they drive me deep into the southwest of the republic. And there, in a small prison, near the Mosel River, my new cover is blown within a short time.

In the middle of a chess game with a friendly, eloquent arms dealer, in the rec room of the station, a report about me is on the communal television, high above our heads. The arms dealer squints and stares at me. He doesn't say anything, but it's over.

I'm quickly relocated to the north. And again, it's a high security station. This jail area was conceptualised for former Red Army Faction members, but since the post-graduate terrorist group has been leading a shadow existence, they've been filling the cells with people like me. Unfortunately, my cell has a tiny, triple-barred skylight with a milky cover of armour plastic. All of the guards have alias nicknames. And their private vehicles have fake licence plates. This station is so secure that they could have just as well hidden me away in a galley kitchen on a nuclear sub in the deepest parts of the ocean. Or on a space station.

From now on my life will be determined by a cryptic algorithm. I'm imprisoned in house X. Twenty-four hours a day, complete isolation. Seven days a week. I run laps alone in the courtyard. Sixty-five paces in a circle. One hour a day. The rest of the day I'm locked in my cell. The nearest wall is six metres high, targeting someone in the yard would require a high-angle gun outside. I never, under any circumstances, run into other prisoners. And the officers employed here seldom speak more than three sentences with me when they give me my meals. I'm alone. The quiet of the days is only interrupted by the hourly 'living checks'. Here, there's no more running away. All of that lies behind me. Now these walls are my home. Walls, smeared with leftovers of food that have long dried, and brown, streaky traces of shit.

My greatest enemy here is time. And its obvious danger is in its sheer volume, an endless emptiness that cannot be filled with anything. Practising Carnegie helps. Reading helps. Fist fight-ing helps. And writing too. And running on the spot, running to nowhere, on a spot of thirty-by-thirty centimetres. And, of course, during weeks and months, the many thousands of push-ups and running kilometres in a sixty-five-step circle also helps. And when all of these things have been done, day for day there is still time for a plentiful rest. I sit on the chair and look out the window, far above me. Behind the milky, cloudy bulletproof pane of glass I think I can recognise shadowy fragments of cloud. And are the small, circling dots there birds? I sit on this chair and look up to the light-coloured spots that must be the sky.

Nothing is happening in the station. Behind the doors insu-lated from speech there is quiet with an iron fist. Only now and again, the officially decreed silence is disturbed by screaming. A confused, wild, desperate scream from one of the neighbour-ing cells. Sometimes the screaming turns into a whimper. Or a pleading. No, this here isn't Zaire. The cells are free from rodents. Day to day, there's enough to eat. And there is Northern German decency, not a single guard would allow themselves to commit the atrocities of the Congolese; such a thing would be simply unthinkable.

The enemy in this place isn't torturers. The enemy isn't hunger. The enemy can be found in your own flesh. And war rages there every day with merciless relentlessness. And here, practically everyone has gangrene, in the head. 'We shall fight on the beaches, we shall fight on the landing grounds, we shall fight in the fields and in the streets, we shall fight in the hills . . . for without victory, there is no survival.' Every child knows this quote from history class. It's from Churchill, 1940, in expectation of the Nazi invasion of the British Isles. Without victory, there is no survival. Only, the Nazis had already landed and set up camp on the beach of my imagination.

'Why get up?' the collective of accusers moans. And laughs gloatingly. 'You're useless!' the comrades in my head whisper. 'Stay lying down. Why eat?' I don't know. 'What's the point of training?'

Yes exactly, what's the point? After my sentence I'll be an old man anyway. And even more likely I will die in here. The prospect of this regularly floods me with panic. I'll run away from it, every instinct in me still present is screaming: 'Run, run for your life.' I'd like to pound on the door like a crazy person and scream and cry out, like the others here. But then they'll come and get me and inject me with some stuff from the emergency psychiatric clinic until I'm like 'concrete', a zombie. And they'll bring me outside of the protective isolation unit. And so I'm allowed to choose between insanity and security.

My shaky fingers clutch the bedframe. *We shall fight on the beaches.* The accusers laugh. They've brought an ally with them. It's my companion from my childhood days. The old, unbeatable frenemy in my head.

'You're a poor crazy person. You still think that you can stay alive here. You have to leave everything behind you,' the trusty voice murmurs. 'Lay down to sleep. You earned it,' it flatters me.

I want to sleep. Time passes when you sleep. But at night, the collective of accusers is awake. Now the voice from the mattresses is whispering to me too. Naturally, they are wonderful old promises. The old lies: 'I'm there for you. I'll always be there for you.' But I'm not nine years old any more. This isn't a tower block. And there are no streetcars here that I could throw myself in front of. 'Let go, you just have to let go. It doesn't have to be so hard.'

This voice in my head is worse than shit on the cell's walls. It's worse than panic and fear and the abyss. And sometimes, I think that this demon is the voice of time itself. Here endless days are stuck together with endless nights. To weeks. And months. To an awfully long, pre-Christmas quiet.

'My love!'

The winter has passed. The sun rises every afternoon a little higher. The shadow of the wall, in the courtyard, becomes lower. Today I run my laps with a light heart. Sixty-five steps of joy. I could hop like a kangaroo, drunk from joy, but I don't do it, in the face of my guards. I run my laps because you have to have a routine. Here, routines are everything. But soon after I read my mail. For heaven's sake, I finally received a letter.

*

After my jog in the courtyard, I sit down at the table. The letter is lying there, with that one word. This word is a statement. A declaration. But what else is it? The Amazon could have also written 'idiot' and it would be totally true. Or 'You fucking idiot, you stole our life together.' That would also be an absolutely fitting statement. But instead it reads:

'Dearest! I didn't have any hope of seeing you again. Hold on, I'm coming!'

It's a letter from Namibia. It's aged. It needed nearly four weeks in order to get from Windhoek to Dresden. And then it needed another three weeks to get from Dresden to me. First the letter was in Berlin. This serves as a wrong track for any pursuers. The ones Franz Ferdinand has hired. And also because of the moles in office. From Berlin, a courier brings the secret post north. And that takes as long as it takes. And now the letter is lying in front of me on the chipped surface of the table. There, where there's otherwise just my steel bowl used for my meals three times a day. This letter is likewise food with vital calories for my soul. It's a manifest of affection that's inexplicable to me. 'Hold on, I'm coming.'

CHAPTER TWENTY

Hold on, that's easier said than done. Because the Amazon isn't coming. And there's also no further letter from her. Days go by, weeks go by. After flying high comes the crash. And an ugly impact. Maybe that was her way of giving me back the pain I inflicted. Or it was just a cruel joke. Get over it. Or even better, die! When night falls, I lose the rest of my control. I crouch on the floor of the cell, in the darkness. And curse confused, bitter stuff. I curse her. And curse myself. And cry, quietly, in a balled-up towel. It takes an entire month until I can halfway pull myself together. 'Dear.' This one purulent sore remains. *What goes around comes around.* Whoever sows pain, harvests hell.

The keys scratch at the lock. The latches scrape through their mounts. My cell door swings open.

'Get ready. You have to go,' the guard says.

'To the doctor?' Probably another one of these mandatory physicals. To determine if I'm still portable or already crazy so that I can remain here.

The guard shrugs his shoulders. 'You're being picked up.'

Damn, it's always the same shit. I have to go outside and I probably smell like two oxen on the run. My weekly shower isn't until tomorrow. 'To go where?' I ask.

'How am I supposed to know? No one tells me anything.'

Alright already, I know that. No one tells anyone anything here. Everyone only knows what he absolutely has to. Internal fragmentation. Keeping things secret is supposed to rescue lives. And it does until now. Outside I meet the friendly men from the 'driving service'. As always, they wear their SK4-vests and their machine guns hidden under extra-large jackets. So I'm definitely not part of a folk dance troupe. Or a gathering of amateur archaeologists on an outing. This here is something else. I climb onto the backseat of the Mercedes, the windows sparkle in spruce green today. For each one of the inaugurated, these windows are an unmistakable signal: *Attention, maximum protection! Something tasty is being driven around inside. Or maybe it's a dirty state secret. An attack would be worthwhile!*

Regardless, I comply. Better within this tank than without it. The driver leaves the city and heads over the flat country, through peaceful brick villages with meticulously tended front gardens and red-roofed barns. Somewhere in the middle of nowhere there's an authority building and the Mercedes rolls into an underground garage with a dull hum. From the basement, we go up to a windowless hallway with likewise windowless cells.

One of the cells is fitted out like an office, it's probably used for interrogations. They make me sit down there. I sit and wait. I wait and stand. The time feels flat, like chewing gum that's been used for too long. I pull a notebook over to me and start to draw a horse.

In kindergarten, during the time at my grandfather's, when I was five years old, I made a name for myself as a gifted drawer of horses and rainbows. In any case, my skills haven't developed in any noteworthy manner since then. And so, I draw a rather shapeless horse. With antlers. Why? Because I can. It's a buck-horse. A horse-buck? Before I can finally categorise my creation, the cell door opens with a creak.

'I said I was coming.'

The Amazon grins. I'm speechless. She takes a step into the room. I don't make it from my chair to her. My legs refuse to do their duty. Shit, this is not how I imagined it. I let my head hang low, suddenly without any courage. It's as if my stupid legs are rooted to the spot. The Amazon approaches me. She crouches before me, takes my head in her hands. That's not good. This touch leads to my tears running down my cheeks and chin in a steady stream. And from there, they drip onto the official floor. I don't just draw like a kindergartner. I also have kindergartener emotions. So this is all wrong. I didn't plan it like this.

'I didn't expect this,' I squeeze out with difficulty.

'What didn't you expect?'

'You ... you ...' I can only stammer. And cry. '... to see you ... again!' The Amazon is probably rethinking her part now. An imprisoned and now also mentally dissolved lover, that's really like a jackpot in the lottery.

'You must be crazy,' the Amazon dryly comments. 'Even if they hid you on the moon, I would find you, my friend.'

She turns my head up. Our gazes meet. 'You never abandoned me.' I try to turn my chin away. My attempt fails.

'Look at me!' Her grip is like iron. 'You never abandoned me. And I won't abandon you either.'

Oh God, this is all so embarrassing. I'm so embarrassing. I

lament and cry. And this woman has more balls in her pants than I do. She flew halfway around the world for a loser like me. Either she's crazy, dim-witted, or she is a saint.

I'm saved. The Amazon's visit resonates through the days. The demon doesn't come around. The collective of accusers has finally shut up. I feel weightless. Easy. Almost free. The days line up. Many, many days add up to a new mountain of time. And sometime all the euphoria lies beyond the mountain. At some point all the happy hormones are used up. And the demon is back. He strikes unsuspectingly. And harder than ever before.

'Go to the sink and chop out your teeth.'

This time the demon doesn't use a voice, it camouflages itself simply and extremely effectively as a thought. An urge. As a bizarre, irresistible desire. Fucking shit. Such weird shit. And why now? Finally, I have the ultimate reason to live. To hang on. In the months before, I was already exhausted. And starved inside, down to my bones. But now everything is different. Up to now I had to be convinced to eat a spoon of lukewarm mashed potatoes. With every piece of wannabe meat. And with the grey, cooked vegetables. But now I lick all the shit from my plate, every bread crumb. And every last drop of fat. Because that's what it means to survive. Eat every plate. Every lap and every push up. Every page read and every page written.

So why now? Maybe the demon works like malaria, it can hide for a long time and wait. And like malaria, the demon is a parasite. Ineradicable, it clings to the flesh of my soul. And waiting for its chance. For the moment, when the clueless victim least expects it. The demon has developed itself monstrously. The voice is gone, but the urge, the thought, is a far worse affliction.

When I go to the bathroom at night, I don't even risk looking at the sink, which glows auspiciously in the sparse light of the courtyard. I stare stubbornly straight ahead and aim blindly for the toilet bowl.

When have I reached the limit? When do I no longer have it under control? When do I step into action? When I look in the mirror, the demon shows me its strange face. It looks at me. Its mouth is a bloody, toothless hole.

'I wondered why you didn't come to me a long time ago.'

My condition seems to be familiar to the area manager. As if he knew that I stood at the sink early this morning, with my hands gripping the edges, throwing my head back in a wide, sweeping movement. Then for a whole hour, I crouched in the narrow gap between the toilet bowl and the sink, I cried and whimpered.

The area manager sends a doctor to me. She finds me in the courtyard, running in circles and mumbling to myself and giggling and crying about something. The film in my head has finally ripped, it's twisted and knotted. Now it's only projecting confusing images. Crazy thoughts. The doctor who hurried to my aid works in forensic psychiatry. She hardly needs ten minutes to take my medical history and writes me a tactical nuclear weapon from the arsenal of psycho pills.

I sleep eighteen hours straight. Numbed from a chemical coma, I don't notice that I have to go to the bathroom, and I pee the bed. The demon is still there, but a giant, rubbery mass separates us. He can't get to me any more than I can get to reality, to the here and now. The pills are made for people with psychosis, compulsive disorders. People who cut off their fingers and poke out their eyes because the voices in their head ordered them to. The pills from the doctor help, but salvation has its price. Within weeks, your brain becomes dependent and soon you have the first dead sections. It's like backburning a forest. Entire areas are razed, one parcel after another turns into a graveyard of lost synapses. Gestures and facial expressions become slower. And soon I'll be a zombie.

It's the choice between the plague and cholera. I can mutilate myself at the sink or, bit by bit, turn into the undead. I don't toss a coin. I take the pills.

The present. The stove cellar.

Just another hour until they come and get me. Or is it two? I run up and down. The tiles are warm. Every metre ahead is accompanied by a soft smacking sound, when the sweaty soles of my feet get off the ground. With every second or third step, I close my eyes and let the movement carry me. The short, blind floating feels disturbingly light, weightless. The excitement tickles me inside like laughing. A power surge. I try to imagine a forest. I wander among shadowy treetops, over rich green, juicy moss. It doesn't work.

The door opens. The people who brought me to the interim cell and are now here to pick me up for the trip, are experienced comrades. When they say 'Go', then I go. And when they want me to stand still, I do that, too. Why is there so much worry in their faces today? Usually, after a few moments, coarse, friendly, meaningless small talk flies back and forth between us. Now there's only silence.

I sit in the car next to junior. While the tank rolls out of the underground garage and all the others in the vehicle are occupied with their stuff, I use the opportunity.

'What's wrong?' I ask in a whisper. The boss, in front on the pillion, immediately notices. For a moment, he lets it hang in the air, then he nods to junior in the rear-view mirror, concise and clear.

'The guys in Dresden have received something from an informant.' Well, that's nothing new. That's a part of the job. It's often just nonsense, but not always.

I shrug my shoulders. 'And?'

Junior doesn't exactly look happy. 'Apparently, your special friend's connections reach further than we thought.' This claim doesn't reveal much, but the serious look on junior's face provides the necessary subtext. I quickly become alarmingly warm under the bulletproof vest.

'How far then?' I ask carefully, although I don't really want to know the answer.

Junior wheezes while he directs his gaze out the window. 'Apparently they reach the unit that is taking you over today and will be responsible for you.'

Excuse me? I must have misheard. But before I can answer anything, the car turns down a short tunnel and rolls out into an empty arena. Past the tribunes and the launcher.

On the grass, at the penalty spot, a Bo 105 helicopter is already expecting us. The Messerschmitt is a medium-sized helicopter, with that typically round bumblebee belly. There's no long greeting; the helicopter immediately lifts off the ground and the infernal noise of the motors prevents any further questions.

Yet junior's words echo inside me while we climb and climb until the stadium beneath us seems like a lovingly created doll's house. The little Bo ploughs ahead, it hops in the gusty north wind that pushes us forward. Thank God I didn't eat anything yet. The fields are postcard green. The tractors on the fields look like toys. And the steel-blue sky lies above the fields and forests and country. This flight could be so beautiful, if junior, who's sitting to my left, didn't look so goddamn serious. And stressed.

'Stay in the here and now,' Carnegie advises.

And so I try to enjoy the floating despite everything. After about a two-hour flight, the pilot lands the machine. I recognise the hills on the edge of the city. I recognise the familiar slopes above the Elbe. In low flight, we follow the winding line of the river.

'Two more minutes.'

The voice of the pilot crackles over the radio like the sound of an old phonograph. Junior wakes up immediately to eager business. He takes a matt black shiny roll out of the backpack that's hanging behind the pilot's seat. It's an MPK with a folding handle. Junior places the magazine in the submachine gun and underloads it. He's also using a double-staple. Then he sticks another magazine under his jacket. What's going on here, a goddamn remake of a battle?

Junior's hand touches my shoulder. 'Listen. If something's going to happen, it'll be now.'

I stare at him disbelieving. 'And what should I do?' My hands are bound and pinned to the bulky vest with a screw carabiner. And then there's the feet restraints. That's the rule. With the bulky, heavy vest and the restraints I'm as agile as an overweight hippopotamus.

'Crouch down behind the pilot seat, understood?'

I nod because I've understood the order. But that won't help much. The pilot switches over to us. He followed our conversation on the radio and now turns his head back: 'I'll keep the helicopter hovering. If necessary, we can hop from the landing plate over the trees on the street. But you have to hold on tight. In the case of an emergency start, we won't be able to close the doors.'

Then he brings the helicopter down further. I recognise the area. It's the vast area of my old football club, near the slaughterhouse. There are five or six connecting training fields and a small stadium. The small, worn landing plate at the edge dates back to the GDR. There's already a convoy of dark sedans waiting there. The pilot pulls up so low over the columns that the men standing next to the vehicles duck their heads. The helicopter makes a sharp 180-degree-turn and lands. Or maybe not. It nearly touches the ground, but we're still hovering. The motors roar under the full load.

Junior rips open the side door and jumps out. He hold the MPK hidden from view. The weapon is so tiny it nearly completely disappears behind his leg. He yells something to the men standing next to the vehicles. His words are torn apart by the noise of the blades. Two-one-thousand. Three-one-thousand. Agonisingly long seconds pass. I can hear the guardian angel-handymen of the bushy-bearded God hard at work, clattering eagerly with their tools.

Finally Junior climbs back into the helicopter. He secures the MPK and puts it away. Then he unbuckles my seatbelt. 'Congratulations!' he says relieved and grinning, and I know what he means by that. 'We'll pick you up afterwards.' Then he pushes me out to where the welcoming committee is waiting.

From the ice they are freed, the stream and brook,
By the Spring's enlivening, lovely look;
The valley's green with joys of hope;
The Winter old and weak ascends
Back to the rugged mountain slope.

Goethe's *Faust*. How I hated that thing during my schooldays! Then I read it voluntarily in one of the worst prison holes. The silly dungeon scene suddenly contains a hint of solace. And a prophesy of salvation. In Goethe, there's a rescue. Will I also be rescued?

I'm standing in a prayer room. The room is located at the end of a long, bare hallway. And the hallway is behind a door. And the door is behind the gates of a cloister. In the middle of Dresden, hidden in a side street.

'Are you becoming a nun now?' I grin over at the Amazon.

'Maybe, if you become a monk,' she grins back at me. She looks very beautiful. Her stubbly hair has grown a few millimetres and seems fuller than usual.

'Yeah, how about a professional reorientation?' I must bicker with her, it's just too much fun. The Amazon waves her hand in my direction, as if she was trying to shoo a fly. The burdensome fly, that's me.

'Be careful with your suggestions. Otherwise, I'll just take one of them, instead of you.'

She points to the row of heavily armed men, framing the prayer room like a silent boys' choir waiting for their cue. They're as fitting for this occasion as an elephant at a high jump.

'Hmm, you won. I'll be quiet.' I wasn't really planning on it, but the backdoor to the room opens. A small, wrinkled woman appears. 'I wish you a good day. If my proposal meets with general approval, then I'll start right away.' The woman arranges some papers on the table in front of her. 'So, what does the bridal pair say to that?'

For a minute, I feel the desire to turn around and check whether she means someone else. But no one is there and so there is no doubt: we're the bridal pair.

CHAPTER TWENTY-ONE

'You must pack! Now!'

The security guard comes storming up the stairs, holding a piece of paper in his hand.

I look up from my book surprised.

'Why?'

And above all, what for? Sudden transfers mean trouble. The guard holds the paper under my nose: it's a fax. Isn't that strange? Anyone who has to go in isn't allowed to leave. But anyone who isn't allowed in any more is quickly put out on the street, as if he'd broken in here. That's the law. It would be illegal to keep me here any longer. And what was once a just punishment, in the name of the people, is suddenly an officially enforced deprivation of liberty. The courts don't joke around about that. And because a representative of the free state judiciary has declared my imprisonment over, I'm being put out on the street.

Barely ten minutes later, rushed through various procedures, I'm standing in the visitors' car park in front of the jail, with a backpack on my shoulder. The parking lot is empty. The wind is blowing a light-brown McDonald's paper bag softly back and forth on one spot. A black cloud scrapes the sky. Where to now?

My odyssey led me through twelve prisons. There was pretty much everything there, from hellholes to brand new buildings. Isolation in the north. Bible reading groups in Waldheim. I wander, accompanied by officials, across a hallway to some examination. And I meet those ex-red-light-heavyweights whose night clubs I raided on behalf of Franz Ferdinand.

I wander, accompanied by officials, across another hallway in another prison. And there I meet the vampire who shot at me together with his comrades. And who not much later took part in the murder of Gomondai. I stumble from one disaster to another and I ensure full employment for an entire army.

Twice I'm supposed to be set free, twice the prosecutor's office takes action against me. They needed me as a chilling example, for whomever. Or will people tell primary school students my story in the future, the story of the man from the poster, as a cautionary tale? I'm the former poster boy of the Messiah. And because of his imprisonment, he got into the catchment areas of one of his arch enemies.

The guy raves to me about the power of his office. From the top down, it's easy for him to adjust some screws and set things in motion for my case. I'm a chess piece on a board that's way too big for me. The transfer of the supposedly vengeful red-light-heavyweights to my accommodations, which were already plagued by violent excesses, could neither be explained by incapability or ignorance. The same could be said for the vampire.

Someone high up hoped that we, the mob, would massacre each other. I'd either be injured after the attack, crippled or dead.

Or I successfully defend myself. And then the other people will be injured, crippled or dead. And there will be a juicy 'second helping' for me. And in the best-case scenario, I'd die in prison after all.

But someone, very high up in the bureaucracy, made plans without the powers above him, without the supreme boss of the bosses. God has his officers restlessly do their work, for whatever reason. The vengeful red-light-heavyweight unexpectedly converts to a conventional life. And an official, a former GDR special forces soldier rescues me from the vampire. But after all these years, I can't say what saved me from the demon. It was hardly my lack of judgement nor the circumstances. Despite doubting him, the bushy bearded God appears to not be finished with me yet.

I'm standing around in the car park as if I'd been ordered there but not picked up. Or to be more exact: as if I *hadn't* been ordered there. The unexpected freedom feels great. And empty. And strange. I think about the past months. About the release in Dresden. The abyss named Waldheim was finally behind me. In Dresden I get a brand-new, blue one-piece work suit and I hire myself out in the institution's gardening and landscaping department.

Day after day, I'm loaded onto a truck and driven somewhere. And there I weed, hack and dig. I also sweep the walkway in front of the entrance of my former department. And with the metal tongs at the end of a stick, I pick up the rubbish that the south wind blows across the officers' car park. I entertain the thought of putting a paper bag on my head to disguise myself. But as an in-house assistant, I'm not allowed to feel shame and so I endure the astonished faces of my former colleagues with an averted gaze and grinding teeth.

Shortly thereafter, the tide breaks over the city and I'm no longer commanded to sweep the walkway. All hands on deck! Everyone helps with the flood of the century. Me too. The part of the front that I am supposed to defend is at the Ministry of the Interior. My mother works behind its venerable walls, in some light-filled cubicle. Stacking sandbags there is the absolute height of my humiliation. It doesn't get any worse. But it's a small price to pay for release and that's why I gladly pay. At least I'm alive, after all this madness, and can still stack something. And since I no longer have to worry about the practical implications of my fellow inmates' hateful fantasies, I have a lot of time to think in the evening, after work. The train of my guilt leisurely enters the station.

I often think about the old married couple now. The man appeared before court. And appallingly, he looked like my grand-father's twin brother. It was only there that I realised what I had done. Only then did the real dimension of the harm I had caused become tangible. And the suffering I caused. And the inevitable nightly horrors that this suffering produces.

When the vampires attacked the bus with the scouts and guides, I was outraged. And not long afterwards I became a monster myself and in my megalomania I assaulted old people. Whenever I think about my grandfather's twin, boiling hot shame floods my small, measly universe. During such occasions, I plan to never forget that I got a good deal. As long as I was occupied with my own survival in the prison hell, full time and with constant heartache and panic, there wasn't much room for such thoughts.

The guilt train can only now drive in. Only now is there movement in my head. Understanding is pitifully slow, but it happens. And that's why I, the former policeman, brand-new gardener, street cleaner and sandbag carrier, swallow my humiliation wordlessly. I do what I'm told to do. And pay back what I owe to the karma bank.

The flood becomes a moment of revival in Dresden. Half of the city stacks sandbags, even through the night, until they're completely exhausted. The other half makes sandwiches and tea for the workers on the front.

I've never experienced Dresden like this. So lively. So united. So colour-blind. Unfortunately, a flood doesn't last forever. After the water subsides, most people return to their own problems. No one had ever seriously made an attempt to examine the cracks in their inner world. No one has ever stretched out a real hand of reconciliation. There were always just promises. And most of those are quickly revealed to be soulless phrases or destructive lies. For a few days, the flood gives us all a chance to live the best version of ourselves. Then the structure of our solidarity falls apart, just like the utopian paradise of the 'Colourful Republic Neustadt' fell apart back then.

And now they've shoved me in front of the gate. For what purpose, exactly? I almost miss my servitude. My regulated daily routine. My strictly commanded 'from where' and 'to where'. I've been at odds with my mother for a long time now. It's actually the same as always, just interrupted by short ceasefires. By a lunch at mother's favourite restaurant. Or her tearful visits to the prison. And at some point she just died.

It feels strange. My arch enemy just left. Without a final battle. Without any final explanations. Upon reflection, my mother drank herself to death. I know from our few conversations that her love for my father never let her go. Just as is often the case when something can't be lived out to the end, it becomes idealistic, unreachable, hardly connected to reality. When my mother was twenty-seven, the love of her life was taken. Senseless and unfulfilled. The firewater-devil helps against the worry, but this comfort is short-term and dearly bought. With joy. Hope. And a big piece of the thread of life.

My mother is dead. The arch enemy is gone. And Moïse, my dearly missed brother is too. He died only a few months after my mother, in a small town in the Black Forest. The death notice is the first thing I've heard about him since he disappeared over twenty-five years ago. It seems like he and mum made a date to die.

As if they'd peacefully settled their years-long conflict in death. The members of my family are united again, at least they are in my imagination. They've only somehow forgotten me, in this parking lot, for whatever reason.

Even the Amazon is gone. For years, while behind walls, I only lived for this idea. For this one moment. For this idea: walking out of the big gates and falling into her arms. We thought that would be enough. We thought that the holy promise would be stronger than all the obstacles. And enemy forces. And fatigue. The Amazon is truthfully the bravest of all the brave women in my life. But the threat of a ten-year separation did not fail to have an effect. Ten years, calculated from the torture barracks in Zaire up to the very last day of imprisonment, back then sometime in the infinitely distant future, in another millennium. Ten years. This threat is about a mountain of time, of a real, truthful fucking Mount Everest.

After our wedding, we had seven-and-a-half years of that. Seven summer suns. And exactly as many long winters. A grim army of endless days. The Amazon is made of steel. Or something harder. After five years we still wandered around in the desert. At some point, the last reserves are used up. At some point, the last battle has been fought. And the last loss suffered. And then you have to admit the hopelessness of an undertaking. Whoever can't let go at this point is going to fall into the abyss without trace.

The Amazon had to make a choice. Actually, it wasn't a choice, rather it was just the execution of a long-held decision. And one day, when she flew home from a job, she found her apartment door open and ajar. And the drawers and cupboards had been searched. Nothing was missing. Her grandmother's valuable jewellery was taken from its hiding place and placed demonstratively in a line on the kitchen counter. Even after this horror, she wasn't ready to give me up. And yet, it must have been a salvation when her boss offered her the lead on a project in New York shortly thereafter. Two years in the Big Apple. That's what she wrote me. It was a chance. A new beginning. And the end for us.

I cried about that goddamn letter. I ground my teeth and wrote her an angry, stupid answer. Eventually, I agreed with her. Even if I survived my remaining prison time, that was the end. New York was unreachable for me. Not because of the ocean or money for a ticket, but because of my visa. As someone with a criminal record the US will always be taboo for me. So the

Amazon disappeared behind the ocean and behind the wall of the immigration office. This letter was a farewell forever.

I stand in the empty car park of the prison. It's summer. The wind blows through the rich green, full-leafed treetops on the other side of the street. I just head somewhere with my backpack, free of any urgency. I cross an old, abandoned access road. There I stop and look at the broken strip of asphalt. These wall ruins belong to the former Soviet garrison. And in turn its front side borders the old terrain of the riot police.

That's where, fourteen years ago, I took my first steps, together with Hemmerle. I was a nineteen-year-old, trained child. Stuffed with gaps in my knowledge and with flimsy idealism. They stuck a man-child into a uniform. The country needed guards and I needed a country. A homeland. And then my life twisted itself into a ball that I can't completely unravel to this very day.

I stand on the broken access road, my former barracks is just a stone's throw away and now it's a completely different universe. I turn back towards the city. And I walk along the wall. Away from the barracks. Away from the prison. There's nothing more for me to do here.

Bonn, mid-July 2021

'Up, up, the fox said to the hare, don't you hear the hunter blowing his horn?' I call through the closed bathroom door.

Behind the door, it's suspiciously quiet. No rumbling about. No laughing. No noises of a sisterly wrestling match. I knock on the door as a precaution, the quiet unsettles me. Everything indicates a dwarf conspiracy. And although I press my ear against the door, I can only hear the rustling in my head. Shit. Should I just go in? Or do I have to lure them out? What would bring the best results in this situation? Suddenly the door swings open. Feli sticks her head out.

'We're still brushing—' with a lightning-fast movement, she uses her hand to catch the toothpaste sloshing out of her mouth '—teeth.'

She shakes her head disapprovingly, displeased with my attempts to disturb them.

'Leave us alone.'

Protesting, I point to the face of my watch.

'You should have been done with that a long time ago. Thirteen minutes, twenty-three seconds. How long do you need to brush three baby teeth?'

Feli makes an indignant face. She looks pretty funny with all of the foam in her mouth. And somehow cute. 'Did you stop the time?' She spits into the sink. 'That's definitely against the convention for children's rights.'

Shit, I shouldn't have told her about that. In the meantime, my children act like little lawyers during our discussions. Whatever, I have to pretend to control the situation.

'Now's no time for political speeches. It's time to go to bed.' Actually, most of all I'd like to have a shift change. I'm nervous because of their mother, my wife. That's why these two bunnies need to go to bed.

'I peed my pants. Accidentally.' Una announces the news calm and collected, like the announcer for the stock market news.

'Sweetheart, you're standing right next to the toilet.'

'Still. It just happened.'

For my little one, this exhaustive explanation is enough. She's already taken off her wet pants anyway. Downstairs is open air season. I look for the pants but can't find them. Great. At some point they'll turn up again. The magic of a household with children. Bunched up and mouldy, we'll pull it out of some corner in a hundred years. I still ask, though:

'Where did you take off your pants, sweetie?'

'I don't know any more.'

She immediately starts crying. Damn, I shouldn't have asked. 'Everything's OK, Una! We'll find the stupid pants tomorrow.'

She's not really content. The wet pants were, of course, her favourite pants. God in heaven, have mercy on my nerves. But I'm glad our girls are at least safe and sound back at home. In the meantime, outside the sky is black and grey, and water is storming out of it. More and more notifications pop up on my phone. Even tiny drainages turn into torrents that carry everything along with them. Still no message from my wife, but the overloaded network is still delivering my messages.

'Dad? You wanted to read us the story.'

To these two, the deluge outside doesn't matter at all. They have finally arrived in the family bed and are loudly demanding their favourite story.

'Which story?' I ask innocently. 'You are both probably much too tired for a story.'

'No!' they cry in unison. Alright. I read to them from the kangaroo chronicles. The children love the part where the therapist jumps around on the couch and makes bird noises. And I love the communist kangaroo.

'When is mum coming? Mum is supposed to read to us.' Their mother can do the part of the therapist even better than me.

'Soon, girls.'

'But when?'

'Soon.'

'When exactly?'

'In twenty-one minutes and thirteen seconds.'

'Really?' Una looks over at me suspiciously. She points her finger at me. 'You're laughing. I saw it.' I quickly close the book and hold it in front of my grin.

Soon the girls are asleep. I listen to their steady breathing in the darkness. Feli is lying next to the wall with her stuffed animals. Una has twisted herself up in her blanket. An arm lies on my head. Better safe than sorry. Not that the parental servant has run off. I gently wriggle out of the knot. The hazy look of the sleeping girls has a calming effect. But the big 'girl' of the family is missing.

CHAPTER TWENTY-TWO

'Did I do something wrong?' Management looks at me. Do I really want to discuss this? That's what this look says. No, I know that I've done nothing wrong. Exceptionally nothing this time. In the studio of a four-star hotel in Dresden, I'm giving courses in physical fitness. If I can do something well, it's that.

'Mr Meffire. Please don't take this personally. Your job is not to complain.'

Aha.

'But you must understand that it would be socially responsible to ensure that your history does not ruin the reputation of the business.'

Someone is appalled just by my sheer presence. A valued hotel guest. And the customer is always king. The polite hotel management doesn't have a choice. She compliments the ex-con right out of her luxury accommodation.

These are the new stories of my daily life. Still, better than solitary confinement, that much is certain and remains irrefutable. But 'being free' is also about 'being seen'. The existence of being put in a box. And the vagueness. And these conflicting rules, according to which everything functions. 'Being free' means being able to do everything. But somehow also not. It means being allowed to go anywhere, or at least to not really be welcome in those places.

On my first day after being released, after aimlessly wandering through half the city, I turn up at a surprised acquaintance and borrow her car for a trip, even though not even I know where I'm going. When I turn right, I overlook a cyclist. The bumper touches the rear fender. The cyclist moans and keeps pedalling. My panicked, mumbled apology and my deathly pale face appear to be punishment enough. Fuck.

Soon thereafter I start working as a fitness trainer. I can do it, so I do. In the classes, I get lazy, desk jockey city folk to do the bare minimum of movement. But the large fitness chains are run half-heartedly, as if the staff are amateur doorsteppers, hoping to reel the public in. The companies don't care about their clients' progress. The best customer is one who signs the most expensive contract and then, after the first euphoric feeling, barely ever turns up. Or best of all, never comes back again. The only thing that counts are signed contracts. And maintained contracts. And when the co-workers in the sales team fulfil their quota, they're celebrated as if they'd found the cure for cancer. As a trainer, I'm a necessary evil for the business. I'm a disruptive cost factor and a necessary studio folklore, nothing more. The luxury hotel is significantly more committed in terms of caring about health, but they don't tolerate my presence for very long.

One step forward, one step back, that's freedom. I rush from studio to studio and also give private lessons. I run and run. But soon my debts catch up to me. There's child maintenance I didn't pay. And then there's the thousands of Euros for court costs and damages. Even the loan for my old car hasn't completely been paid off, although the car no longer exists. It's an unexpected blow when they empty my bank account to repay my debts. A month's wages disappears into thin air. Just about one hundred sweaty training hours. My bank account is frozen. The money for goods and rent is gone. No one seems to care about what I'll live off. I beg acquaintances for support. I pay old debts with new ones. Freedom? No one prepared me for the fact that everything that I work for will be taken away from me again. Freedom? What freedom? I showed evil years ago, and correspondingly the money I harvest today is scarce. And full of weeds. *What goes around comes around.*

'Listen, Sam.' It's Simone, my oldest connection to Neustadt, from the pre-revolutionary days. 'Are you looking for a job?'

'Is the pope Catholic?' I ask in response.

She laughs. 'Everyone needs a trainer, I hear. Do you want to sign up?'

Of course I want that. Somehow my life appears to revolve in cycles. I look out of the window of my apartment in the tower on the seventh floor. A one-room box from the housing association. It's not possible to find something smaller or more affordable. But at night I have an unbelievable view of the city lights. Deep below me the Great Garden gapes like a cursed place in the middle of the city. There I am. Grown up in the tower blocks. And now I'm back there again. Once you're in the tower blocks, you're always stuck in the tower blocks?

'Are you still there, Sam?'

'Of course.' I can't afford to say no. 'Where do I go?'

The whole affair turns out to be a building site. Simone's assessment was right in this case. It's a training job. Though it's one of the folks from the youth welfare. It's now my honour to do gymnastics for hours for badly behaved kids. The official label is 'Experiential Pedagogy through Intensive Sport Exercises'. This job comes with a non-negotiable work description: *Stick it out. Stay there. Don't run away.* And it's not always easy to do that every day.

The kids see me as one of them. I'm someone from an emotional gulag. That means we can regard each other at eye level and build the first bridge, even with those with whom you can never build bridges and whom you normally can't engage in any fun. Job after job. Welfare youth after welfare youth. And always more youth welfare. Teenagers who sometimes seem like children. Children who sometimes seem like adults, and whose flesh and soul have been mutilated. Little wolves. Or even bigger ones. And now and then really hungry, really vicious wolves. I keep them moving. I keep moving. I listen. Really I am caring for the hopeless. Often they are cases for psychiatry. Often they're also guaranteed cases for the cemetery.

At some point I end up in the so-called IPMs, individual pedagogical measures. In fact, these are court-ordered deprivations of liberty. I bring, pick up and accompany everyone that's dangerous. I'm attacked with faeces, plates, with kitchen utensils and pieces of furniture. With just a few bumps and bruises, I get out of there with mild injuries. A colleague gets stabbed with a knife between his chest and his shoulder. In another incident, a colleague gets some of his chest muscle ripped away.

A new wave of cheap chemicals first sloshes across the ocean, then over everyone. Usually, it's crystal. It's a phenomenon whose existence no one in the far-away chancellor's office in the capital city of Berlin wants to speak about. And even less about its origin. Crystal, this awesomely efficient dirt, creates a lot of violence. And an absurd amount of extreme violence. High speed capitalism always brings more existences into being that aren't winners. People who don't have anything to offer for sale besides their own flesh: to be beaten, to be fucked, to be tortured. Young flesh for money. Money for crystal.

Crystal cuts devastatingly through all classes. A state representative is caught with it in a bathroom in parliament. After that, there's a brief, public outrage. But no one wants to know anything about all of the dead tired, secretly sniffling doctors. And nothing about the lawyers. And of the nurses. And policemen. Crystal, that's the former 'tank chocolate' with which the godforsaken moustache armed his soldiers as they went to the final battle. Into the grave, over in Russia. And to their deaths. Crystal, the resurrected methamphetamine in the democratic resurrected Germany. The goddamn Führer must surely be laughing about that in hell.

These are desperate times. And desperation always brings an irrational longing for simple answers and quick cures. The minor, psychotic, violent remainders of this confusion end up with me. Will social work be effective against system deficiency? To ask this question is taboo. And that's why I can't afford to ask this question.

At some point I become a waste product of a law that requires specific qualifications for jobs with special tasks. New people are urgently needed in youth work. But still, career changers like me are no longer allowed to work with troubled young people. That's what the cartel of the responsible organisations decides. Why do certificates count more than real-world experience? To me, all this seems like an evil plot hatched by old, male bureaucrats behind closed doors. Of course there are semi-legal loopholes through which institutions suck in people like me. But the risk of being caught is real and ultimately isn't worth it any more. So once again, I'm standing before the abyss.

I need a new job, something that brings enough money in for rent and food. I'm working as a stocker in a health food store. And as a furniture removalist for a carrier, at least long enough until I can no longer get upstairs any more because of the fluid in my knees. I work as a steel buyer for a Ukrainian trading company. I work as a careers adviser. I work as an assistant and badly paid intern. And somehow things go exactly as one would expect. You can take the guard from the wall, but you can't take the wall out of the guard. At least not the longing for it.

I land at the door again. During the day I walk from carrier to carrier with my own concept for youth outreach. And from work group to work group. I get a lot of approval and little money. The carriers are big and slow. The authorities responsible for them are even bigger and even slower. So I earn my rent at night. I guard a fetish party. I guard construction sites. I help the escorts at a pompous wedding for a pop star queen. I keep watch on a warm summer night at a knee-high fence, directly in front of the diva's bedroom window.

I work throughout the years in diverse student clubs and alternative dives. And several hundred times I muck about with some comrades. Ugly and intense. With sociopaths and career fighters. With chemically alert superheroes. And maybe, perhaps, the bushy beard god made a teeny tiny mistake. At least when it comes to the structure of the male brain. Because nothing feels as real as my time at the wall. The community of brothers. And the fight. Nothing awakens such an intensive liveliness in the here and now. Protecting, fighting, suffering.

Maybe I've become a junkie without any chemicals and am ruined for normal life. How else can you explain that after Alberto Adriano's murders I joined up with some guys and go on tour with them, as a bodyguard for Afro-German top acts? Folks that you can normally admire on music stations like MTV and Viva, are undertaking an educational and concert tour in the darkest, most dangerous corners of the East German forest. The hate-filled vampire mob waits for our tour bus in every city like a herd of true hardcore fans. No one with my past and two cents of understanding would get involved in something like that. But I do it anyway. Serving and protecting. The wall makes you addicted. That we even make it to the final concert at Alexanderplatz in Berlin, alive and unharmed, is a complete mystery.

Years later, already deep into another life, I still won't let myself be cured of idealism. A guy from the tri-border area of Germany, France and Switzerland wants to become chancellor. I assist someone who assists the bodyguards of the Federal Criminal Police Office. Once again I'm behind a messiah. Or in this case, someone who would have liked to become one, but who is light years away from the stature of the Saxon original. Yet regardless of him, I'm ready again to throw the shell of my body onto the scale, for this gifted producer of empty promises and vain hopes. Although I don't owe these guys anything. You can take the man from the wall.

Later still, in February 2018, I will learn how fast it's over with my shell of a body. During an attempt of non-violent civil courage in a streetcar, motivated by my naive illusion of being a helper, I stumble upon a rampaging boy on drugs. And I nearly pay for my self-deception with my life. My upper jaw is stuck through with a multifunction tool. The attack misses vital nerves and organs by a hair's breadth.

All this is still years away, in the future. I'm back in Dresden. It is 2004. I'm standing in my tiny apartment, after coming home from somewhere. I stare down the street at the park. Behind me, my refrigerator hums loudly and discontentedly. In its old age, it doesn't like to be empty and therefore lacking purpose. And down below, in front of the house, there's a homeless man sitting next to the rubbish bins. He is sitting there again. Even his life seems to move in cycles. Seeing this toothless man there, again and again, pierces through all of my scabs. I let myself be moved. But always doing the same things leads to similar results. I have to stop. Get going. I have to clean up my construction sites and my goddamn head. I have to put the puzzle pieces together. And finally start something and actually finish it.

Maybe I should leave here. Go somewhere where I don't have a name or a history. Somewhere where the only thing that counts is what I can deliver. And nothing else. How does it go in that fairy tale with the town musicians? *I always find something better than death.*

CHAPTER TWENTY-THREE

Train stations are like human beehives, interspersed with a lot of honeycombs, and restlessly busy. I don't like train stations. And I especially don't like train stations during rush hour. On weekends. Or in the evenings. Or on holidays. And since I have to travel through train stations a lot, from somewhere to somewhere, this proves to be a challenge.

Today I choose the spiral method of approach. First, I ascend the stairs to the square in front of the cathedral, then I circle the huge building once. Finally, I descend again to get to the station. I've brought my backpack that I love more than anything else. It's wonderfully inconspicuous, and with it, in my business shirt, I could pass for a bank employee to a lot of people. Or a clerk from the city administration. And with my bag I could be on my feet for twenty-four hours uninterrupted, without needing anything else: I have calories squeezed into concentrates. Water. A medipack. Emergency communication. Several chargers. Cold protection. Rain protection. A multi tool. A change of clothes. And everything is beautifully organised and securely stowed in compartments. The only thing I'm missing is a foldable tiny house. Or a spaceship you can blow up, like in *Adolar's*

Fantastic Adventures, this one disturbing, funny, comic series from Hungary.

This backpack is my second home. It provides me with everything, except for the tiny house. And the rocket. This backpack is my life insurance. And today I may need it more urgently than ever before. I sneak on a loop over the platform in front of the cathedral. And then once around and once through the train station. Then I take a stand not far from track 9. There's a large wall at my back. And I have a good view in all directions.

Nothing's going to surprise me today. Whatever comes down this platform, I'll be ready. But the hardest thing of all is waiting. And the nervous flickering in my stomach. And the goddamn adrenalin that can't go anywhere. I stand in my position below track 9. The people rush down from the platforms and past me. And in another direction, they rush up the platform as a very obese woman with blue-black skin and two very sweet, lively twins with pigtails, is struggling with a pushchair loaded to the brim. This physical stage is apparently the general fate of parents. You're transformed into a pack donkey. And a double shift worker drone. For a moment, I fight with myself. Then my guilty conscience wins. I leave my spot and walk towards the woman, who's staring down the platform with a desperate look while she's trying to tame the twins.

'Excuse me?'

I address the woman from a suitable distance and with a loud voice in an attempt to drown out the infernal noise of commuters and the rattling announcements over the loudspeaker. The woman turns to me astonished. Her gaze is slightly annoyed.

'May I help you?' I say while pointing to the pushchair, and then up the stairs. The woman's face brightens to a smile.

'You don't have to do that, it's heavy.' She waves me off. 'Too heavy.'

'I'd like to help.' That's a lie. And I don't have any time. So without further ado, I grab the pushchair and I heave it onto my hip. What the hell does this woman have in this stroller? The thing weighs at least forty kilos. And because of the damn bulkiness it feels twice as heavy. After twelve steps, my heart is beating hard in my chest. After another twelve, I'm close to having a heart attack. Shit. Why didn't I comfortably wait in my spot and just watch the woman in all this madness? Really and truthfully, no good deed goes unpunished. I stop for a moment, now my head down, struggle to get air and try to ignore my fingers which are burning as they hold on to the stroller.

Out of the stroller, three sacks of potatoes smile up at me. And red beets. And pickles in jars. And frozen pork chops. And five thousand other things. For heaven's sake, that's enough food for a month. I'm done for. Just like the frozen pork in the plastic packaging.

I finally make it almost to the platform. Directly behind me, the mother huffs as she walks up the stairs holding the twins' hands. I focus on the last step. My hands burn. My back is burning. Goddamn. But whatever. *Up, up and away!* I tighten my muscles, then I place my left foot on the next stair. The stroller, weighing a tonne, swings off my hip; I reach for it and grunt with effort.

And then it happens. She passes me. She walks down the stairs coming towards me. Her, who I'd recognise in any large crowd. First, I see her Terrex half-boots coming down the stairs. Then the typical jeans and parker. She could have been anything in this outfit. She could have been commuting for any possible reason. For a world tour. For street music. Or as a PhD student. I immediately recall our first meeting. How she sat across from me with cards and smoking a cigar. And how her gaze meets mine.

First I see an incredulous expression on her face. She sees me. With a stroller packed to the brim. And an overweight mother. And twins. But her astonishment only lasts a short while, then it turns into a grin.

'Well, you should've told me you couldn't make it today because you're taking a trip with your family.'

I try to stammer something quickly, but I don't succeed. I desperately struggle for air.

'Now don't have another heart attack. I'll just go back up and wait for you upstairs,' she says to me, grinning.

'Thank you so much.' The mother of the twins is visibly relieved.

'I'd gladly do it again.' Maybe not today, but another time. The twins grin at me wildly, they point in my direction with their little fingers and babble something incomprehensible. After a few steps holding on to their mother's hand they lose interest in me, and the small, cute pigtailed heads get lost in the hustle and bustle. The Amazon sidles up to me. She's laughing.

Then she pulls me to her.

'Well, do you always have to rescue the world?'

'Ah, if only I could do that.' And then I add: 'My last attempt wasn't so successful.'

The Amazon waves me off. 'Crisis as an opportunity.' For a moment, she looks at me seriously.

'You fell into a terribly big pot of shit. It happens.' She kisses me. Really quickly and self-assuredly, somehow as if no time had passed. As if we had only said goodbye to each other that morning in our apartment door. Her kiss smells like the lemon-ginger-candy in her mouth. And like her.

'Come on, let's go. I thought you invited me to eat?' She smiles again. 'Or was that just a pretext?' She pokes me in the ribs with her fingers. It rather hurts. But it also feels good. We settle down in a tiny Japanese soup shop not far from the train station. The interior dates from the last century, the walls are yellow with cigarette smoke. Nevertheless, the guests crowd tightly together, because you can find original soups here, beyond the usual imitations and compromises. Here, sweaty cooks work behind a fogged glass pane scooping the unique soup into bowls. I love this place.

'So you live in Cologne now.'

I shrug my shoulders but don't say anything to that. I'll have to admit to her soon that I still guard doors and people, because the money in youth welfare isn't enough, not even in the West. I'll have to tell her that I sleep in a warehouse behind an old recording studio, somewhere in the suburbs, on a mattress, on the floor. I'll have to tell her that I've got the crazy idea of writing a crime novel. More specifically, a series of crime novels. On single-side printed wastepaper from the copy shop around the corner. And that the writing feels so goddamn right, so long overdue and fitting, even though I don't earn anything with it. Yes, I'll soon have to tell her a whole lot. Including something about my newly won freedom. Freedom? The West hasn't been much more merciful to me than the East. But nevertheless at least I've finally arrived. And I'm slowly becoming my own person. That probably sounds completely silly for a thirty-six-year-old man, but I'm indescribably proud of it.

'Hey, Earth to idiot! What are you thinking about now?' The

Amazon sticks her finger in my ribs and grins contentedly. 'You're probably thinking about how quickly you can get into my little recreation area.' I raise my hand quickly, but I'm still holding a spoon. The Amazon's front gets splashed with a little soup. Shit, I had already forgotten how direct she can be. The Amazon calmly looks at her stained jacket.

'That was really mature. You'll definitely get a chance to enter my recreation area, friend,' she decides while grinning. 'But I need to know something beforehand.'

The grinning has suddenly disappeared. This here is serious. I lay the spoon carefully onto the table. Nice and slow. Nice and orderly, as good as my shaky fingers can manage.

'You really want something to happen? Between us?'

I avoid her gaze and follow the course of her veins down her toned arms.

'What do you mean by that?' I can't manage to get anything more out.

'I mean that a lot of time has passed. A lot of time. You've had to get by during this time. I have too.'

What can I say to that? What should I say to that? I don't want to upset her. Just not that. Not today.

'I was on the outside. You weren't. I met with other people. You didn't. I did my own thing.' Her gaze is hard and fixed. 'Ask me. You can ask me anything. But don't blame me for being free. Because then this won't work.'

I know. I've long known everything she's saying. I have long since levelled all these allegations against her. I have long cursed her and given up. And myself too. I remain silent. Maybe that's the best.

'Do you know why I'm here today?'

I shake my head, while the tears run down my face and into my soup.

'Screw their lying morals. Screw them!'

Her fist slams the table. The bowls shake and sway in protest. Heads turn around, but no one risks saying anything. Not when they see the Amazon.

'Screw them! Think about our wedding vows. Do you still remember them?'

Of course I remember them, you dumb cow. *Of course* I remember. It's a quote from the Book of Ruth:

Where you go I will go, and where you stay I will stay. Your people will be my people and your God my God. Where you die I will die, and there I will be buried. May the Lord deal with me, be it ever so severely, if even death separates you and me.

I cry. I cry like I've never cried before in my life. I don't care about the people around us. I don't care about the soup. Nothing matters to me. I have to get it out. I've seen so much in the years. Loyalty wasn't often part of that. I bring my hands to my face and cry. The Amazon cries, too.

'Now stop crying you girl,' she finally says to me. 'And screw the soup.'

Through my tears, the Amazon glows like an unearthly appearance. 'Come on, let's go to my place.'

She slams a few bills on the table and pulls me out of Little Japan. And she keeps her promise. Regarding her recreation area. And also regarding our wedding vows. Later, when we're lying sweaty in our rumpled hotel bed and she's asleep, I scribble onto the writing pad on the minibar:

You have to take the dust
out of the rush,
then the sea rushes again.

You have to take the dust out
and put the magic back in.

Allow
the rushing to enchant us again,
once more.

We have to take
the dust out our ears
and our hearts,
then the ocean will rush again
and enchant.

Long live the Technicians' Health Insurance. They pay for a whole series of sessions with a head doctor. He's apparently a specialist for when one's completely twisted and broken upstairs. But how's that supposed to work? Can the guy do magic?

'So you want to . . .' the man looks at the note 'take the rushing out of your heart?'

Oh shit. I shouldn't have shown this guy my text. It sounds silly when he says it like that. I still nod. I reached the practice through a nondescript hallway. The premises have the appearance of a Tax Advisory Office, with couches for patients, ugly houseplants and a tiny kitchen. The brain repairs happen on the ground floor. That's how I'm able to observe, behind curtains from the couch, how people on the street with better functioning brains go about their errands. Here, I'm supposed to understand how broken I am. And why. And how my condition can be alleviated. And the insurance mechanic, with his doctorate and all the diplomas on his wall, is supposed to hold my hand during this self-realisation. But I'm actually only here because of the Amazon. Because something has to change. I can't lose this woman over some nonsense again. Cupid's arrow hits me right in the head. For the same girl. Again. Oh well, there are worse reasons to go to therapy.

Three sessions later: 'If your suffering is supposed to have a purpose, then you have to try to go into the world of your feelings.'

'The world of my feelings?' How deep then, please? I understand the intention, but I'm doubtful about the implementation.

'Are there no alternatives?'

Why can't I use logic? Causality? How objective can you be, when you're paid to tell people that this is the only solution? I twist around like an eel. I give the magician my objections. I give him alternative theory to chew over. Carefully pieced together crap. Until I have to admit to myself in the fifth or sixth session that all of the loss I've experienced just can't disappear in thin air.

I've never dared to complain about my father's absence. All the dead. The death. Like my grandfather's, for example. And maybe I really tried to fill my old father's wounds with pieces of my enthusiasm for the Messiah. Or my grandfather's wounds? Franz Ferdinand was also a kind of 'father'/grandfather. He died too, shortly before we could have a pre-arranged conversation. My lawyer, dead. Apparently by choice. Even though he was successful and in the middle of life. My karate trainer, my Budo idol and friend, dead. My first therapist, dead. The wife of Thomas, my colleague and friend, dead also from cancer. Thomas, dead, on the way to a meeting with me. I have exactly as many doubts about his choice to die as I did about my lawyer. My mother. Dead. And my brother, too. That's a tonne of farewells. And missed opportunities. What a massive pile of crap.

'What am I supposed to do with that?' I ask the magician.

'With what?'

'With death?'

'What do you want to do with it?' Can't this guy speak one straightforward, non-cryptic sentence? Just once without this goddamn psycho babble . . .

'I'd like it to stop.'

'Like what to stop?'

Yeah, what exactly? 'The dying. The dying needs to stop.'

The magician nods. Maybe I'm on the right track. 'I don't want everyone to just disappear from my life.' The magician's pencil scratches on the paper.

'Why do you want that? Have you ever asked yourself that?'

Yeah, why exactly? I have to think about it.

'Why do you want the people around you to stop dying?'

Anything that's good dissolves into this air. In lies. And in death.

On the other side of the window, normal people rush to their normal things. I puzzle over how they do it, how they live their lives. Their joy. Their pain.

'I would love to finally arrive somewhere. To finally be at home somewhere,' I answer the magician. And cry.

'I'm going to leave there.'

Some time has passed. Each week, I lie on the couch. Today

I'm hoping for some more of his advice. Actually I'm hoping that's he'll take this decision from me. Or he'll talk me out of it. Or the opposite. Actually, I don't care.

'So you want to leave, this . . .'

'Uniter.' I help fill in the gap. 'Well, it means "together as one", and it's a kind of self-help group for all kinds of people who have something to do with security.'

His face remains neutral. If he's read anything about this matter, he's keeping it to himself.

'Why do you want to leave?'

So things are going to go like this again? I do all the work and he gets paid for it?

'It's not what I was looking for.' The sports school wasn't right. The Bible reading group of charismatics wasn't right. The neo-anthroposophists weren't either. I didn't find it in the barracks. And definitely not in prison. And Uniter? Not there either.

The magician looks at me expectantly. Then he gives me a push: 'Could it be, that this isn't about where they are or with whom? But why?'

I remain silent.

'Are you afraid of having to take on responsibility?'

I shake off my paralysis. That's nonsense, psychobabble!

'What responsibility?' I bark out. He's acting as if they were giving away high-paying, permanent positions there. But it wasn't like that. So what kind of responsibility?

'Responsibility for yourself?' the magician answers quietly. 'And responsibility for others through your actions. Or don't you see it like that?'

I notice that I can hardly control my anger about what he's saying.

'I wanted you to tell me what I should do. I mean, for once you could just say straight-forward what you think!' Is that really so much to ask! My tone is quite sharp. The magician flinches. 'So you want me to give you the answers?' I nod eagerly. Yes, that's what I want. All this time, bloody hell.

'OK.' The magician lays his pen and notepad down next to each other on his little, round table. Then he bends forward.

'You've used up all of your chances. Wilfully. And you led men to commit crimes. And . . .' The magician uses his forefinger to draw an exclamation point in the air. 'You've caused devastating emotional pain. To your victims. To your mother, of course. And also to your friends. And to yourself. That's what you're responsible for. And I'm firmly convinced that you have long since understood this, at least partially.'

Normally the man says practically nothing. And today it's gushing out of him. Can he please stop? No, he can't.

'Every behaviour is also a crime scene. And you need to find out the motive of the perpetrator. So?' He points with his bony pointer finger in my direction. 'What motivates you? Why are you running away?'

The detective in me is resisting the knee-jerk reaction of the protesting voice in my head. Such miserable shit.

'If you want to work with public bodies, you have to stay away from something like that,' I protest after all, because that's the truth. Uniter has officially been classified as 'suspicious'. Although so far, no one there has wanted to invite me to a Putsch. No one there wanted to drag 'Mutti' before the chancellery and hang the Chancellor herself. Or do some other shit like that. For me, the place is more like a general assembly for security stuff, like a private research group, where people give lectures and organise charitable actions for all those who return from various missions crippled inside.

'Exactly, it's not about who the people are. Or aren't. Rather, it's about what you hope to find there, I'm truly convinced of that.' And after a brief pause, the magician adds: 'And you take that filter in your head with you everywhere. Regardless of where you are and what you're doing.'

If one follows the magician's logic, then once again I was looking for a father. Or at least an order of knights as a replacement for a father, and security. And instead of meeting the Round Table, I met a gathering of handymen. And instead of salvation, I got homework. That's not what I wanted from them. That's why I'm running away. I don't want any responsibility. I want to get away from my mother and her punitive judgement. And I can't let go of the father/grandfather gap. I don't want to be grown up. But finally I can. Then I won't be a puppet any more, no longer on anyone's strings. Not a father-complex junkie. Maybe it's really that banal. That simple. I suck the snot back into my nose. And laugh.

'Why are you laughing?' the magician asks. And that just makes me even more cheerful. I scream with laughter. Freed from everything adult. And with my full throat. Tears run down my cheek.

'I had to think of *SpongeBob*,' I finally manage to get out. The magician frowns.

'The cartoon?'

I nod and wipe the tears from my eyes. 'I had to think about what SpongeBob said to his friend: *We're not ugly. We stink.*'

Bonn, mid-July 2021

All's well that ends well. I think about that, as I hear you walk up the stairs and I hear your key in the door. The rain spat you out again. You're home. You got through the traffic on the outer ring road. The traffic jam couldn't stop you. And Peter probably didn't have the guts to mess with you either.

'Why are you staring at me like a squirrel in love?' I have to grin at you too.

'Stop, you idiot.'

I can't. I would like to, but I can't.

'OK, then keep grinning.' You shove me into the kitchen. 'But make something to eat in the meantime. I'm hungry enough for three brown bears. All they had there was celery sticks and yogurt dip, can you imagine? She's in one of those low-carb phases again.'

I'm so happy that you're back home. I risk giving you a hug, even though I know how dangerous you are when you're hungry. Your kiss speaks volumes. Then you push me away from you.

'Get away! I'll cook us something.' With that, you push me out of the kitchen. 'And please read the mail, because of the September series. They still have questions about the curriculum. Or one or two issues? I can't remember exactly.'

With that, you've dismissed me. And you begin to dash frenziedly from cupboard to cupboard, tidying, rearranging, like a magician. In the office, I open up the mail program on the large monitor. My gaze scans up and down the subject lines without being able to focus on anything. I listen to myself, but even the collective of accusers doesn't have any sensible commentary. Ultimately, I pull a piece of paper from the printer and the pen flies from one side to the next, as if by itself.

You're my beacon in the storm, you healed my doubt,
        with your smile.
I dream of that. Wherever I go, and wherever I am.
I dream about waking up in your lap.
And outside, at the window, a wild choir of
        sparrows sings
an even wilder hymn to life

I stare briefly at my scribbles, then I fold it into a steamboat and in the hallway, I quickly stick it into the front pocket of your messenger bag, next to your phone. Over the years, the steamboat-origami has become an inside joke between us. You get a love letter from me. And I get replies from you. 'Idiot.' 'Lovesick hamster.' Or something similar. We bicker like a married couple. We are a married couple. We're companions. And we've got the girls, too. What's still missing? Everything fits, nothing is missing any more.

Bringing a book from manuscript to what you are reading is a team effort.

Dialogue Books would like to thank everyone at Little, Brown who helped to publish *Sam* in the UK.

Editorial
Sharmaine Lovegrove
Amy Mae Baxter
Jon Appleton

Contracts
Megan Phillips
Amy Patrick
Anne Goddard
Bryony Hall
Sasha Duszynska Lewis

Sales
Caitriona Row
Dominic Smith
Frances Doyle
Hannah Methuen
Lucy Hine
Toluwalope Ayo-Ajala

Design
Nico Taylor
Jo Taylor

Production
Narges Nojoumi

Operations
Kellie Barnfield
Millie Gibson
Sanjeev Braich

Publicity
Millie Seaward

Marketing
Emily Moran

Copy Editor
Karyn Burnham

Proofreader
Edward Wall

Finance
Andrew Smith
Elle Barry